AN ACTOR'S LIFE FOR ME

BY

DAVID ROPER

Copyright

For all the actors I have ever worked with

Contents

Part One
An Actor Toured

Part Two
An Actor Bored

Part Three
An Actor Scored

Part Four
An Actor Adored

Foreword

Everybody seems to have an all-consuming interest in what actors get up to on stage, screen and in real life. David Roper's *An Actor's Life for Me* takes the lid off it all. It is not so much an autobiography more an entertaining chronicle of all the various ups and downs of any actor's professional, personal and perennially fascinating life.

David has been an actor for very nearly 50 years. He has worked in Theatre, TV, Radio and Film - you name it. He first tasted fame in the 70s, starring in The Cuckoo Waltz, a Granada TV sitcom. In the mid-90s he spent 2 years in EastEnders, playing Geoff Barnes, Michelle Fowler's tutor and lover. He was in 'Coronation Street', as Alma Baldwin's boyfriend, Bob Bradshaw, and has appeared in many TV series: 'Harry', with Michael Elphick; 'Heartbeat'; 'The Bill'; 'Holby City'; 'Emmerdale'.

As a freelance writer, David wrote 108 weekly articles for the Brighton Argus newspaper over a period of two years, from 2003 to 2005, and *An Actor's Life for Me* is an edited and updated compilation of those articles.

From the heights of touring in Stephen Daldry's award-winning production of JB Priestley's play, 'An Inspector Calls'; starring in several Pantomimes in Brighton and Bristol; featuring in the film 'The Damned United'; playing The Bishop of Norwich in 'The Crown'; and finally into the depths of unemployment and the rigours of real life, follow David's journey as a professional actor, as a husband and father, and, perhaps most revealing of all, as a dog owner!

With wit and charm, an actor's life is opened up, giving a perceptive insight into what makes an actor tick, what makes an actor angry and, well, - what makes an actor.

AN ACTOR'S LIFE FOR ME

PART ONE

AN ACTOR TOURED

A JOB! A JOB! MY KINGDOM FOR A JOB!

"I've got a job! A seven month-long job!"

Now this may not be cause to crack open the Cava in your lush neck of the woods, but in the desert that is the acting profession it is an oasis of security, believe me, and has chucked me way over the moon. The reason for my excitement may elude you, due to the fact that deep within the mythology surrounding actors there are fundamental and fallacious flaws. Namely, the belief that:

Actors are paid vast amounts of money, equivalent to the Gross Domestic Product of Luxembourg.

They spend their wealth on A-list substances, which they share with B-list celebrities in C-list night clubs.

They wile away their leisure hours in the company of models and starlets with IQs only marginally greater than their chest measurements.

Sadly, this is not the case, and is a somewhat overstated assessment of your average actor's lifestyle, to put it mildly. As luck would have it, you don't have to look far to find one of the major culprits in putting this 'myth' into mythology - you probably come across it every day. Yes, sorry lads, but the Press (well, to be fair, the national red-tops really) must shoulder a good proportion of the responsibility for perpetuating these misconceptions. For one thing, they will insist on reporting largely unsubstantiated and often exorbitant estimates of the amounts of dosh paid to actors. You know the sort of thing:

'After the incident with the banana on 'Richard and Judy', she was axed from her £120,000 a year role in EastEnders, and now faces a civil action in the High Court, brought by the Fruit and Vegetable Liberation Front.' Or…

'He denied paying the prostitute £200 to wear his Manchester United football kit and perform oral sex on him, while he watched a video of the omnibus edition of Brookside. "No way would I do that! For a start, my video packed in at Easter, and anyway, I'm a lifelong Everton supporter. Besides, she would never wear red with her colouring!" he quipped, as he left his £2,000 a week job on the series for the last time, and checked into an exclusive Surrey clinic for nasal rehabilitation.'

Even if those figures were correct, they would represent only the tiny tip of an enormous iceberg. The rest of the profession is lurking down there under the water, waiting for something titanic to strike and lift them out of the icy depths.

But I can't blame the Press for all the bizarre notions that fly around about actors. The Public has cultivated its own wealth of weird and wonderful ideas about us, and they will say and do the most amazing things. Here is a true flavour of what I mean.   Man in HMV shop: 'Didn't you used to be David Roper?'

Rotary Club member at question time, when I was the lunchtime guest speaker: 'When you were in bed with Diane Keen in The Cuckoo Waltz, how did you cope with getting an erection?' Tells us more about him than about me, don't you think? And you can stop right there - the answer is no, I did not!

At a Friends of the Theatre after-show party, a middle-aged woman shook my hand and curtsied! Where did that come from, for crying out loud?

Man in a West Country café: "I know you, 'course I do! You installed my Tele!"

Two dodgy geezers in a Liverpool boozer: "You bastard! We recognised you from somewhere, but we thought you were an undercover copper on the look-out!"

Dishy woman in her twenties outside the stage door in Hull: "My mother used to watch your programme when she was pregnant with me."

Ten year old boy in the street: "Here, mister, what's it like shagging Michelle Fowler?" Believe it or not, I was with Oliver Reed at the time and he blushed.

But this one really takes the biscuit. I was asleep on a train to London, when a woman woke me up to tell me who I was, "Here. You're David Roper!"

Anyway, enough of that. What about this job? Well, I have landed a part (actors always 'land' parts, don't ask me why) in J. B. Priestley's play 'An Inspector Calls'. We are scheduled to rehearse in London and Birmingham for four weeks (it is a joint production with Birmingham Rep.), play there for two weeks and then trot off on a twenty-two week jaunt round the British Isles. It will take us from

Aberdeen in the North to Jersey in the South, and from Norwich in the East to Belfast in the West, although luckily not in successive weeks.

Funnily enough, J.B. Priestley was at school in Bradford with my paternal grandmother; a moderately impressive, if tenuous, name-drop. She described him to me, with typical Yorkshire candour, as,

"A cocky little bugger, with his breeches-arse hanging out."

Many, many years later I appeared in an amateur production of his play 'When We Are Married'. It was put on to commemorate the fortieth anniversary of the Bradford Civic Playhouse, which J.B. himself had founded forty years previously - by gum, you can't fault 'em for timing in Yorkshire, can you?

J.B. Priestley attended that performance, and at the party afterwards I found myself talking to him. I don't think he reckoned much to my performance, and declared my mutton chop whiskers to be 'anachronistic'. However, my grandma, God rest her soul, would be pleased to know that he had obviously worked on his social skills and that his mother had sewn up his trousers. At the same 'do' I met Billie Whitelaw, the well-known Bradford actress, and told her that I was going to Drama School that autumn. "I think you should," she said and wandered off. At the time, with the blinding arrogance of youth, I thought she meant I was so *good* I *deserved* to go. Years later, with the clarity of hindsight, it dawned on me that she probably meant I was so *bad* I *needed* to go. Thanks, Billie.

It goes without saying that I shall miss my home in Brighton while I am away, although I will be back every weekend to polish-up on my hoovering skills.

'Objection, your honour!'

'Sustained!'

Fair enough, I confess. My wife, Andrea, does it all. I wouldn't say she is obsessed with hoovering, but last Christmas I bought her a black one for evening wear.

In order to retain my sanity, and to keep Andrea and our twin boys, Harry and Jack, abreast of what I am getting up to, I thought I would keep a written record as the weeks roll by. We start rehearsals next Monday, so after that I won't be around very mu...crikey! That is less than two days away! I had better start learning my lines!

David Roper

A TICKET TO RIDE

08.32 on a cold Monday morning - the first day of rehearsals for 'An Inspector Calls' - found me at the tail-end of a snaking ticket queue at Brighton Railway Station. My train to London Victoria was due to leave in ten minutes at 08.42, and all the ticket windows seemed to be crammed with back-packers wanting to go to John O'Groats via Land's End, Luxembourg and Luton.

This did little to improve my mood, which had been laid low (and me with it) by a sweet little old lady in her 80s, elbowing me out of the Kiosk queue. What is it with the older generation these days? They seem to think that just because they can slice the top of a boiled egg at 86 it gives them the God-given right to treat everybody under pensionable age like dirt. Whatever happened to respect for your youngers?

With only seconds to spare, I ran to a free window and ordered my ticket - or at least I tried to. In the days of good old British Rail this used to be such a simple task - not any more. Without a degree in Ticketing, it is useless to try and fathom railway prices these days, so I just handed over my wallet and legged it for the barrier.

In the nick of time I got to the platform, and came a respectable fourth in the sprint finish for the 08.42. No podium position for me, I regret to say, but a creditable performance for one of limited athletic ability, and made even sweeter by watching the doors close this side of my little old lady. No, I have not got an irrational prejudice against the elderly, but if God had meant them to travel in the rush hour, he would never have given us Saga Holidays, would he?

As usual, I had dozed off by Hayward's Heath, and must have been sound asleep by Gatwick, as I have no recollection of passing through it. There is a section of track three or four minutes from East Croydon, which was specifically designed to wake the dead. The carriages lurch from side to side, causing any carelessly lolling head to be flung violently against the window. It is either the result of woefully inadequate track maintenance, or else a cunning plan by the rail company's Customer Services to make sure dozy 'customers' don't miss their stop.

I was duly jolted awake and looked around me. Several people gave me weak smiles, which I took to mean that I had been snoring my head off since Three Bridges, and why didn't I just have the operation and give them all a bit of peace.

There is always that little frisson of excitement, I find, on arriving in London, and I felt it that morning as I crossed the cavernous concourse of Victoria Station and walked out onto Buckingham Palace Road, which, by an inspired piece of City of Westminster road-naming, is the road to Buckingham Palace.

Her Majesty the Queen was in, I could tell, as the flag on top of her Palace was flying. Well, it was hanging limply, actually, but it was still nice of her to let the rest of us (and any interested Terrorist Organisation) into the secret of her exact whereabouts. In the current climate, I really think MI5 should have a long, hard think about this, you know.

I always enjoy the walk across Green Park, particularly in the spring, when it is carpeted with the most glorious display of daffodils and semi-clad, spread-eagled Scandinavian tourists. Would that William Wordsworth were alive today...

I wandered lonely as a cloud
That floats on high o'er vales and hills,
When, all at once, I saw a crowd,
A host of prostrate Swedish girls.
Beside the Mall, beneath the trees,
Their skirts rolled way up past their knees.
The English frown on such behaviour.
What bliss to live in Scandinavia!

Sadly, this was January, so I packed away my fantasy and emerged into Piccadilly. I bought my habitual Big Issue from the seller outside The Ritz, noting, not for the first time, the irony of his choice of pitch, tucked it prominently under my arm and strode off. A lot of the articles in Big Issue are very interesting, I must say, but my principal reason for buying it was so that it would be noticed by the dozen or so other sellers that I would pass, thus sparing me that gnawing sense of guilt at not buying from them. Pathetic or what?

By 10.20, two and a half hours after leaving home (i.e. 35 minutes longer than the flight to Alicante), I felt I had already done a days work, as I took a deep breath and entered the rehearsal room…

AN AUDIENCE WITH...

Hundreds of you have written to ask…that is, quite a few people have been asking…all right, if you must have it, somebody asked me once:

"What are Rehearsals for?"

Knowing my rapier-like mind and penchant for witty repartee, you might have thought, mistakenly as it happens, that I replied, "For Rehearsing, of course, Dumbo!"

Instead, I rather pompously and patronisingly pointed out that it was, in fact, the wrong question that was being asked.

Incidentally, being pompous and patronising are the first two characteristics Andrea tried to knock out of me - principally because the poor girl can't spell them - looks like you've still a bit of work to do here, my love, sorry.

A more revealing question would have been (hint of pomposity there, you see.), "Why does a two hour stage play need four weeks rehearsal, when a two hour TV play, with no discernible rehearsal at all, is 'in the can' within two weeks?"

Curiously, the answer lies with the ultimate audience.

You see, for a stage play, the audience is 'immobile', as it were, and sees everything, so the actors must know where the focus is from line to line, as well as being audible and visible all the time.

For a TV play, however, the audience is 'mobile' and sees what the director wants it to see, so the actors have no need to worry about focus, or being visible and audible - the technology does it for them.

Also, TV 'shots' tend to be quite short, so line learning is easier, and you only have to get it right the once. On stage, however, the performance is continuous, so you have to learn all the lines and get them right every night. That being the case, all those lines have to be analysed and learnt in their entirety, and then trotted out in front of a live audience of up to two thousand.

Now that sounds like a lot of people, I know, but when I first worked in TV, I was confronted with the possibility of appearing in front of an audience of 15 million, and it was frightening. The producer calmed me down by pointing out that, apart from the fact that the programme would be pre-recorded, we were not really playing to an audience of 15 million people at all, but to seven and a half million audiences of just two people, each sprawled in its lounge, drinking Special Brew, picking its nose and dropping it behind the sofa, while demanding to be entertained.

It is a bizarre thought that all the technological wizardry involved in making and transmitting TV programmes has, as its ultimate audience, just a couple of people in Wolverhampton, say, who are probably arguing about whose turn it is to make the tea, anyway - but at least, if they are paying attention, you are spared their comments.

A theatre audience, on the other hand, is right there in front of you, and any comments can be embarrassingly audible. I remember that as I made my 'starry' entrance at one matinee of 'Boeing-Boeing' in Wimbledon, a loud voice from the stalls rang out loud and clear, "Of course, I prefer Gerald Flood." The late and much missed Gerald laughed like a drain when I told him years later.

That was nothing, though, compared to what Laurence Olivier must have felt, during an East End kids' matinee of 'Othello'. He had just killed Desdemona and was standing over her, all blacked-up and brooding, when a cockney kid chirped up from the gallery,

"Go on, mate, fuck 'er while she's still warm!"

Olivier's response is not recorded, but I doubt he took the advice.

On this tour, with it still being winter, we are suffering from the bane of an actor's life - the coughing audience. The other night it was like playing at an International Phlegm Convention. They were everywhere! It was so bad that we eventually took to pausing and repeating lines after each hacking interruption.

Coughing, however, may be unavoidable, but the 'chirp' of a mobile phone certainly isn't, and what varied and witty 'chirps' there are to entertain us these days. You are in the middle of your big speech, acting your polyester socks off, when you suddenly get Tchaikovsky's 1812 in one ear and the Morse Code for SOS in the other. And people actually *answer* the damn things! - "Hello, sweetheart, I'm at the theatre…'An Inspector Calls'…not bad. That bloke from EastEnders is in it. He's put on a bit of weight…what?...OK, I'll pop in ASDA's…two litres of semi-skimmed and some Lillets, sure…and you…bye."

There should be a law against it. If it was up to me I woul…oh, hang about, that's my mobile. It must be Andrea. Speak to you next week.

"Hello, sweetheart, I'm at the theatre…"

WHEN DO I GET A DAY OFF?

Question: How many actors does it take to change a light bulb?

Answer: 30,001. One to change the light bulb, and 30,000 to stand around saying,

"That should be me up there!"

What makes that funny is that, although it is outrageous, unbelievable and farcical, there is a grain of truth in it. You know it is not true, yet there is a recognisable truth in it. Such is the stuff of all great comedy.

Take Fawlty Towers for instance. It is also outrageous, unbelievable and farcical, but it is also hysterically funny. Why? Because all the characters are rooted in the truth. They all believe totally in their situation, and can therefore stretch that belief, and with it our belief, as if it were elastic, until it is just this side of breaking point.

Perhaps the best example is Basil beating his broken down car with the branch of a tree - a totally believable emotion taken to a virtually unbelievable conclusion, but in which you still recognise the truth of his anger.

In the same way, the 'How many actors…?' joke exposes their self-obsession and paranoia, by placing them in a virtually unbelievable situation, but in which you still recognise the truth of their envy.

I mention this, not to denigrate my chosen profession (it needs no help from me), but to confess that I too suffer from the same self-obsession and paranoia. The other week, for instance, in the heat of my excitement and self-congratulation, I omitted to tell you how I got the part in 'An Inspector Calls' in the first place.

I suppose that begs the question, 'How does any actor get a job?' 'With difficulty,' is the short answer. Let's face it, I can't nip down my local boozer and pick up a day's work, like a plumber/builder/scaffolder does, can I? Imagine:

"Pint of bitter, Jack. Don't know anybody who wants a bit of acting doing, do you?"

"Funny you should say that, Dave. The Casting Director from 'The Bill' was just in saying he was short-handed in the villain department, and would I spread the word."

"Don't know his number, do you?"

"No, but he'll be back later on. Said he's got to meet the Producer of EastEnders. Now there's a bloke might have something for you - he's Australian, actually, but funnily enough he's quite nice."

It just doesn't work like that, I'm afraid. The fact is, you can't get anywhere in my business without an agent. Lots of people think this means you just sit back, watching yourself in endless repeats, while your agent gets you a job.

Wrong.

An agent can't *get* you a job, but acts as a kind of clearing house. Mine gets information from all the casting directors about what is in the pipeline, sifts through it to see which part(s) I might be suitable for, and then suggests me to the appropriate person.

I then trot off up to London, at my own expense I might add, to meet the director and/or producer, usually at the casting director's office. There, we either just have a chat about their forthcoming production, or I am asked to 'read.' This involves acting out a page or two of the dialogue (after only a few minutes preparation), with the casting director's secretary reading all the other parts. It is at this point that you begin to wonder if you chose the right profession in the first place, as the secretary invariably gives a fantastic rendition, and makes you look a complete pillock.

In the case of 'An Inspector Calls', I had to go through this rigmarole twice. Firstly, for the eponymous role of the Inspector - at which I evidently failed miserably - and secondly, for the role of Mr. Birling, the other male lead - at which I evidently succeeded triumphantly, and was offered the part the following day. Happiness, you would think.

Wrong.

You see, an actor is a strange creature. Not only is he self-obsessed and paranoid, but he appears to be allergic to his own profession. He spends months in enforced unemployment, wallowing in self-pity and watching his mates on TV

David Roper

playing parts he could have done better, then when he lands a job, he complains about the work it involves and how it is interfering with his private life.

That is the stage I am at now, so excuse me while I trawl through the touring schedule to see how many days off I can find.

HOME, SWEET HOME

I am at home for a whole week, and I can't tell you what that means to me. Actually, that is not strictly true. Something I can tell you about being at home is that I have to report all the gossip to Andrea - not that she is a gossip herself, I hasten to add, but the girl does like to keep abreast of events.

Now, this puts me in a very difficult position, as I am the worst in the world at picking up thespic tittle-tattle. It probably comes from being self-obsessed, but I never have a clue when, how, what, where, why or who is doing what to whom. It is a standing joke in our house that if I was doing something I shouldn't, I would be the last one to know. So, if you hear any rumours about me, give us a bell, please, it will stop me worrying.

In fact, worrying was how I started this tour. I was really concerned about Andrea and the boys missing me. How would they cope without the man of the house?

In the event it was me who had the problem. You see, since I endured the agony of their birth seven years ago (if only Andrea knew what I went through!), I've only been away from the twins for about three months all told.

The wrench, as I left on that first day, was palpable. I was virtually in tears as I drove away up Wilson Avenue, and by the time I got to Brighton Racecourse I was ready to turn back and jack the whole thing in. How would I survive over 200 miles away and for 22 weeks, when I was an emotional wreck just over 200 *yards* away and for 22 *seconds*?

In the end, it wasn't that bad. I had great digs in Birmingham (more of digs later), which meant I was happy on a personal level, and the rigours of rehearsals and the production week kept my mind fully occupied.

But you can't beat home, can you? Or can you? From a touring actor's perspective (i.e. as just another set of digs) home can be a mixed blessing, it has to be said. Yes, I am in my own home with family and familiarity all around and no rent to pay - great - but I also have to fill the dishwasher, put the rubbish out, polish the table and sleep with the landlady, and to cap it all I don't get touring allowance!

However, I'll be brave and put up with it. You see, I love my home. Not just the house, of course, but the whole business of being a family. It came to me late in life (I was 45 when we married; 51 when the twins were born). Up to then, my life had been a series of mistakes, mostly mine, but I suppose it's better to have loved and left, than never to have loved at all.

Andrea was fully aware of my chequered career as a star of Stage, Screen and Wedding Reception, and it didn't take her long to knock me into shape. But that is what a woman is programmed to do, isn't it - knock a man into shape?

A man plays the field until he finds the woman most closely resembling his preconceived ideal, and accepts her, warts and all. A woman, on the other hand, plays the field until she finds an acceptable specimen, warts and all, and then proceeds to mould him into her preconceived ideal, starting with the warts.....

"Don't know who gave you those, but you're not coming near me 'til they're gone!"

All that kind of sums it up:

A man sees a woman as what he wants.

A woman sees a man as raw material.

Cynical as all that may seem, I think there is a grain of truth in it. Andrea was no different, and she instinctively saw her role as knocking me into her desired shape. For my part, I was well pleased to have found my ideal, and was quite happy to let her carry on. I had no problem with it, still don't, which is why you must excuse me as I happily fill the dishwasher, put the rubbish out, polish the table and …thank the landlady!

OF HIGHWAYS, HATS AND HITLER

Doesn't time fly? We are on the road now with 'An Inspector Calls', and our four weeks in Birmingham seem an age away – but what a city of contrasts it was.

The first impression is that it has been designed solely for the motor car. It is impossible to get anywhere without going under, over or across a four-lane highway, and even the pedestrianised areas have roads running through them! Perhaps the best, or worst, clue to Birmingham's obsession with the car, and willingness to do anything in its name, is the Five-ways roundabout, which has a plaque on it proudly declaring:

'On this site stood The King Edward VI Grammar School – 1883 to 1958.'

They gave up a school for a roundabout? I rest my case.

I must say, though, having risked life and limb crossing the roads (there are only two kinds of pedestrian in Brum – the quick and the dead), the City Centre is charming, and is choc-a-bloc with Georgian terraces, imaginatively lit canals, tempting bars and restaurants, and enough lap-dancing clubs to keep your mind occupied for weeks.

No, I didn't! For a start, I wouldn't have dared go in! Although, I must confess to a secret desire to visit one of these establishments, or something similar – for research purposes, you understand. It goes back to when I passed a joint in Soho, which advertised 'Nude women in bed – 50p'. Now this was irresistible…almost. What in the name of soft-porn was in there? Whatever it was, how could they offer it for 50p (including VAT, presumably)? I never did go in, but I know a man who did. Suffice to say, the deal involved a slot for your

15

coin, a peephole in the wall and a strong smell of cheap disinfectant – what do you expect for 50p – Dettol?

In Brum I would never have been allowed in the clubs, anyway, as I permanently contravened their dress code. I have never understood these sartorial sanctions, but this one was a pearler: 'No Jeans, Trainers or Hats.' Hats? What can it be about donning a titfer that turns a benign, bareheaded bloke into a horrendous, hatted hooligan? Search me, and they probably would have.

Near the theatre is a large, magnificent War Memorial. Now here's a funny thing – at each corner is a notice, saying: 'No Skateboarding'. Quite what the dead of two World Wars thought about Skateboarding isn't on record, but it struck me that they might have been a tad miffed to think that the fundamental freedom for kids of all races to play in peace was one of the causes they were fighting and dying for, and was here being denied in their name. I am not privy to what Hitler's policy was on Skateboarding, but I bet you a pound to a falling Euro it didn't involve Afro-Caribbean, Asian, Caucasian and Jewish kids doing it together, as they were, quite peacefully, that day.

Among a vast collection of excellent eating places (or 'Eateries', as the new lingo would have it) is a great French restaurant, nestling between a gorgeous, fountained square and one of the many twinkly-lit canals. The food is excellent, the atmosphere suitably French and the waitresses unfailingly attractive and attentive. Therein lies a problem. They will insist on clopping over every five minutes and asking,

"Is everything all right?"

I'd love to say,

"Not really. I've got this psychiatric disorder, which makes me throttle waitresses who ask, 'Is everything all right?' every five minutes." – but I don't. Like the rest of the acquiescent English I simply mumble, "Fine. Lovely, thank you." as if she had done me a favour by asking.

Why do we do it? Whatever you say about the French, and who doesn't, at least they have got their restaurant rules sorted. They don't mistake service for servility, and they don't need their customers to tell them their food is 'all right' - it is excellent. After all it is their job. I mean, you don't get actors nipping into the audience every five minutes, saying, "Is everything all right? If you don't like the play, I'll get J.B. Priestley to write you another."

But, all in all, Birmingham was a pleasure. I was staying with a dentist called Mr. Payne. Honest! His wife told me that they were only a hair's breadth away from calling their son Ivor, before the horrific consequences hit them.

By the time you read this, I will be packing to fly off to Glasgow. Now there's a city that even Birmingham is pushed to rival. I can't wait.

"Andrea! Have you finished my ironing yet?"

David Roper

IN BED WITH THE NIGHT PORTER

A few weeks ago I promised to return to the subject of digs, so here goes.

Contrary to what you might think, actors have to arrange these themselves. On this twenty-two week tour, that means me phoning round seventeen theatres (I'm commuting to five), requesting their Digs List – Hotels, B&Bs, self-contained flats, and people deranged enough to think sharing their house with an actor would be fun.

Rumour has it that in the old days actors would mark digs, where appropriate, L.D.O. (Landlady's Daughter Obliges) for the benefit of those coming after them, if you understand me.

It's OK, Andrea, nowadays, with drink-driving and all, proximity to the theatre is the main issue, and next to '10 minutes on foot to Theatre' you are more likely to find L.T.P (Landlady Tells Porkies), meaning that it may be 10 minutes for Linford Christie, but a good 45 minutes for the likes of you and me.

I tend to vary my digs, with a preference for the self-contained flat, as eating out on tour can be terminal for the old wallet, and cooking for myself can save £s.

That didn't hold true, however, when I took a room in a house in Nottingham many years ago. I'd expected to eat out every night at great expense, so was pleasantly surprised when the landlord said, "Shall I lay you out some food for after the show?"

Great, I thought! A sandwich or a bit of cold meat and salad would go down a treat after a few pints. When I got back on the first night, I could hardly believe my taste buds.

The kitchen table was heaving with a buffet that wouldn't have disgraced The Ritz. Prawns in aspic, slightly pink filet of beef, oranges in brandy – the lot. That's the only touring venue where I've ever left the pub before closing time.

At the other end of the scale, was the B&B where the landlady had such a Hitlerian regime that when she said Breakfast was at 8.00, she meant Breakfast was *at 8.00*. I ill-advisedly nipped out for a paper one morning at 7.55 and returned at 8.02 to find that I had missed it.

If I recall correctly, she also had just two House Rules:

No ladies in the upstairs rooms.

No solids in the downstairs lavatory.

Goodness knows what the consequences would have been if she'd collared you, as the bit of crumpet you'd clandestinely cajoled up to your room got caught short on the way down.

On the subject of bogs, there is a bathroom in Inverness that is close to my heart and will forever live in my memory. The landlady was evidently obsessed with things horticultural, and had surrounded the said bog with such a vivid and varied collection of plants, flowers and ferns that it took me all of five minutes to find it.

Once seated, however, I found it rather pleasant and peaceful, until I discovered that there wasn't a single piece of toilet paper in sight. Short of embarking on a mini-safari through the adjacent jungle, trousers round my ankles, and having nothing more than two postage stamps (2nd class) to hand, as it were, my only option was to put the leaf of a large Brother Candytuft *(Phalaenopsis)* to a more mundane and practical use than the decorative one for which it was intended. It did the job quite well.

Even the more upmarket world of hotel life can be confusing and stressful. Consider this intriguingly comma-less notice on the door of a hotel bedroom I once occupied:

'Place your order before 2.00am if you want breakfast in bed with the Night Porter'

Were the Management really prepared to offer this intimate extension to their Room Service, I wondered, or were they merely two commas short of a grammatical sentence? All week I waited, but he or she never turned up. Pity, really, I could have done with the company.

David Roper

But it is the Midland Hotel in Manchester that has pride of place in acting mythology. In the seventies, its Fire Alarm system would go off regularly in the early hours, and dozens of bleary-eyed actors would pile out into St. Peter's Square. I remember Peter (Last of the Summer Wine) Sallis telling me that, far from being an annoyance, he found it was the only way he got to meet up with all his old friends.

Actually, we are playing Manchester later on, so I'm off to book in...well, you never know who I might bump into.

MK = H9x(S4 + N2)

Milton Keynes - two words that have come to symbolise the ultimate suburban nightmare. But how true is it? I set off to find out during our week there with 'An Inspector Calls'.

It wasn't a promising start, I must say, even before I got there. My landlady said, "Turn right at the H3/V9 roundabout, first left and park behind the BMW."

You see, Milton Keynes, or MK in the local patois, has cornered the world market in concise, if somewhat ridiculous, road names, and holds the world record for roundabouts. There are 15 surrounding the central area of only half a square mile, and within that there are 43 car parks, 25 streets (named variously: North 2nd to 14th, South 5th to 10th, Upper 2nd to 5th and Lower 2nd to 10th) and nearby sits a gigantic arena called, in a triumph of hope over desperation, 'Xscape!' (The innumerable road signs, for whatever constitutes 'Xscape', do give MK a decidedly temporary atmosphere.)

Standing in the middle of it all, as I am now, it feels as though I've been dumped at Gatwick during an Air Traffic Controllers' strike – long empty avenues, glass-fronted buildings and people wandering around looking lost, as indeed I was.

I asked a bloke where the main Shopping Centre was. He replied, "I am No. 2. You are No. 5.", and wandered off to talk to Patrick McGoohan. Well, he might as well have done. Everybody I approached for directions either hadn't got a clue, or said something incomprehensible, like, "Hang a left at the H6 end of S10th, head up towards H5 and you can't miss it."

I couldn't live here. I'd never see the wife and kids again. It's taken me 15 years to grasp the difference between North Road and North Street in Brighton, without having to grapple with fourteen of the damn things.

Having said that, walking around MK is not unpleasant. There's a feeling of space, lots of greenery, it's easy to park and cross the road – you can see a car coming half a mile away (the Romans would have loved it here) – and the Shopping Centre, once located, is crowned with a branch of John Lewis.

Now, for Andrea and me, John Lewis is the merchandising equivalent of Mecca, and we are devout pilgrims. We journey miles, like kids with tickets to see Santa, just to have our store cards swiped and run up massive bills. What the South East has done to upset John Lewis, I don't know, but there isn't one single branch within a 30-odd mile radius of Brighton – now there's an idea for the West Pier.

Back in life's departure lounge, MK, overlooking runways H5 and V6, I bumped into a couple of the locals (L3 and L4) and their dog (K9 – sorry about the easy pun). They told me that, once you've succumbed to the idea that the whole of life is mapped out for you on an enormous grid system, living here is fine,   You see, I'm working in the 'Theatre District', next to the 'Food District', across from the 'Shopping District', adjacent to the 'City District', surrounded by the 'Residential District' and only a short hearse-ride from the 'Crematorium District'. You know where you are, you see.

In death, as in life, MK is ordered and compartmentalised - see a show on Monday, eat out on Tuesday, shop on Wednesday, bank a cheque on Thursday, pass away peacefully at home on Friday and get cremated on Saturday. What more could you ask for? And all with easy parking.

To escape, last night I tried for a pint in the 'Rat and Parrot' – it's real name, God help us – but the bouncers wouldn't let me in because I had a bottle of wine in a plastic bag from Waitrose (John Lewis again, see?)

"Sorry, Sir, we don't allow alcohol – this is a pub." I couldn't be bothered to argue my way through the logic involved in this statement, so I nutted the bigger one, slammed my knee into the other's groin and wandered off humming "If I can help some…body…"

To be fair, I can see some advantages in MK's layout and sense of order, but its fundamental trouble is that it has no centre, no soul, no blood running through its veins – essentially, no heart.

If a camel is a horse designed by a committee, then MK is Brighton created by a team of Town Planners.

I long to be back in the queue outside our car park in North Road…or is it North Street…or North 8th Street…or…damn, they've got me at it now!

ACCENT ON IRRESPONSIBILITY

Sorry, folks, but it's the week for getting things off my chest, or rather down from up my nose where they are forever getting lodged - dog owners, cyclists and Moira Stewart.

Let me set the record straight - I like dogs. What I don't like is that they have got a lethal weapon at one end and no sense of responsibility at the other, and that is where my beef with dog owners lies. You've met it:

"It's OK, he won't bite you."

Has the dog agreed to this? Has it signed a binding agreement? Has it seen 'Lassie'?

As for the 'business' end, well, I don't want to put my foot in it, but how much more doggy-doos can this planet take before it veers off its orbit?

I live near East Brighton Park, officially known as The East Brighton Dog Poo Depository, and it is a minefield. Watching a football match there, I thought the winger was practising his dribbling skills, until it became clear that he was actually steering a course through the innumerable piles of recycled Pedigree Chum.

True, many responsible owners do remove Rover's 'little message' (a dollop of gratitude for that) and, for all I know, they may even collect them, mounted in glass cases marked: 'East Brighton Park – 17.9.02' or 'St. James' Street – 23.1.03' or, God forbid, 'Nanny's Lounge – 25.12.02'. What a Christmas Day that was!

But it is the irresponsible among them who get my goat. Mark my words, you selfish dog owners, in an increasingly litigious society, it won't be long before one of you gets sued to the tune of £1 million for causing 'actual bodily harm' to a poor child who did a roly-poly through Rover's poo and picked up some horrendous eye disease!

Now, cyclists - *not* the aerodynamic Tour de France types, who flash silently through Alpine villages on their way from Bordeaux to Paris (haven't they heard of the N10?) - *nor* the family variety with their outsized crash helmets and a baby strapped precariously to the pannier like a parcel - *not even* the suicidal ones, who creep up on your inside as you turn left at the traffic lights, and then disappear in your rear-view mirror, mutely mouthing obscenities from their prostrate position on the pavement.

No, the ones I am banging on about are the Schizophrenic sorts, who can't decide whether they are a pedestrian or a car, but believe they have the inalienable rights of both and the fundamental responsibilities of neither.

They flout the law by riding full throttle on the pavement, taking corners on two wheels (OK, it is all they have got, but you know what I mean) and endangering the life of any old couple foolish enough to emerge from the Post Office at the wrong moment. Even on the roads, these cowboys wilfully ignore every rule in the Highway Code - and many that aren't. They tear through red traffic lights as if colour blind, they go the wrong way round roundabouts and up one-way streets, and they resolutely refuse to use cycle lanes. Woe betide you, though, if you dare to walk in the said cycle lane, as they appear from nowhere and berate you for taking up their God given space.

Psychotic cyclists beware! The day will come when some Government will wake up to your dictatorship of our pavements, and declare war on your irresponsibility and propensity for mass destruction - with or without a U.N. Resolution.

So, what could I possibly have against Moira Stewart? Not a lot, to be honest, but what there is irritates me beyond measure. She is clear, pleasant and audience friendly, but, and this is difficult to explain in print, she will insist on adopting the accent of the country of origin of any proper name that happens to pop up on her auto-cue. I am not talking about *pronunciation*, but *accent*.

Take the sentence, 'In Grenoble, today, Francois Mitterand resigned'. With a nod to French pronunciation, Grenoble would be Grenobler, and Mitterand would be Mitteron. Let the fragrant Moira loose, however, and they become Grrrenobler and Meetterrrorn, heavily accented.

Why does she do this? It is totally unnecessary and wildly pretentious. I think the answer lies deep within Anglo-Saxon linguistic insularity and insecurity. We all know we are crap at languages, or merde, as Moira might have it, so her

25

subtext is, "Listen, I know how Johnny Foreigner talks, even if you don't, so cop this, mon brrrave!"

Oh, cripes! My worst nightmare has just passed the window! Moira on a bike, taking her dog for a dump in East Brighton Park!

LOST IN TRANSLATION

You find me having coffee and a Danish inside my favourite building in Glasgow – Princes Square.

What a changed city this is since I first came in the Seventies. There was so much crime and violence about then, even the police cars had to creep around in twos.

I read yesterday that Glasgow is now one of the safest cities in the world, which doesn't say an awful lot for the world, but it is comforting to know that, statistically, I should survive the week in one piece.

Since being voted European City of Culture, if that is not a contradiction in terms, Glasgow has undoubtedly smartened up its act. One of the secrets of its success, architecturally at any rate, is that the authorities have resolutely refused to bulldoze any of the beautiful Victorian stone facades.

With its exterior intact and an interior blended tastefully into the original walls, Princes Square is a prime example. It is full of up-market clothes shops (so up-market nothing is priced, but there you go), cafes and restaurants and features a Foucault's Pendulum, swinging back and forth and proving that the Earth rotates, or so it says.

I am staying in Renfrew Street, which is full of B&Bs and small hotels. The odd thing is - they all advertise the 'Famous Scottish Breakfast'. Call me picky, but the only discernible difference between the 'Famous Scottish Breakfast' that I was presented with this morning, and the 'Famous English Breakfast' I am used to, was that I was eating it north of the border.

It was no more Celtic than ours is Anglo-Saxon - the tomatoes were Spanish, the pieces of dead pig were Danish and the sausage, as always, was undercooked and of unknown origin. Only the egg and the waitress were possibly Scottish, and even then I couldn't be sure, as neither of them said a word.

I put it all down to Scottish Nationalism. Don't get me wrong, I think the Scots and Scotland are great, and good luck to them in their fight for a stronger national identity. I just sense that they feel compelled, quite unnecessarily, to overstate that national identity, as compensation for centuries of domination by the English.

Stand by for: 'The roast beef of Old Scotland'; the 'typical Scottish Rose'; 'Scottish Tea'. After all, we're already subjected to 'Yorkshire Tea', which, as we all know, is produced from that well-known northern Tea Plant – Infusionia Eeebygumia.

Oh yes, how well I remember, at my grandmother's knee, being told tales of her toil, lugging large loads of leaves across the vast Tea Plantations of Tadcaster and Pontefract.

On my way to Princes Square, in Buchanan Street - a quite splendid pedestrianised avenue - I stumbled across a small army of men at work behind a sign saying:
CAUTION!
Chewing Gum Removal in Progress

Now this is a relatively recent phenomenon, and evidently has spawned a whole new Industry and created limitless job opportunities. Scottish school-leavers no longer fear unemployment (sorry, Jobseeking), but rather they rush headlong to join the burgeoning queue of prospective Gum Removal Operatives, snaking its way along Sauchiehall Street. They wait patiently, secure in the knowledge that the more globs of gum they gob onto the pavement, as they queue, the greater their chances of getting a job clearing it up - the perfect Job Creation Scheme!

Much has indeed changed in Glasgow, mostly for the better, but one thing remains constantly confusing - the virtually impenetrable Glaswegian accent.

In a common or garden boozer the other evening, there was nobody behind the bar, and only two middle-aged male customers. With that canniness unique to the Scots, one of them sensed that I had come in for a drink, and said:
"Jockstrapping your willy's a sin to Cilla."
"Pardon?"
"Jockstrapping your willy's a sin to Cilla."

Having no phrase book to hand, I had to ask him to repeat this extract from the Blind Date Contestants' handbook four times, before it dawned on my untutored ear that what he was helpfully trying to say was:

"Jock's the chappie you're wanting, he's in the cellar."

Our ensuing conversation was a Russ Abbot sketch made flesh. After several abortive attempts I managed to translate "You appear wankin?" into the more acceptable "You up here working?", but after my second pint I started to get the hang of it.

"Seen yonder bollocks?" (Seen you on the Box?)

"Trite!" (That's right – not bad for a first attempt, I thought)

"You a nectarine?" (You an actor then? - my favourite one, I admit))

"Yam." (I am)

"Warts arse senior?" (What have I seen you in?)

"Och! Arse in suspenders, yes, I go." (Oh, I was in EastEnders years ago.)

I was particularly enamoured of my use of the indigenous 'Och', which seemed to go down well with him too. I downed my pint, and with a cheery "Kat Slater!" (Catch you later!), I wandered out into George Square, flushed with pride at having mastered another language in under twenty minutes.

"Omagh gunners! I've just no tits!" (Oh, my goodness, I've just noticed!) Foulcault's ruddy Pendulum has stopped swinging! Either it is closed for maintenance, or the Earth has stopped rotating and I am about to be flung off into outer space! Speak to you next weee.........!

David Roper

REVIEWING THE TROOPS

The audience response to 'An Inspector Calls' has been excellent. Well, it is a tried and tested play, and this innovative production has been performed for ten years to rapturous receptions all over the world, so something is right.

It's fantastic to be in a successful production, and makes our job that much easier. So much so, we've all been getting excellent personal reviews as well, and it's every actor's dream to have the papers on his side.

You see, we have a love/hate relationship with the press. We love them when they are nice to us, and hate them when they are not, but we detest them when they ignore us! There is one thing worse than being recognised - *not* being recognised.

The great Press paradox is that they bend over backwards to give birth to a new 'star' and trumpet his/her arrival, only to joyfully join in years later, as the knives go in and the bleeding corpse of a career lies in the gutter alongside the Press that put it there.

OK, I confess! I am not a great fan the Popular Press (The Sun, Mirror etc.). I prefer the Unpopular Press (The Independent, Guardian etc.). Is it a coincidence that the former are tabloid size, while the latter are broadsheets, at least for the moment? If I were unkind, I'd say there is a linear correlation between those sizes and the brain power of their respective readers - but I'm not, so I won't, and the local Brighton paper disproves it, of course.

I have thought long and hard about why people read 'the tabloids' - the workings of an idle mind, eh? My conclusion is that reading them is the literary equivalent of 'rubber-necking' at road accidents, and is an example of the Greek notion of 'the purging effect of tragedy', which amounts to the same thing.

Witnessing the fall, demise or destruction of another human being (real or imagined) from the safety of a car, sofa or theatre seat reinforces your sense of security, and makes you thankful for what you have got. The Germans, of course, with due etymological efficiency, have encapsulated it in one word: schardenfreude. Do you know, I never realised that the tabloids were so altruistic. But then, as someone once said:

"Before I got my Social Sciences degree, I used to read The Sun. I still read it, of course, only now I know why I'm doing it."

Others profess to read it for the sports coverage - oh, yes? Incidentally, for really good sports reporting try The Daily Telegraph. Its football section is comprehensive, although it does have a tendency to be over-complementary to right-wingers and over-critical of strikers.

But back to my subject: many actors refuse to read reviews, and those who do always have the same response. If it's a favourable review about them, they'll say:

"I didn't think I was all that good last night!"

At a stroke, self-deprecatingly inferring from the review how great the reviewer thinks the actor is, while self-importantly implying that greater things are possible.

If the review is bad, though, you will hear:

"He didn't understand the play, of course, and it's only one person's opinion, anyway!"

You see an actor is like a dog. He responds playfully to praise and slavvers all over you, but recoils curtly from criticism and curls himself up in a corner to cry. So, next time you see me, do us a favour – pat me on the head and give me a bone, it will make my day. Thanks.

Critics themselves are not above criticism, of course. The story has it that one of them sneaked out of a Church Hall amateur production of 'Hobson's Choice' just before the interval, and went to the pub to write his habitual complimentary review. He delivered it next morning, and it was on the streets by lunchtime. He had particularly praised the leading man's performance in the second act, blissfully unaware that the Church Hall had burned down ten minutes after he had left.

The shortest review I have heard of was for a play called 'Queen Elizabeth slept here' – it ran to all of 3 words – 'So did I!'

I have had some wonderful reviews, and some damn awful ones - ranging from 'David Roper treated us to the best piece of acting ever seen in this theatre' all the way down to 'Mr. Roper desperately needs to work on his unconvincing drunken acting' and 'Roper's Scottish accent was appalling'. But the worst review I ever had was when playing the lead in 'Noises Off' - the reviewer never even mentioned me! How's that for making an impression?

Hang about! Andrea's arrived with a copy of The Sun. I better have a quick look…at the sports coverage, of course!

JOBS FOR THE BOYS

When the show was in Brighton a few weeks ago, our twins, Harry and Jack, were in it with me (we recruit four or five kids at each venue). Since then they have enrolled for drama classes - at their own request, I might add, in case you think we are pushy parents.

In the car the other day I asked them what they wanted to be. Jack said, "An actor." and Harry said, "A footballer and an actor." I pointed out this might prove difficult when an away match at Old Trafford clashed with the Saturday matinee in Inverness, but he didn't seem to think it a problem - "I'd have an understudy, wouldn't I?"

Alternatively, I suggested, he could always get himself sent off in the first five minutes, like Jack did the other week, as a result of two highly contentious and dangerous flying tackles. I have no idea where he gets that kind of behaviour from - I blame the parents.

The thing is, do we want them to be actors in the first place? OK, I have survived in the business for well over 40 years, but it has been ruddy difficult at times, ask Andrea. She has often gone days without buying a new outfit.

Objection!

Sustained!

I apologise, your honour, I mustn't have a go at the defendant, especially as she has just phoned me to say she has scratched the car - again. Unbelievably, she actually got someone to help her this time. Unable to get out of a parking space, she charmed a passing workman into doing it for her, and between them they etched scratches on the driver's door like the tail of Hailey's Comet.

But to the point. Acting is a roller coaster existence. Sometimes I have worked for years, but at other times I have done one day's work in 18 months, and that is hard.

Quite frankly, I think the boys would be far better off with a career in plumbing. Now there is a steady, well paid, cash in hand calling, if ever there was one. You work when you like, charge what you like and meet the most charmingly gullible members of the public.

Plumbers are like Consultant Surgeons these days, only more expensive. They get paid for just turning up, and therein lies their great trade secret – the 'turning up trick.' It works like this:

Customer phones at 10am with problem. You'll be round at 5.00pm.

You don't turn up.

Anxious customer phones at 6pm. You are in Eastbourne, at a flooded Old Peoples Home, but you will be round at 8am tomorrow.

You don't turn up.

Desperate customer phones at 9am. You had your tools stolen last night, but you'll borrow a mate's and be round at 12 noon.

You don't turn up.

Frantic customer phones at 1pm. Your mate's wife has gone into labour, and he is at the hospital with his tools, but you will get them and be round at 6pm.

You switch off your mobile, and turn up at 7.25pm.

Delirious customer almost wets herself at seeing you. She happily calms down to watch Coronation Street, willingly pays you whatever you ask and enthusiastically recommends you to all her friends.

To be fair, getting away with this is not down to plumbers, but is predicated on supply and demand. There is a national shortage of them (30,000, I read), but demand for their services is rising. Result: the market is theirs, and prices increase. Solution: either reduce demand (impossible, unless we all take our washing down to the river), or increase supply, by training more plumbers. So why aren't we doing this? Answer: because we are obsessed with academic achievement and league tables, leading to an over-emphasis on paper qualifications and an under-emphasis on 'the trades'. A-levels are there for the taking, and Degrees are 10 a penny, sorry 10 grand each. Soon we will all have letters after our names, and Gilbert and Sullivan will be proved right: 'When everyone is somebody, then no-one's anybody.'

Hence the attraction of steering the twins towards plumbing, regardless of my own academic background, which has consigned me to being the most useless member of the family, in any practical sense.

The boys have obviously got a talent for the trade. They constantly leave taps running all over the house, and regularly stuff the Loo with reams of bog roll.

"Harry! Jack! The washing machine's leaking!"

"Sorry, Dad, we're busy unblocking the Loo, but we'll be round at six."

That's my boys!

David Roper

FOOD FOR THOUGHT

This is nice. I have just settled myself down in a Pizza Express restaurant opposite Cardiff Castle. I can't actually see Cardiff Castle, but it is good to know it is there.

To get here I walked through Bute Park, a large and beautifully laid out grassy area adjoining the aforementioned Castle, and through which the River Taff meanders soothingly. The magnolia trees are in full bloom and, this being Wales, as you will have guessed, the whole place is carpeted with – yes, another good guess - daffodils.

I had a really peaceful stroll, gazing at the river from the footbridge and walking through the arboretum. Watching the gardeners tending this idyllic scene, I was reminded of a version of 'An Ode to a Garden' that Clifford, a friend of mine, penned:

'God gave us the trees and the flowers
And all things that truly have worth,
But you're nearer to a hernia in a garden
Than anywhere else on Earth.'

More of Clifford's wit and wisdom later.

My poetic mood continued, and the Muse visited me as I stood gazing at one massive Oak:

'I'm standing here, a quite intelligent bloke.
You're standing there, a gnarled and knotty Oak.
I have a brain, can think and so give thanks
I'm not like you and thick as two short planks.

OK, you're bigger than I'll ever be,
But you will never be as smart as me!
You'll never have a chat with all your mates.
You'll never drink from cups, or eat off plates.
You'll never see inside the Castle walls.
You'll never star in 'An Inspector Calls.'
But maybe I'm not really all that clever,
'Cos, like as not, you'll thrive and live for ever.
In centuries men still will see your wonder,
But me? Well, I'll be dead and six feet under!'

Bute Park is festooned with bi-lingual signs (English and Welsh, needless to say), and it's obviously national policy that everything, from Ambulances to Zoos, must be signed in both.

Now Welsh, like Polish, is one of those unpronounceable languages and contains words which look like something Carole Vorderman has just stuck up on the 'Countdown' board.

No, I am not going to have a pop at Welsh. I just wonder why Wales and England have such startlingly different languages, so I did a bit of digging. What follows will either fascinate you, or bore you to tears – take your pick.

In most European countries there are lots of words you could guess the meaning of. You know the sort of thing: in French – un repas = a meal or repast; in Spanish – mucho = a lot or much; in German – uber alles = over all. Not so in Welsh. For example: the English word - International - translates in Welsh as - Ryngwladol - by no stretch of the imagination is there any common ground there.

It seems that Welsh is of direct descent from the Brythonic language of Roman Briton, whereas English is descended from a collection of languages, due to various invasions over the centuries.

As a result of those invasions, the Welsh nation (the original Celtic English) was driven westwards and they split up into several communities, among them Welsh, Cornish and Breton (in the Northwest corner of France). To this day, apparently, it is still possible for a Welshman and a Breton to understand each other, albeit with a bit of effort, and it is easier for a Welsh speaker to learn Breton than it is for a Frenchman.

There, that wasn't too bad, was it?

Ah, you must excuse me, as my Napolitana pizza, with extra anchovies, has just arrived. You know, I really am a great fan of Pizza Express, and I seek one out wherever I go. The thing about them is that they've somehow cracked the secret of all being exactly the same, yet seemingly totally different from each other. They have exactly the same menu, system, general design and quality of food, but each of them has a stamp of individuality in either the building, décor or layout.

Many of them feature live music - jazz or classical, typically. As a matter of policy, I am not too keen on any extraneous noise in a restaurant, apart from the inevitable slurping and burping and waitresses working. However, Pizza Express present their music in such an understated way that you can enjoy it or talk over it with equal ease.

I wonder if they will give me a lifetime supply of Napolitanas (with extra anchovies, please) for this glowing recommendation? Google me with offers asap.

THE ROOT OF IT ALL

It turns out that three of us in the cast of 'An Inspector Calls' were trained in Bristol. No world shattering coincidence, granted, but enough of one to kick off a trip down memory lane.

I was at The Bristol Old Vic Theatre School from 1969 to 1971, arriving just a couple of months after my 25th birthday.

Short pause while you work out how old I am…got it?

Most of the other students were in their teens, so I was very much the 'father' of the school. This was compounded by the fact that I was also married - not to Andrea, I hasten to add, which was just as well, as she would have been nine at the time, and I would have been arrested.

My two years there were fantastic, once I had got into the swing of things. You see, I had given up a career in Accountancy, qualifying in 1967, and the switch to Drama School was necessarily something of a culture shock. Swapping double-entry book-keeping for drama and ballet exercises took a bit of getting used to, I can tell you. Old habits die hard, as they say, so in the early days I would turn up at the School in the collar and tie I had been used to wearing at the Office - prat!

Within three weeks of starting, half a dozen of us were co-opted into The Bristol Old Vic Theatre Company itself as spear carriers and to play small - OK I admit it - *tiny* parts in Macbeth. I was cast as Seyton and had the line 'The queen, my Lord, is dead.' I thought I did it really well, and could not for the life of me understand why I was not mentioned in the reviews - the arrogance of youth.

Funnily enough, that line has gone down in acting mythology. In an East London Drama School production of the play (with the late, great Kevin Lloyd as Macbeth) the line, for some reason, had been changed from 'The queen, my

39

Lord, is dead.' to '*Your wife*, my Lord, is dead.' - probably to do with the Director spotting that Macbeth was not yet king, I suppose, so his wife could not be the queen - fair enough.

The actor playing Seyton duly made his entrance, but the line-change had confused him and he transposed the line to:

"*My* wife, *your* Lord, is dead."

Kevin thought for a sec and said,

"Is she? What about my wife?"

"Oh…errm…she's dead as well," said Seyton, realising his mistake and, at the same time, more or less forcing Kevin to utter the immortal line:

"There's a lot of it about, isn't there?"

I just wish I had been there.

A lot of the work at Drama School revolves around stripping away all the idiosyncrasies, inhibitions and imaginative barriers which build up in all of us over the years. In a phrase, it is about 're-learning how to play.' Look at any group of children and you will see how uninhibited and imaginative they are. They will turn a cardboard box into a castle, or a settee into a shop, and really believe in what they are doing.

As we get older, we lose this ability in the maze of grown-up responsibilities, rejections and rationalisations. In other words - we put away childish things. Drama School is largely about dragging them all out again. After all, acting, at its root, is just pretending - to love; to hate; to laugh; to cry; to…whatever.

It is a cliché that drama classes are all about standing around pretending to be a tree, but we actually did it, and it does have a relevance. It makes you aware of your body's capacity to contract and expand: to curl up small (as you might in fear); to stand tall (as you might to be dominant). It also leads the way to opening up your imagination and, more to the point, closing down your inhibitions.

I must say, though, our first attempt was somewhat inhibited in itself, as it was on the day the windows were being cleaned. There we were, thirty butch blokes and leotard-clad lasses, giving an improvised demonstration of collective arboreal growth in front of a Bristolian window cleaner, who must have thought we were all stark raving mad.

There is a practical side to drama training, of course. I learned to fence, ride a horse, dance (after a fashion), sing (all right, let's forget that one) and 'talk proper'. However, it has to be said, I did not come across many scenes in EastEnders where I was asked to have a swordfight, on horse-back, while singing and dancing, but one of these days…. watch out for it!

ANYTHING YOU CAN DO...

Having a lot of time to myself on this tour I have rather rashly taken to thinking. Now, this is never a pastime to be taken lightly, particularly during those difficult male menopausal years, which I fear are upon me, but it has led me to unearth a great discovery - there is a difference between men and women!

It has been bothering me for years, on and off. I knew there was something different about them, but I could never quite put my finger on it, if you get my drift.

I am not talking about the obvious piddling little things, like wearing or not wearing a dress (and that is a grey area down Church Road of a Saturday night, believe me), nor that a woman is incapable of going to the loo without turning a basic human necessity into a mini girls' night out. Can you imagine a bloke saying,

"I'm off for a pee. Do you want to come, lads?"

Why do women always have to go en masse? It is not as if they can stand side by side having a good old chinwag, is it? They have to sit in their separate cubicles and dish the dirt by shouting under or over the partition, I suppose.

No, what I am talking about are the deep-rooted differences:

Why can't men do more than one thing at once, whereas women cope with kids, cooking and phone calls all at the same time?

Why can't women park cars and read maps, whereas men, as we all know, perfected the three-point turn in order to exit the womb head first?

Why do men always have the exact money ready at the supermarket check-out, whereas women spend two years fumbling through their entire make-up stock, as the queue lengthens into infinity?

Why are women so disinterested in traffic-jams, whereas men get out of the car, chat to all the other blokes and return with the astounding news, "We're in a traffic-jam! Chap in front is from Ipswich. He's going to Taunton. On the

A30, would you believe! I told him 'use the A303, mate.' He wouldn't listen. Mind you, he's driving a Skoda, so what do you expect?"

I think the reason for these things lies deep within our primeval past, when men were hunter-gatherers, needing to navigate and be single-minded, and women were child-bearing home providers, needing to cope at home and be flexible.

It makes sense. A few years back an American couple, on 'Punch and Judy's' daytime TV chat show, or whatever it was called, said there was now scientific proof that differences in various parts of our brains meant that men and women were genetically predisposed to being good/bad at certain things. Their underpinning contention was that we should all accept this situation, and not fight ourselves and each other over an unalterable fact of life.

I think they have got a point, you know. I mean look at Andrea and me. In our house, it is manifestly true that I find it impossible to do more than one thing at once. I am forever saying,

"I can't talk about that now! I'm chopping an onion!"

Andrea, though, can easily talk about complex issues, while fending off the kids, making a Shepherd's Pie and watching 'Neighbours'.

However, when it comes to driving and maps I find it a doddle to relate the one to the other, but Andrea hasn't a clue. The only thing she is certain of, geographically speaking, is that it is not a good idea to drive south out of Brighton, except in a boat.

Whenever we travel any long distance, I find it impossible not to have a map in my mind of where we are and where we are going. Andrea couldn't care less. All she needs to know is how long it will take, and what is our E.T.A. at the next loo. She couldn't give a toss that to get to Birmingham, say, you need the M23, M25, M40 and M42 (unless there's road works round Banbury, when you'd use the M1 and M6, naturally). To me this is the stuff of life; to Andrea it is just so much mumbo-jumbo.

The point is we are both right about these things, and it all supports that American couple's thesis. Men and women should embrace their respective talents and limitations, and learn to live with them and with each other.

So, I hereby swear that I will make no more jokes about Andrea's driving and map-reading, and I will try my utmost to do more than one thing at....

"No, I'm sorry, love, I can't open a tin of ruddy Marrowfat peas! I'm writing, can't you see!"

Well, one step at a time, eh?

GOD'S A YORKSHIREMAN?

In the good old days everything was closed on Good Friday (today). Not anymore. I am in Ipswich on a Bank Holiday, and the only places closed are the banks!

I have just emerged from W.H.Smith's with The Times. There was a box to put the money in - instead of queuing - and I admit I had an urge to do a runner, just for the hell of it, but I didn't. My Methodist upbringing still exerting its influence, I guess.

On the front page of the paper is an article about the Archbishop of Canterbury, Rowan Williams, washing the feet of twelve of his congregation, echoing Christ's demonstration of humility in washing the feet of the Disciples at The Last Supper. Church finances being what they are, our Rowan might have been better off turning the water into wine and flogging it off, but it was a nice gesture all the same.

Boy, does that bring back memories for me! In the seventies, I played Christ in 'The Passion' at Exeter's Northcott Theatre. Being quite well-built, it was obvious my Christ hadn't stinted himself at The Last Supper, which made hoisting me onto the Cross somewhat heavy going for the soldiers crucifying me. One of them was played by Brian Capron (latterly, the dastardly Richard Hillman from 'Coronation Street'), so I suppose that I was his first victim, and it was his first stab at murdering the innocent.

He had to hit me, kick me and spit at me, but never once did he hurt me. The only night it didn't go quite according to plan was when his pretend spit actually materialised and landed. I don't want to spoil your breakfast, but having somebody's 'stuff' dribbling down your face isn't my idea of a fun night out at the

43

theatre. But I forgive you, Brian, assuming you're reading this - and if not, why not?

I also had to wash the Disciples feet, and it was a humbling and revealing experience, I must say - don't some actors have dirty toenails!

Years later, in 'The Mysteries' for the Royal National Theatre, the positions were reversed. I was one of the Disciples, and so was on the receiving end of the foot-washing by Christ (Karl Johnson). The trouble was, being incredibly ticklish, I couldn't stand him touching the soles of my feet. On the first night I was hopping up and down in fits of agonised laughter.

The strange thing was, far from spoiling the moment, this exhibition of physical vulnerability made it that much more poignant and human. The audience loved it. After all, statistically, one of Christ's Disciples must also have had ticklish feet, or was Judas just giggling at the thought of what he was going to spend the money on?

In that production, the late Brian Glover (from Barnsley, Yorkshire) played God. That's the third time I have used the word 'late' in describing a fellow actor - was it something I said?

That reminds me of a story about the late (there I go again) Tony Hancock. Brian Murphy was touring Australia with the stage version of 'George and Mildred', directed by Tony Clayton. One night they were in the pub next to the theatre in Sydney, and the barman said:

"Do you know, I was the last person to speak to Tony Hancock before he went off and committed suicide."

Quick as a flash, Murphy said,

"What exactly did you say?"

Back to Glover as God. My parents came down from Yorkshire to see the show, and I asked them what they thought. My mum said:

"Quite good, but one thing was wrong. God was never a Barnsley man."

Being in those plays took me back to the roots of theatre - religion and the church. To this day, Anglican and Roman Catholic services are still essentially theatrical productions, involving elaborate costumes, music and dramatic delivery, set in sumptuous surroundings, and telling a gripping story.

My Methodist background involved little of that. We had a plain Hall, hard seats and some bloke at the front telling us to stop having lascivious thoughts. But how could I not, sandwiched as I usually was between Judith Hebblethwaite and Susan Crabtree, both smelling, headily of 'Revlon - beauty on a budget' perfume?

Neither of them was sex-on-a-stick, but in those days, sitting thigh to suspendered thigh was about as close as you could get to 'number ten' in our numerical scale of sexual attainment. All we could look forward to was squeezing a girl's hand, snatching a tight-lipped peck (no tongues for us) and rushing home for a sly cup of cocoa and 'Riders of the Range'. Ah, the good old days!

David Roper

PERMISSION TO LAND

Arriving at the airport, it was obvious that Aberdeen is somewhat unique. I don't know the collective noun for helicopters (a rotor?), but I certainly could have done with it as I watched several of them hovering gracefully overhead. It seems as though everybody gets around by chopper in this place. Even the hospital on the way into the City Centre has its own helipad prominently displayed by the roadside - how cool is that?

The City Centre itself has the obvious signs of a great past, a lucrative present and a secure future – granite buildings, restaurants and bars, and an off-shore oil supply that will outlive us all. What more can you say about a city with all that?

Quite a lot, actually, and Aberdeen is so proud of it all that there are lists of its fifty greatest achievements posted all over the place. Here is a small selection:

330 restaurants

busiest civilian heliport in the world (told you)

first Iron Lung – 1933

water polo invented – 1863

first self-seal envelope

Far be it from me to criticise a city that has welcomed me, fed and watered me, and entertained me with such largesse and friendliness, but I have to say that in the great catalogue of human ingenuity I don't reckon water polo and the self-seal envelope rate too highly as contributions to civilisation.

Having said that, many aspects of life here are indeed eminently civilised; not least of all the licensing hours or lack of them. On the first night we went to the theatre's local boozer, The Noose and Monkey. It was…ah!…

...I must pause here to explain that this establishment is not part of some ludicrously named chain, but is so-called because of the isolationist and xenophobic leanings of the good burghers of Hartlepool. Why that particular port's population should have been singled out for such a memorial lies in the fact that, during the Napoleonic Wars, they dragged ashore the sole survivor of a wrecked French ship - a monkey. Having never seen or heard a Frenchman before, and as the monkey was of human proportions, but didn't understand English and was incomprehensible when it 'spoke', they concluded that they had captured a grossly unshaven French sailor, with an excess of body hair and somewhat dubious personal hygiene. Therefore, they summarily hanged him as a prisoner of war. Good job for them that the Geneva Convention had yet to materialise, leave alone the Animal Rights Movement. Why this particular Aberdeen brewery felt moved to adopt the name is a mystery to me.

Back in the pub it was two minutes to eleven, and nobody had called last orders.

"What time do you close?"

"Midnight, usually."

Wow! Not only that; the local chippie stayed open until 3.00am, so you could mop up that midnight pint with haddock and chips as you staggered home. Civilised or what?

But there is one crucial area where Aberdeen really scores and can claim to be the smartest, most pristine and financially clued up city in the UK - the state of its pigeons. It is a well-known fact that if you want to get the flavour of a place study its pigeons. Actually, I just made that up, but it could well have a grain of truth in it. You see, being at the bottom of the food chain, pigeons always accurately reflect what is above them, and the Aberdonian pigeon population is, per force, well-fed, immaculately clean and unerringly polite.

As I sat in Castle Gate, on the Thursday of our visit with 'An Inspector Calls', twenty of them were being fed by two middle-aged ladies. One of them waddled over (a pigeon, that is, not a middle-aged lady) and politely waited at me feet for a scrap of food.

Unfortunately, I had nothing to offer so, with a sympathetic nod of the head, he puffed out his chest, cooed enticingly and waddled back to try and mate with the nearest female. I think he had missed his chance, as she was pecking idly at a post-coital fag end.

At that moment an enormous skinhead seagull was given clearance to land (so big, Air Traffic Control must've spotted it), and proceeded to mug two pretty

47

pigeons of a discarded piece of wholemeal bread - cholesterol being high on their agenda, of course, in such a healthy environment as Aberdeen.

Pigeons do bring problems, naturally, and they will drop things on your head from time to time, but as a reflection of the real Aberdeen - friendly, spruce, well-heeled – they should have pride of place on the city's Coat of Arms.

Ooops! It is getting late, and I fly back to Gatwick in the morning, so you must excuse me. Early start and all that - the helicopter to take me to the airport is due at 7.30 am. Night, night.

FAME IS THE SPUR

Salford Quays, where we are this week on our tour with the play, is Brighton Marina in a cloth cap. It has the executive houses and apartments, the designer outlets, the restaurants and bars, and lots of water (in this case, the Manchester Ship Canal). What it lacks, though, is people, but I suspect Brighton Marina would be hard pushed to attract many if it were not for the sainted ASDA.

Considering that Salford Quays' very existence is due to the Lowry Theatre, named after L.S.Lowry, whose paintings are teeming with 'matchstick' men and women, it is ironic that it is so devoid of the real thing, matchstick-thin or not.

Why do they build these places in the middle of nowhere? As I sit here, the sole occupant of the dozens of benches, looking across the water at the Manchester United stadium - I have never been as close to so much money in my life - the penny drops. Salford Quays is a tax-efficient investment for footballers with too much loose change in their pockets - of course! Also, trust the BBC to cash in on a good thing. Since I first put pen to paper, they have moved up here lock, stock and studios.

Two miles away are Manchester and Granada TV, which both played a pivotal role in my early career. I started as a fully-fledged actor at the Library Theatre, Manchester, in 1972, and my first TV role was for Granada TV in 1974. I was in 'Coronation Street' playing the copper who arrested Eddie Yates for nicking tins of corned beef from the corner shop. Walking into the 'Coronation Street' make up department and seeing all those famous faces I had known for years, lined up having their slap put on, was nerve wracking, I can tell you. I knew them by their character names, of course, so it was weird to hear 'Ken' calling 'Deirdre' Ann, and her calling 'Ken' Bill. But even they could get confused. In one episode, apparently, Bill Roach ('Ken Barlow') came into The Rovers, where Doris Speed ('Annie Walker') was serving, and said, "Hello, Doris, half of bitter, please." Nobody noticed he had used her real name, and the episode was broadcast, so I understand.

'Coronation Street' stories are legendary and often involve Doris. Years later, Harry Kershaw, one of its formative producers, told me that when they were on a promotional tour of Australia he was desperately trying to find the Press Officer, called Norman. He knocked on Doris' hotel room door and called her name. Back came the reply,

"Harry, I'm getting into the shower and I'm stark naked. What is it?"

"Terribly sorry, Doris. Is Norman with you?"

Back in the make-up room I took my place, and a couple of minutes later a bleary-eyed Doris herself sat down beside me. She looked in the mirror, squinted at her reflection and said to the make-up girl,

"Glenda, there are two eyes somewhere in that lump of dough, and it's your job to find them."

On the set the cameras were rolling, and my big moment was imminent. I was to catch Eddie in Bet Lynch's flat. Nerves were jangling though, as I pulled instead of pushed, and the door knob came off in my hand - I couldn't get in! The Floor Manager gave me an almighty shove, I burst in at a rate of knots, somehow managed to get my two words out, and the Director complimented me on a fantastic entrance. Such is the happenstance of TV acting.

But Manchester and Granada's most important contribution to my career was without doubt 'The Cuckoo Waltz', which brought instant fame to Diane Keen, Lewis

Collins and me on 27th October, 1975. At 7.30pm on that autumn Monday nobody knew who I was, but by 8.00pm nearly 20 million people could recognise my face, and by the next morning my life had changed forever.

It is difficult to describe what that kind of sudden visual fame feels like. Over the intervening thirty or forty years I have got used to it, so has Andrea, and it has become part of our everyday life. Wherever we go, even abroad, the chances are that somebody will know who I am.

Curiously, that kind of exposure often gives way to a feeling of isolation. People, who might otherwise talk to you, shy away because they don't want to 'intrude'. Now that is very considerate and much appreciated, but sometimes, for the twins' sake mostly, we wish we were just another family and could have the pleasure of making friends like everybody else. It is no big deal, but you know what I mean.

So, next time you see me wandering the streets, and you feel like saying 'Hello', don't be shy - I don't bite!

David Roper

ARE THEY ROSE-TINTED?

This is the hardest article I have had to write, as you find me in a raw and emotional state. I am wandering the streets of my home town, Bradford, and the memories are flooding back.

I am walking down Ivegate, a steep flagstoned street in the city centre, retracing the steps I took as a toddler on May 4th, 1945, clutching my mother's hand and proudly watching my father marching in a VE(Victory in Europe)-day parade shortly after the end of World War 2.

My father wasn't a General or a Commando or a Dambuster. He never got a VC or fired a shot in anger. He was simply one of the countless millions who fought, in their own way, to make the world a better place for me to live in, and I am immensely proud of him for that.

He was quite small in stature and was a gentle man, not someone you would immediately associate with great courage or fighting ability (albeit that I once stumbled upon his after-shave. It was called 'Pagan Man'). Where his courage lay was in providing for my mother and me.

Between leaving the army in 1945 and the Coronation in 1953 he saved enough to buy a house with a bathroom (a luxury in those days), and insisted that we had a two-week seaside holiday every year - a remarkable feat of domestic economics in those austere post-war years.

He'd often take me for a walk after Sunday lunch, and we would talk about anything and everything. He didn't really tell me things, rather he would encourage me to exercise my mind and argue - boy, did we argue! In a word, he taught me how to think.

52

Our last conversation, in typical fashion, ended in a 'heated discussion', but we would not have had it any other way. I miss you - you argumentative old bugger.

Just round the corner from Ivegate is where I used to work as an accountant, and I am standing in the doorway that I last came through all those years ago, when I left for good to become an actor. Across the road is the shop where I bought my first Durex ('rubber johnny' to us, 'condom' to you). I had little hope of using one, of course, but in those days the mere possession of a 'packet of three' gave you a certain kudos, as you casually revealed it, nestling in your wallet, when it was your turn to buy a round. In one of those ironic twists of fate the place is now a photo-copying shop, advertising 'Reproduction at reduced rates'. Nothing changes.

Bradford, by the way, is like Rome (come on, stop laughing), built on seven hills, and used to be immensely wealthy because of the Wool Trade. There were once more Rolls Royce cars registered in the Bradford area than anywhere else on earth, bar Beverley Hills. Its fall into poverty began in the fifties, with the introduction of synthetic fibre, it went into terminal decline in the sixties, and finally expired sometime in the seventies.

It is now a monument to under-investment, lack of foresight and myopic local authority planning, which has turned a once beautiful city into a municipal litter bin and the roosting place for half the world's starlings. The old Talbot Hotel, where we would drink in the 'Gentlemen Only' bar (tells you how long ago it was), now houses a mobile phone shop, and is something of an architectural Ena Sharples, shrouded as it is in an enormous wire 'hairnet' to discourage our feathered friends.

You often hear ex-pat northerners wistfully wittering on about being born 'up north' and how their roots are really there - I suppose I am doing it myself. So I hear your perceptive question,

"If it's so ruddy wonderful up there, what are you all doing supping Chardonnay in Wine Bars in Camden Town and The Brighton Lanes?"

Nevertheless, the truth is I always come back 'down South' with at least one example of that perfectly delivered and delightfully unconscious wit, unique to the North.

I remember strolling up to the Traveller's Rest pub with my Dad one day, and we passed the local Ironmongers. You know, the sort of place that would have a shiny dustbin, two lawn mowers and a clapped out paraffin dispenser outside, with a man in a standard brown overall inside, whose sole purpose in life was to humiliate you.

"Make your mind up, son! Do you want a 4-inch tappet grommet, countersunk, or a 3-inch badger bolt with a female end? "

I asked Dad if 'brown overall man' was still around.

"No, he died. Fell into his breakfast last Tuesday."

"Oh, dear. What was it?"

"Rice Crispies, I think."

Life doesn't get funnier than that - thanks, Dad.

CALM AFTER THE STORM?

What is Belfast?

Look at a map and it is like any other city. There are streets, Post Offices, toilets, churches - all clearly marked. Walk around and there are houses, restaurants & bars, litter, people - it is like anywhere else.

Only when you drive through Newtonards, say, and see whole sides of houses covered in colourful and complicated sectarian murals, proclaiming allegiance to, in this case, the Loyalist cause, do you realise that Belfast was and still is a divided city.

Quite what divides it these days, though, is anybody's guess. I have heard it said that the whole religious and political struggle has degenerated into some kind of Mafia-style turf war, if it wasn't that in the first place, and that Belfast has become like the Chicago of 'The Untouchables'. Just who is supposed to be the Al Capone figure, I don't know, but I can't really see the likes of a UK Prime Minister as a 21st century Eliot Ness, can you?

In a commendable, if somewhat morbid, stab at private enterprise, local taxi firms now run sightseeing tours past those sectarian murals on Belfast gable-ends, and around landmarks in its tragic recent history, and I think that is a bit weird. It is as if 'The Troubles' was merely some kind of long running Soap Opera, with the 'set' and 'locations' now open to the public - a sort of Granada TV tour of 'Coronation Street', but with a cast of thousands, many of whom put their lives on the line to star in it, only to be mercilessly written out for ever.

The truth of the matter is that everything does seem calm and peaceful at the moment, although on the way to a radio interview I got a hint that all was not settled when we passed Stormont (seat of the Northern Ireland Assembly), and the taxi driver crossed his fingers. No, he didn't, I lied, but when I come to think of it that is pretty much a symbol of the feeling you get here - a city with its fingers crossed.

I haven't got a clue what the people here have really been through these past thirty years or more, but, my God, they haven't let it get them down. I have never met a friendlier and more good-natured bunch of people in all my life. Whether that is due to inherent Irish hospitality, or a result of the current release of tension, I don't know, but it is a pleasure to be surrounded with it, I must say.

Opposite The Grand Opera House, where we are this week with 'An Inspector Calls', is The Crown Liquor Saloon, Belfast's most famous pub. It is all stained glass, ornate wooden booths and marble-topped bars, and it looks wonderful. The whole place is illuminated by gas-light, which is cute, but makes it rather stuffy, dark and difficult to count your change (somewhat of an anathema to a Yorkshireman).

Don't tell Andrea, but The Crown also has its own web-cam, and it is possible to log on and check what your other half is up to. As the thin end of the wedge goes, this is fairly alarming. It is bad enough knowing that every street you walk down is covered by somebody's CCTV, without having to tell the truth about how many pints you have downed because the missus has witnessed every gulp.

Who knows, though, perhaps Television has here finally found its true vocation. Reality TV shows are all the rage, CCTV footage of crimes, bad driving and almost anything you care to mention appear to be compulsive viewing, and now we have the web-cam, the ultimate in real life TV.

Is this the future? Are we all destined to forsake The Rover's Return and The Queen Vic for evenings huddled round the tele, watching a load of people getting slowly sozzled in the pub round the corner? We could even watch the folk next door, while they watch the people in the pub round the corner, who could be watching us, watching them. I reckon all that is not far away, given man's primeval desire to be on television.

But bedtime beckons. Since I am in Ireland, it behoves me to end with an Irish joke, but I am not going to - so there. Instead, I am going to finish this article, put on my jimjams and pour two bottles of Guinness down the toilet - well, it will save me having to get up in the night for a pee.

NO END TO IT ALL

'An Inspector Calls' (JB Priestley's masterpiece) lasts 1 hour 45 minutes and has no interval. Those statistics may not seem particularly significant to you, unless you drink a lot and/or have a weak bladder, but to an actor they are of monumental importance.

What they mean is that once the play has started, the next stop is the end, and that end, with a 7.30pm curtain up, will be 9.15pm, promising a good two hours drinking time, or a flying start to the Saturday night journey home, whichever turns you on. Believe me, there are unemployed actors, not a mile from where you sit, who would cheerfully lop off a right arm to be in such a short and booze-friendly play.

I mention this because we have reached that stage in the tour, after sixteen weeks on the road, when we are losing sight of how lucky we are to be working and are beginning to wish our lives away. At each venue a large notice has recently appeared, pleading 'Roll on Llandudno' (our final destination). In our defence, it has to be said that most tours last about twelve weeks, so ours, at twenty nine weeks (four weeks rehearsal included), is somewhat off the scale.

But our feelings are not uncommon amongst actors. You see, touring is interesting, varied and often exciting, but it is above all relentless. No sooner have you packed up, driven home through the night and unpacked, than it's time to pack up again and hit the road to the next venue.

This week, though, it is half term and Andrea, Harry and Jack are with me in Malvern. We have rented a country cottage, and the weather is great. Also, the boys are in the play with me, which means I get to be with them all the time (great for me), and Andrea gets to be without them for three hours every evening (great for her - every mum knows what I mean by that).

It is a strange feeling being on stage with my sons, and it makes me feel so proud I could cry. I daren't look at them (I'm not supposed to anyway) because if I did I would end up a blubbing wreck - soppy date!

Yesterday, we went on our first ever trip to a Safari Park, somewhere in the wilds of Worcestershire. Driving through the animal enclosures, the boys were over the moon; lions, tigers, wolves, giraffes, elephants - all only feet away. Admittedly, they were mostly either snoring, farting or defecating (the animals, not the boys), but it was still fascinating for them to see all that wildlife at such close quarters and to realise that they had so much in common.

As we inched our way forward in the traffic jam, passing the Bengal tigers, it occurred to me that this would go down really well on the M25. Why not ring London with one enormous Safari Park? Charge a pound to get on and, at a stroke, millions in revenue would be raised and, instead of fuming at the delays, we would all be entertained and have no need to scream at the kids, misbehaving in the back. I propose that this should be done immediately.

Back to touring. There is the play itself, of course. Last night was our 134th performance, and it is inevitably starting to wear a bit thin. You find yourself slipping into a kind of theatrical Automatic Pilot. Lines just tumble out of your mouth without any discernible connection to the brain that stores them. The danger is that, from time to time, this Automatic Pilot will disengage and you'll 'wake up' to find that, for the life of you, you can't recall a particular word.

It happened to me the other night. At one point, I have to say,

"And I should think so! Damned impudence!"

I have said that line over 100 times, but could I dredge up the word 'impudence'? Could I heckerslike. I knew it began with 'imp...' and ended with 'ence...', but the bit in the middle was lost to me. The brain works at fantastic speed, but in the milli-seconds before I opened my mouth the only word mine could manage was 'impotence'. I was about to endow the character I was referring to with a totally unjustified sexual condition, when my brain miraculously found an alternative, and the line came out as,

"And I should think so! Damned *impertinence!*"

Great word. I reckon JB Priestley would have been proud of me. Thanks, brain.

IT NEVER RAINS

Everything was going so well. I had kissed Andrea, Harry and Jack goodbye and had set off for the beautiful Georgian City of Bath for another week of treading the boards. I had my habitual twinge of sadness as I left them all, of course, but the sun was shining and I was feeling quite good as I eventually accelerated off the M25 slip road onto the M4.

Then I remembered!

At the weekend, I had borrowed my father-in-law's lawn mower, and as I took it out of the boot to return it, an enormous great spider disappeared under the back seat. Oh, my God, where was it now?

Suddenly my journey took on nightmarish proportions. Was it crawling up my leg? Was it down my collar? Or was it creeping across my crotch? I could see the headlines, clear as day:

SPIDER LANDS ON ACTOR'S FLY

Car abandoned in middle lane – 25 mile tailback on M4

But I was very brave and made it to Bath, along with my passenger presumably, without incident. Thank goodness.

My digs there were fantastic. The whole ground floor of a Georgian terraced-house on The Circus all to myself. So I settled in to enjoy the week, and the feel-good factor returned.

Then it happened!

One of the cast decided to leave, and we had to rehearse his replacement every day.

Bang went the pleasures of Bath. Nothing against the new cast member, of course, and we all rallied round, as actors always will, when 'the show must go on'. It did knock a dirty great hole in our social life, though. Still, there were always the late evenings and after-show drinks to look forward to, so I felt good again.

Then I met them!

The bar staff from hell. The first lot were in a bar nearby. Two forty-something ladies who evidently had pressing engagements elsewhere, as they spent the whole time glancing overtly at their watches every thirty seconds, like two people waiting for a bus that was overdue. It seemed rude to disturb their concentration, although when we did they looked so startled you would have thought we had just landed from Mars.

In the end, we left them to it and moved on to the pub next door. Wrong! The staff there had obviously missed out on the 'How to make a customer feel welcome' classes at the Bath Charm School. The barmaid looked as if she were in the middle of some traumatic emotional crisis and was about to burst into tears. This was proved to be untrue, in case you think I am being harsh, because her whole demeanor changed and her face lit up with a beaming smile the instant 'time' was called.

The barman, on the other hand, was quite open about his attitude. He put his coat on at 10.15, ignored everybody and started cashing up the second the clock hit 10.30. The whole atmosphere made you feel like an intruder. I bet there are burglars who've experienced a deeper sense of welcome than we did.

Third time lucky, we thought, and found ourselves in a common or garden boozer, where the staff had cottoned on to the idea that a smile costs nothing and can reap enormous rewards. Well after closing time, I went to bed on several pints of real ale and the feeling that maybe things weren't quite so bad, after all.

Then I discovered it!

My car had been vandalized overnight. This is Bath, for crying out loud. Things like that don't happen here. I have parked in the seedy back streets of Bradford, Birmingham, Manchester - all over the place - and not a mark on it, but one night in this most un-seedy and salubrious city, and my car gets done over. What is the world coming to?

It's an ill-wind, though. You see, it would have cost me the thick end of sixty quid to securely park for the rest of the week - there really is not much space here - so the fifty quid to replace a window (the only damage) and the Garage's kind offer to keep my car under lock and key for the rest of the week for free, turned out to be something of a result.

But, all in all, Bath, beautiful as it is, had been a chapter of disasters. The only consolation I could find was in the hope that the vandals who broke into my car did so with the express intention of stealing the spider - or did they?

Watch out for the headlines.

David Roper

THE CHRONICLES OF ROPER

What is it about the sea that fascinates us so much? I am sitting outside a café on The Hoe, perched high above Plymouth Sound, watching the yachts, ferries, tankers and Royal Navy cruisers ploughing in and out of the harbour.

I have sat here every morning and just stared out to sea for ages, trying to work out why I find it so…well, soothing, I suppose.

Maybe it is because the sea is where man originated, and I am being drawn back to my primeval roots; maybe it is because I feel dwarfed by its enormity and humbled by the thought that the water I am looking at belongs to the same body of water that crashes onto Bondi Beach in Australia; maybe it's because I live on an island and belong to a seafaring nation; or maybe it is just the gentle pace of it all - the rhythmic lapping of the waves; the stately progress of the Plymouth to Roscoff ferry; the jaunty bobbing up and down of the crisp packets and plastic bottles.

Whatever it is, I am very happy to be here and it is a great way to spend my birthday. Yes, you've missed it again!

Looking back at all those years, it is fascinating to find what pops up in my mind. 1949: I am five and am walking to school on my own (you could do that then). For no particular reason, I start to wonder what it would be like to be blind. I close my eyes, set off along Midland Road, Bradford, and walk slap bang into a lamp-post. Being a quick learner, I conclude that being blind is no piece of cake.

1954: I am nine and walking home from school with Susan Whiteley. She is a bit of all right, and everybody fancies her (whatever any of that means). I feel this sudden urge deep within my short trousers. I don't know what it is, or what to do with it, so I kiss her on the cheek. It frightens me a bit to sense something going on inside me that I don't understand, so I have a word with my dad about it, and get my one and only piece of sex education,

"Right, the thing is…just keep your fly-hole buttons fastened, lad!"

1955: I am eleven now and have won a free scholarship to Bradford Grammar School (a fee-paying day school). The kids in our street scoff at my new uniform and call me a snob. I get so fed up with this that I tell them they are right and that every Tuesday and Thursday we have 'snob' classes to teach us how to treat kids who are educationally subnormal, like them. To my amazement they accept this and never tease me again.

1961: I am seventeen and have just failed all my A-levels miserably. My parents try to hide their disappointment, but I can see it in their eyes. They don't give me a hard time, but I feel I have really failed them and I vow to make up for it.

1967: I am twenty-three and have qualified as an Accountant. My parents are really proud of me. Almost immediately I give it all up and swan off to be an actor. It is as if I have finally proved my worth to them and to myself, and can now do what the hell I like, so I do.

1988: I am forty-four and after nearly twenty years as a professional actor, two and a half marriages (one was a live-in lover thing) and so many different addresses that my mother has a separate book for them all, I am desperate for some form of stability. And then it happens! I see Andrea working in The Colonnade, the pub/bar next to The Theatre Royal, Brighton. She is a vision in pink and white, with a bum to die for. She must be at a bit of a loose end, because she agrees to go out with me. I just can't believe my luck.

OK, it is a one-night stand, well more like a one-night sit actually, as we are in a restaurant, and I only get about as far as I did with Susan Whiteley, a quick peck, if you recall, so neither of us thinks it will go any further. How wrong can we be?

1995: I am fifty-one, have been married to Andrea for five years, and the twins, Harry and Jack, have just popped out (in that order). Am I a lucky man or what?

The twins grew up, as kids will, and last Monday Harry told me he had looked up 'sexual intercourse' in the Shorter Oxford Dictionary, and could I explain it, so I do.

"Right, the thing is…just keep your fly-hole buttons fastened, lad!"

Not a lot changes in life, does it?

A LOVER'S TALE

Last week I mentioned how I first met Andrea, and that it became the longest-running one-night stand in the history of British theatre.

Sensing the desire for a touch of titillation among you, and to deny The Sun of the pleasure of printing it, I have decided to reveal the sordid details of our affair.

So pin back your lugholes!

I start by disappointing you. On our first date I behaved like a real gent (Andrea's words, not mine). A bit of a surprise, I agree, as I was 44 at the time - an age when fore-play has more to do with golf than girls, and when men tend to conduct their love lives like amateur rugby players, all 'kick and rush' merchants. Admittedly, I did push things along on our subsequent dates, with promising results, I must say (a deft pass from a loose scrum, followed by a skilful Gary Owen, leading to a low tackle and a converted try - you rugby buffs can translate), but the week ended with us parting...but not for long.

I was back within a fortnight and was delighted to find that Andrea welcomed me with open arms. It looked as though we might have something going here.

True, there was a 16-year age gap between us. No, she wasn't 60, try the other direction, she was 28! People have asked us if we worry about the long-term implications of such a difference in our ages. Well, to quote Clint Eastwood, when he was asked the same question about marrying a much younger woman,

"If she dies, she dies!"

So began our courtship (with Andrea, not Clint). I would commute, as often as I could, from where I lived in Berkshire, or Andrea would come and stay with me, whenever she had the time. It all made us feel like teenagers again.

I don't suppose there are many people who can identify the exact moment when they 'fell in love'. I certainly can't. It crept up on me until it seemed the most natural thing in the world to be with Andrea all the time. She became part of me and my life to such an extent that I eventually couldn't imagine being without her – I had 'fallen in love', I guess.

Andrea, on the other hand, professes to know the exact moment when everything 'gelled' and she knew that I was the one for her. No, it wasn't as we gazed into each other's eyes; nor was it during a romantic moonlit walk; it wasn't even after a deep and tender kiss. It was, she insists, when I served her chicken, stuffed with lemons and topped with crispy, streaky bacon, at the table I had laid, al fresco, next to the outside lavatory of my house in Berkshire. I know how to woo a girl, don't you worry!

The table setting was my own invention, so I can reasonably take credit for that, but the meal itself was a stroke of luck, I confess, and the location was dictated by the lay-out of the garden. What I didn't realise was that I had somehow managed to bring together Andrea's three greatest desires all at the same time: a man she fancied, a meal she adored and a toilet she could fall into. I wouldn't say Andrea is obsessed with toilets, but if she passes one without passing water, she feels as though she has snubbed an old friend.

The end result was that she fell hopelessly in love with me, as I was with her. I proposed to her in Newcastle - romantic fool that I am - at the last night dinner of a play I was in. Most of her family were there, as was my agent. Trust an actor to have his agent around when entering into a new contract.

We were married at Brighton Register Office, with the reception at a seafront hotel, and it was fantastic, marred only by my new brother-in-law, Mick, ordering £34.50's worth of sandwiches on my tab, for which he still owes me, by the way. How could anybody do that to a Yorkshireman?

As Andrea and I gazed out of the Honeymoon Suite that night, through the scaffolding that covered the hotel, and onto the rotting remains of the West Pier, we kissed passionately. She drew me slowly towards the bed, her hands caressing my aching body and whispered in my ear,

"I'm dying for a pee!"

David Roper

WHO'S DROPPED ONE?

One day, when I was at the Bristol Old Vic Theatre School, I told an American student there that I had once spent a week exploring the Norfolk Broads. He replied,

"Are English women really so accommodating?"

I recount this fairly mediocre joke to introduce the fact that this week our tour of J.B. Priestley's 'An Inspector Calls' is in Norwich, which, as the locals rightly insist, rhymes with 'switch', not with 'porridge'.

It is also where our production company is based, and the other night the management took us out for dinner to an Indian restaurant. It was a very pleasant evening, but its aftermath has been catastrophic and disturbingly long lasting. At the risk of putting too fine a point on it, the long term effects of the food on many of us caused the sales of toilet paper in the Norwich area to rocket, leave alone the fact that the show gained a certain urgency for a couple of nights.

This is the third time on the trot, if you'll pardon the expression, that we have been treated to a meal 'on the house', and it is a bit worrying. Not because of the effect on our internal workings, but because managements just don't do that kind of thing. It turns out that our's has done so by way of a compliment to us for what they consider to be a particularly good version of this production.

In fact, Stephen Daldry, the production's originator, who also directed 'Billy Elliot' and 'The Hours', was so taken by us that he has given his stamp of approval for our transfer to the West End. If, or rather when, that happens, you will be able to say you were the first to know, but keep schtum, eh? Thanks.

For the moment, though, we have to wait and content ourselves with watching Wimbledon on the TVs in our dressing rooms. The trouble is the ruddy matinees are seriously getting in the way of our afternoon tennis viewing. So keen are some members of the cast on keeping abreast of the scores that I have been cajoled into relaying the state of play during performances (I have a 15 minute gap in the middle).

This afternoon, for instance, my character, Mr. Birling, could be heard muttering to his wife and daughter, "4-3 to Serena!" (hardly a line J.B. Priestley was likely to have written). Unfortunately, the actor playing the Inspector overheard me and it threw him into getting his lines all wrong. I was in a bit of hot water for a while, but have since apologised and promised never to behave in such an unprofessional manner again.

To be fair, we have all been remarkably disciplined over the months, with very little mucking about and the minimum of corpsing. For those of you unfamiliar with the term, corpsing is when an actor has an uncontrollable fit of laughter, usually brought on by something going wrong or happening unexpectedly (thank you, Denis Norden). Its origins are unknown, but may be rooted in an actor giggling while playing a corpse.

Corpsing is at once exhilarating and excruciating. You know you shouldn't laugh, but you just can't help yourself and feel as though you are about to explode. In a comedy or farce you can usually get away with it, as the audience is in a light-hearted mood and, provided they have some idea of why you are doing it, will accept a modicum of giggling. But in a serious play it is a different kettle of fish. The very mood of seriousness can make even the silliest incident seem like the funniest thing you've ever witnessed.

I remember watching Shakespeare's 'Troilus and Cressida' at the Bristol Old Vic. The Greek and Trojan armies, each represented by half a dozen naked men, were ranged against each other. Ajax (I think) stood between them and should have shouted out, "Greeks and Trojans!" However, it came out as "Treeks and Grojans!" What the audience thought of a dozen grown men in fits of laughter, their shoulders heaving up and down, along with various other parts of their anatomies, is not known, but they must have thought it a strange twist to the confrontation of two great armies.

Our greatest corpse, I must tell you, was a couple of nights ago, when one of the children in the on-stage crowd that we co-opt each week, farted at a decibel level wholly inconsistent with her size. Hysteria ensued. It's an ill wind, though - sorry about that - and we just thanked our lucky stars that this embryonic Norfolk broad hadn't eaten at the same Indian restaurant as the rest of us. Close call!

David Roper

A HOLIDAY SAGA

Sometimes an actor's life on tour can be a real pleasure and this week is one of them. We're in St. Helier, Jersey, and Andrea, Iris (her mum), Harry and Jack are with me. The boys are up to their necks in the play, Andrea is up to her neck in the pool and I am up to my neck in debt on my credit card. What the hell! It is like being on holiday.

We are staying half-board in a hotel near the theatre. Most of the other guests are on SAGA holidays…and before you say it…yes, I feel quite at home.

They are an odd bunch, though. It is 10 o'clock in the morning, as I write, and there is virtually nobody about. Where do they all go? They congregate like seagulls after a fishing boat for breakfast and dinner, and then mostly disappear. The ones who stay, lounging around the pool, look not so much half-board, as half bored.

No, I am not being ageist. The reason for their ennui is that one of their number, Charlie, has taken it upon himself to visit each of the others, like a consultant surgeon doing his rounds. Every morning, just before midday, he strolls from lounger to lounger, chain-smoking and drinking lager, endlessly recounting the story of his countless strokes, which curiously, not to say miraculously, had nothing to do with chain-smoking and drinking lager.

At his approach, manicured matrons dive into their Danielle Steele's, and copies of The Sun pop up with military precision…but to no avail. You see, Charlie's other mission in life is to gain an encyclopaedic knowledge of everybody's everyday life and itinerary, which he toddles off to impart to his wife in excruciating detail:

"That couple from Middlesborough are off to Ramsbottom's fish and chip shop again. He must be mad eating all that fatty food! I'll get another pint…toss us a fag."

St. Helier is a bit of a disappointment, quite frankly. We had expected it to have a pretty little harbour with bars, restaurants and expensive yachts moored bow to stern. No such luck. There is a massive marina, commercial area and ferry port to the west, and a coast road runs right alongside the beach to the east…not a bar or bistro in sight.

From both these sides there are views of a central headland, housing a Territorial Army barracks, a power station and an abattoir. Ah well, at least we know we're well defended and that our electricity and meat are fresh.

St. Helier's best feature is the Precinct, a pedestrianised street full of shops, restaurants and bars, with roads and alleyways running off it - a sort of longer, larger and, it has to be said, livelier version of The Lanes in Brighton. Through this Precinct is the way we walk to the theatre, and is also where the boys discovered that Jersey is full of jewellery, mini-skirts and school girls in high heels and white ankle socks (sometimes all three together). As school uniforms go, this was a bit of an eye-opener for them, as they are used to the more sober dress of the mainland. However, their demand that we immediately move to Jersey to continue their education was turned down flat. Who do they think I am…John Nettles?

Which brings me neatly to Jersey's affluence. Magnificent houses line the bays, and most of the cars are less than a year old, with open-topped sporty models being ten a penny. Also ten a penny are *Advocates* (lawyers/barristers, I guess). Why Jersey is home to so many, I don't know, as crime is fairly minimal and Bergerac must have lived through a really bad patch. I can only assume that these *Advocates* are employed, at great expense, to construct impenetrable property laws and off-shore company legislation, which they then charge enormous fees to deconstruct again.

Hello! Feeding time must be nigh, as the sensible shoes of the SAGA army are shuffling towards the dining-room. It is an awesome sight - this phalanx of waving blue rinses, oscillating cellulite and static-filled Bhs nylon shirts, advancing to devour the salmon terrine (with lemon wedge), roast chicken (with stuffing ball) and Black Forest gateaux (with Jersey cream, naturally). Only one of their number stands apart. Yes, you've guessed it. It is indeed the fount of all knowledge, cholesterol-concious Charlie, chain-smoking and drinking lager.

David Roper

Maybe he has got a point. If the lager hasn't got you, the gateaux certainly will!

THE FINAL CURTAIN

It has arrived! The last show on the last day of the last week of 'An Inspector Calls'.

We started rehearsals on 30th December, opened in Birmingham on 24th January and have toured from Aberdeen in the north to Jersey in the south, from Norwich in the east to Belfast in the west and a score of places in between. We have ended up in Llandudno, where I now sit having a coffee, waiting to trudge to the theatre for the final performance - number 191, for those of you of a statistical bent.

Time to take stock, I suppose. It has been a long, hard but mostly immensely enjoyable seven months. Sometimes, it is true, I have wished it would end there and then, and I've hated being away from Andrea, Harry and Jack. On the other hand, I have adored it when they were all with me, and the boys were in the play. Thinking back to Birmingham, it is hard to believe that I went into the first matinee more or less in the dark, and now I will be coming out of the last performance, blinking into the evening sunlight.

We have endured fire scares, power failures and personal tragedies. We have shared our meals, our dressing rooms and our lives. We have played to 1500 rowdy school kids in Stoke, and 25 snoozing pensioners in Jersey. Mobile phones have gone off in the middle of shows, hearing aids have whistled through our speeches and we have twice had to utter the immortal line,

"Is there a doctor in the house?"

We have had some fantastic reviews and some lousy ones. In Belfast I was described as, "…letting the side down by playing Mr. Birling as if auditioning for a Monty Python sketch." Cheek!

We have had some great digs and some terrible ones. Seven of us rented log cabins on a hillside near Truro and loved it, someone took the penthouse suite in the most expensive hotel in Belfast, and Martin, my understudy, and I managed to root out the world's most disgusting B&B in Otley. There was no door on the one and only dribbling shower, the same cornflakes that were ground into the carpet on the first day were still there on the last and the breakfasts appeared to have been cooked in WD40 - 'Catch a sausage, win a Metro' would have been The Sun's headline.

In Llandudno we have taken over a whole hotel and the landlord is extremely accommodating. Apparently he asked some actors what they really wanted. "Breakfast 'til midday, drinks 'til dawn and after show sandwiches 'til we burst." And that is what he provides, plus lifts to and from the theatre if it rains. Amazing. He has served drinks 'til 5.30am and then breakfast from 8.30am for three consecutive days. He nods off around 3.00am, but is happy to be woken up to dish out more booze. However, last night nobody could rouse him and he appeared to be clinically dead. Not wishing to take advantage of this, we tucked cash into his hand for drinks and left him to it. Next morning he appeared fresh as a daisy, having been out for two punnets of strawberries for breakfast - a remarkable man!

I now take you on 24 hours. It is Sunday and I have driven back to Brighton after that final performance. Last nights are emotional affairs, and ours was no exception. After all, we had become the sort of 'family' that only touring for a long time can produce, and our personal and social lives had become inextricably intertwined. Now we were having to say goodbye to each other. Some we would see again, some we wouldn't - some we would want to, some we wouldn't.

When the final curtain fell, there were handshakes, hugs and kisses, and not a few tears. Then it was time to pack up the costumes and the set, the make-up and the memories, turn our backs on our 'family' and head for home.

Like everybody else I had mixed emotions, as I was driving away passed the theatre this morning. I was genuinely sorry that the world we had created for ourselves was disintegrating, never to reappear. But I was also aching to get back home to my real world, never to kiss goodbye to Andrea, Harry and Jack again - until the next time. Whichever of those worlds I thought about, it got me in the throat. It always does.

Nevertheless, there is no doubt about it:

"It's an actor's life for me!"

AN ACTOR'S LIFE FOR ME

PART TWO

AN ACTOR BORED

David Roper

BACK IN HARNESS

"I'm unemployed," he said dolefully.

Yes, it comes to us all, and at the end of seven months on the road with 'An Inspector Calls' it was time to face the reality of it and to pick up the pieces.

It appears a lot happened while I was away.

A 'comedy terrorist' made fools of our Head of State's security services and wandered into Prince William's birthday bash at Windsor Castle, as if it were Debenhams. Come to think of it, he might have had more trouble at Debenhams. He would probably have been thrown out before he had even got as far as the Clinique counter. However, on sheer initiative this man, whoever he was, should obviously be made head of the Royal Protection Squad without further delay.

Tony Blair picked up enough air miles, in his pursuit of statesmanship status, to fly off on holiday to Sir Cliff's pad in Barbados (Congratulations to him).

And the grass in our garden is so high, Harry and Jack have demanded mobile phones to keep track of each other.

I also returned to the news that the invasion of Iraq has yet to turn up any of the weapons of mass destruction, which were its justification in the first place. This is rather worrying. As much as everybody, including most of Iraq by the sound of it, is over the moon to see the back of Saddam Hussein and his regime, there may yet be trouble ahead for our Tony. Apart from having to explain how he inadvertently did the right thing for completely the wrong reason, he is also apparently having difficulty convincing the President of the United States that the GB plates on our cars are not indicative of the 'special relationship' and do not stand for George Bush.

Tony and George are also struggling to find a needle in a haystack, or rather a dictator in a dream world - Saddam himself. I know it is too obvious for words, but have they actually tried directory enquiries? I have, and can now reveal that Saddam Hussein is holed up in a motel in Massachusetts. An anagram of his name confirms this: 'Hidden - Mass., USA.' Osama bin Laden, by the same token, is languishing anagrammatically in North Eastern Pakistan: 'Islamabad? No, N.E.!'

Coincidently, Tony Blair, like me, has also been on tour, playing second lead in one of JB Priestley's lesser known plays, 'An Arms Inspector Calls'. The plot involves an Arms Inspector, the Kingdom of the Baddy and his Weapons of Death, which may or may not exist, and Tony and his boss, George, who have their own Weapons of Death, but, as they are goodies, that isn't a problem. Tony is great with the media and persuades everybody that Secret Elves have told him that the Baddy has hidden his Weapons of Death, which is why the Arms Inspector couldn't find them and which conclusively proves that they exist. The play is a comedy and is still running.

Then again, some things haven't happened. The West Pier has still not been finally put out of its misery, and why not, we all ask. To Brighton's eternal shame, the thing has been in the background of every Party Conference TV report in the living memory of most Parliamentary backbenchers. Charges against successive Councils of committing pierslaughter, by reason of diminished salvageability, are eagerly awaited.

On a more serious note, the big news on the domestic front is that while I was away, treading the boards, Andrea sold our house. We had agreed to do this, I hasten to add, lest you think her to be a mere creature of impulse.

"What shall we do today, boys? I know, let's flog the house!"

What this means, of course, is that we are now going through one of the most stressful events of our lives, dwarfing everything else. We are having to deal with solicitors and estate agents, surveyors and mortgage providers, all of whom speak their own largely incomprehensible language, and we are having to think in terms of sums of money that, quite frankly, frighten the pants off us. We have to change our address and telephone number, and have gas, electricity and water readings all coinciding. On top of all that, we're faced with clearing out the accumulated junk of the last seven years.

The good news is that our problems make Tony's troubles pale into insignificance. Be honest, which would you prefer: questions in the House or simply house-moving?

A LITTLE NIGHT MUSING!

There are certain unfathomable questions that have exercised the minds of men since the beginning of time. What is the meaning of life? Is there an end to the Universe? Why are so many TV programmes presented by Carole Vorderman?

But perhaps the most puzzling of all is: What on earth do actors do between jobs? The short answer is: they worry. They worry about where their next job is coming from, where their next cheque is coming from and where their next meal is coming from. The worrying starts even before they have finished the previous job. Will they ever work again once it's over? It all goes back to what I mentioned many weeks ago - the actor's paranoia, although in this case there is some justification.

I was at this stage last Monday morning, after two weeks out of work. I had woken up at 3.30am - when the human spirit is at its lowest, so they say. You must have been through it. It is that time when everything in your life takes on horrendous proportions. When that leaking tap in the downstairs loo seems like the greatest tragedy mankind has ever had to face.

Everything in my life was parading before me, and it all seemed impossible to cope with. That mess in the garden shed was like the aftermath of an earthquake, Southern Water's latest bill was the size of a small mortgage and my bank balance was draining away like bath water. I tried to clear my mind and think of nothing, but only succeeded in reminding myself of what lay ahead on the job front - nothing - and the whole sorry cycle began again.

By 4.00am I had had enough and went downstairs for a cup of tea. I switched on the TV to take my mind off things, but all I got was ITV's

'NightScreen', where they play incessant music and display their forthcoming drama presentations. To a normal, sane insomniac this might be interesting, but to a paranoid, out of work actor, at four in the morning, it was just a cruel reminder of all the programmes I had failed to get a part in.

"I went up for that! Why, for the love of God, did they give it to him?"

I was forced to take refuge in BBC1, but was immediately plunged into the horrors of man's inhumanity to man by BBC News 24. Mass murder, child abduction and arsonists setting fire to Western Europe, just for a laugh, did little to lift this lad's spirits, I can tell you, particularly when repeated every fifteen minutes by a newsreader, who looked about as fed up as I was.

As dawn was breaking, I turned over to BBC2's Learning Zone, only to be quickly made aware of my total ignorance of 'I.T. in the Modern Workplace', or some such, by a smug anorak with a beard. Were all the people who present these programmes born looking exactly the same, or have they miraculously grown to conform to some stereotypical image laid down by TV Centre? Their Christmas parties must be a hoot.

By this time, you will have gathered, my mood was necessarily pretty black, and it was not improved by flicking the remote and stumbling on Channel 4's jolly little offering - 'Killing Fields of Kazakhstan'. Some programme controllers really know how to put the boot in, don't they!

Staring out of the kitchen window, as Brighton and Hove began its day, I watched the gainfully employed heading for their secure jobs, and wondered why I put myself through it. Yet another morning was slipping by, along with my life, and the phone was ominously silent.

'I'm unemployed,' I muttered to myself, a tad more dolefully than usual

Then Harry and Jack wandered in, having peacefully slept the sleep of the unmortgaged.

"Dad, will you play a game with us?"

"In a minute. I've got things to think about."

"What things?"

"You wouldn't understand. Adult things - work, money."

"You can have ours. It's only money. Come on, play a game."

Do you know, there's nothing like a good session with the kids, playing SSX Tricky on Play Station 2, to make you realise what a self-indulgent wan..plonker you really are. My whole life instantly changed. The sun was shining, the birds were singing and to top it all - they let me win. Thanks, kids. I love you.

SOAPS ON THE ROPES

I have been bringing myself up to speed these past few weeks with all the TV I missed during seven months on tour.

For instance, I had totally lost track of what was going on in 'EastEnders' and 'Coronation Street', both of which I've appeared in, as it goes. It is really interesting to look afresh and 'compare and contrast' them from both a punter's and an actor's point of view.

From a wide perspective, there are the obvious differences in location, accents and style, but it is curious how fundamentally similar they are. There seem to be certain structural rules that have to be obeyed - e.g. there has to be:

1) A geographical setting where most of the community of characters live, work and can bump into each other. Albert Square = The Street.

2) Within that setting, places where the characters can meet, outside their own homes. The Vic; the 'Caff'; mini-market = The Rovers; Roy's Rolls; corner shop.

3) Continuity and change of cast. Meaning, there are long-standing core characters. Ian Beale; Pauline Fowler = Ken Barlow; Emily Bishop, who draw in a succession of short-lived transient characters. Geoff Barnes = Bob Bradshaw, both played by me. Trust me to get the short-lived straw!

4) Within the community, characters which have specific, dramatic roles to play. These characters appear quite different on the surface, but all have identical functions. The hard-nosed businessman, who can be ruthless, but often gets his comeuppance: Ian Beale = Mike Baldwin.

The matriarch who has been through the mill and dishes out advice to the youngsters. Pat Butcher = Rita Fairclough (as was)

The man who tries his best in his work and personal life, but always seems to fail. Barry Evans = Curly Watts.

The woman, often living on her own, who opens her mouth before her brain is in gear. Pauline Fowler = Audrey Roberts. And so on.

A quick look at 'Emmerdale' seems to back all this up. It has the village, the pub, the shop, Eric Pollard, Marlon, to name but a few, all corresponding to one of the above.

Also, every Soap seems obliged to introduce a 'rogue' family from time to time. The Slaters = The Battersbys = The Dingles. These start off being quite feisty and aggressive families, but eventually are embraced by the community and by the audience, too, and somehow become lovable.

So what is it like to appear in the Soaps? Here again there are similarities and differences. The day to day work is very similar, as the schedules are relentless, with little room for manoeuvre if something goes wrong. Everybody working on each show, in whatever capacity, is welcoming, supportive and highly professional. I enjoyed working on both 'EastEnders' and 'Coronation Street' immensely.

The differences, though, are quite marked and, curiously, have nothing to do with the shows or the cast and crew, but everything to do with geography - the internal geography of the buildings, and their geographical location. What I mean is this:

Firstly, the 'EastEnders' building has no large communal area, so you tend to meet only those actors who are in your scenes. When I was in it, there were actors who I didn't see for months, even though we might be in adjacent scenes. 'Coronation Street', on the other hand, has an enormous communal area, through which everybody has to pass and where the actors hang out. Consequently, you are almost bound to meet all the cast called that day, whether you have scenes with them or not.

Secondly, 'EastEnders' is made in Borehamwood, or Borehamstiff as I came to know it, which is in the middle of nowhere, and a good place for it too. As a result, everybody tends to drive straight off after work to their homes all over London, and there is no social life to speak of. 'Coronation Street', however, is made in the centre of Manchester, surrounded by all it offers, and many of the cast live/stay within walking distance. As a result, the social life is comparatively lively.

What it all boils down to is this: solely because of geography, 'Coronation Street' feels more of a social experience, whereas 'EastEnders' feels more 'nine to five'. Neither one is better than the other: they're just both the same, but different. Got it?

To be honest, I didn't intend to bang on about all that when I started to write this. I intended to have a look at all the new TV programmes that I had missed, but I hope it has been interesting.

David Roper

NOT SUCH A DAFT IDEA

Doesn't time fly? A couple of weeks ago, during that heat wave, it was difficult to believe that we were celebrating Harry and Jack's 8th birthday. Funnily enough, it was blisteringly hot when they were born, too. Poor Andrea was cooped up in a south-facing hospital side ward that you could have grown tomatoes in.

Now, every time the boys' birthday comes around, or Christmas for that matter, I always get a wee bit twitchy. Not because of us having to arrange the party, or because these occasions are always such a shock to the old wallet - have you got kids, or do you still have money? No, nothing like that. The reason for my nerves being on edge is the thought of all those ruddy presents that will inevitably need assembling. You see, along with changing light bulbs, cleaning cars and setting fire to 100 quid's worth of reconstituted dead pig on a barbecue, it is written that 'toy assembly is a dad's job.'

A few years back we bought the boys battery-powered trikes. They were quite small things and only went at one mile per hour, but they were made up of 144 separate bits. I am no expert but I bet some motor cars have less parts than that.

It took me all day and half the night to put the bast…blighters together. Andrea had to shut the lounge door to stop the boys being subjected to the torrents of questionable language that are a necessary fact of life in assembling kids' toys, as every dad knows. When I had finished, I discovered I had also proved that other inescapable fact of life;

'After putting together any given child's toy, there will always be two unidentifiable bits left over.'

And there they were, staring at me defiantly, so I put them in the drawer with all the other unidentifiable bits I had amassed over the years, and went to bed.

This year I had the unenviable task of creating a Power Rangers De Luxe Wild Force Megazord. For the uninitiated among you, this is quite simply a collection of plastic animals that *easily* clip together to form one large Megazord, which is a character on the TV show. That is the theory. In practice, it is a collection of plastic animals that *refuse point blank* to clip together in any discernible way whatsoever, and is designed to reduce any dad who touches it to a gibbering, chain-smoking, obscenity-hurling wreck. The kids eventually took pity on me and assembled it in two minutes flat. They then happily wandered off to play with the cardboard box it had come in, and which they evidently preferred. Such is a dad's lot.

The thing is, all of this blood pressure-inducing frustration could so easily be avoided by the simple expedient of including 'kid's toy and equipment assembly' as an integral part of all ante-natal classes. It makes total sense.

Our classes, quite properly, took us through all the easy stuff - birthing techniques, anaesthetic options, breathing exercises etc., and went on to explain post-natal problems, like how to handle baths, burps and bums. Not a single word, you notice, about how to avoid trapping your fingers when erecting the double-buggy in the pouring rain outside ASDA's - nothing on how to fix a teddy bear mobile to a 12 foot high ceiling with a bent drawing pin and no ladder - and, worst of all, total silence on cot construction, trampoline technology and the bane of my life…Bey-Blade building.

This is a serious omission and leaves gaps in a chap's knowledge that can make bringing up baby a far greater technological challenge than even NASA has ever had to face. I have seen grown men reduced to tears by the braking system on an Action Man bike, and what dad hasn't been driven to opening a bottle of Mighty Murray White at 3.30 in the afternoon by the mere sight of a toddler's slide laid out in pieces on the back lawn?

It is time something was done. If the ante-natal classes won't help, then I suggest that we dads get together and put an embargo on all unfathomable and unassembleable presents. We should call ourselves Dads Against Fathomless Toys - DAFT, for short. Join here!

David Roper

THROUGH THE TRANSFER WINDOW

"Go on, lads! Off you go! You can do it!"

The very words, or at least a loose translation of them, that every commanding officer, from Bonaparte to Bush, has used to exhort his troops to march off and do their duty. But this is no battlefield in war-torn Western Europe, or on the dusty plains of Southern Iraq: this is no struggle to dominate a continent or to liberate a country: this is far more serious: this is football.

The scene is a pitch in Northern Saltdean, where the Saltdean Tigers under nines B-team is engaged in a 'friendly' against the under tens. The voice is Andrea's, shouting at the top of her lungs, as Harry (striker) and Jack (defender) battle it out on the playing fields of Saltdean United Football Club.

I must pause here to tell you that this is the woman who swore on her Next catalogue that she would never - I repeat, never - stand shivering on a touchline and screaming like a fish wife.

To be honest, though, I was never much of a footie fan either. Well, I was born and brought up 100 yards from Bradford City's Valley Parade ground, when they were in the 4th division (north), so I didn't have much to go on. My only claim to fame in the football world is that I was its very first hooligan. Me and my mates got in free at three-quarter time one Saturday in 1951 (we used to collect empty fag packets to flick against the wall). My so-called *friends* bet me that I daren't run onto the pitch and pick up the ball. Not one to baulk at a challenge, I rose to the occasion and did that very thing. The stadium erupted, as I was picked up by a goalie the size of a house and deposited back where I came from, with the sternest of warnings never to do it again. My dad and granddad were in the crowd. They both disowned me on the spot.

Back in Saltdean, Harry had just scored the B-team's first goal of the season. He punched the air in celebration, Andrea leapt two feet off the ground and I started wondering which member of Junior S-Club 7 he would be best advised to marry in order to advance his career. Well, you have got to think ahead, don't you?

A few years ago, when the boys started football, it was obvious, even to our untutored eyes, that there was some really good play going on. Call me partisan, but there are people who will back me up, when I say that we have witnessed lots of matches equally as thrilling in skill and tension as many a professional one.

There are fundamental differences, of course. The pitch and the players are smaller, there is no off-side rule, the referees favour a liberal interpretation of the rules, and the crowd consists of only a dozen or so parents, knocking back flasks of coffee as if there is no tomorrow.

But in all other respects the kids behave like true professionals. They argue with the manager about being left on the bench and sulk, they are ruthless with their sliding tackles (Jack was sent off last season for two particularly vicious ones) and they have their own inimitable ways of celebrating a goal. The tradition of pulling the shirt over the head is still popular, although some haven't quite got the hang of it and do tend to bump into each other like demented dodgem cars.

Harry and Jack have also somehow managed to negotiate themselves a fee. This is based on the number of goals scored and is in the nature of a productivity bonus. It is OK for Harry, of course, as he is up front and has a chance of scoring, but for Jack, as a defender, it is infinitely more difficult. He rather deviously got round this by demanding wage parity and by quoting my words back at me,

"It's the whole team that scores a goal, you know, not just one person!" Big mouth.

As a result of their inadvertent introduction to the free market economy, we have to cough up two quid for a goal, five quid for two and a blank cheque made payable to 'Cash' for a hat-trick.

If they ever cotton on to transfer fees, we're finished!

David Roper

CAVIAR TO THE GENERAL

As I write, Brighton is in the middle of yet another refuse collection saga. I thought all this had been sorted out months ago. I don't pretend to know all the ins and outs, but I do know that they refuse to take my refuse. Piles of black sacks litter the streets, the seagulls think all their Christmases have come at once and as a result, we deeply regret having those prawns for dinner last Saturday.

The country is also on the brink of a national postal workers' strike. If these two disputes coincide, we will really be in for a shock. Letters will spew from little red boxes throughout the land, and in Brighton these will mix with rat-infested rubbish, making gazing at the West Pier just about the best view in town.

In a bid to avert this appalling situation, and to reconcile all parties, I propose that the refuse collection services and the Royal Mail enter into a merger, forming one co-ordinated nationwide company called Combined Refuse and Postage (CRAP).

The basis for this revolutionary 'marriage' is quite simple. Refuse vehicles go out empty and come back full; postal vehicles go out full and come back empty. Combining the two and creating a multi-purpose mail delivery/rubbish collection vehicle would ensure 100% use of capacity, therefore reducing costs. The resultant savings would be passed on to the workers in the form of increased wages, and to the customers in the form of reduced Council Tax bills.

The scheme would also mean daily - I emphasise *daily* - rubbish collections, and additionally save a small fortune in Royal Mail shoe leather. While the postman hops off to deliver your letters and parcels from the front section, the refuse collectors hop on to sling your rubbish and recyclables in at the back - hey presto, happiness.

Another advantage would be…

I don't believe it! South Today on BBC1 has just politely informed me that the dispute is over. To add insult to injury, and at the exact same moment, a gang of refuse collectors is merrily gathering up our two weeks of accumulated rubbish right outside the kitchen window. Couldn't they have waited until I'd finished this? Honestly, some people!

What it means, of course, is that instead of finding an ingenious way of solving the insolvable and reducing redundant workers, I find myself having to find an equally ingenious way of solving the insolvable problem of a redundant article.

So, I will do what any self-respecting writer would do in the same circumstances - plagiarise other writers. In this case, though, it is not so much a case of nicking what they wrote, but nicking what they didn't write, or rather didn't intend.

For example, did The Guardian Business Section sub-editor, when headlining a report on a conference about lamb from New Zealand, really mean to intrigue us by writing, 'New Zealand lamb talks'? And, when the wife of the jockey, Lester Piggott, was unfortunately injured in an accident, did that same sub-editor have his pen firmly in his cheek, when he created his headline, 'Piggott's wife in stable condition'?

It is without doubt, though, that the reporter on a Midlands newspaper was the victim of a disastrous series of printing errors, when his article on a recently deceased Colonel described him as, 'the *battle-scared* hero of Tobruk'. The felony was compounded the following day in the corrections column, when the paper contritely announced, 'The Colonel should have been described as the *bottle-scarred* hero of Tobruk'. At the third attempt they got it right: '*battle-scarred* hero'.

My all-time favourite misprint, though, also has a military connection, and can still make me smile. A celebrated General had sadly passed away. He had obviously been an inspirational leader of men and had been instrumental in spurring his troops on to hold their positions in the face of the enemy. The report on his death was given a suitably reverential tone by the obituary writer, concluding with a list of the General's achievements, ending with, 'The General is best known for his crucial *fart* in the Battle of Gibraltar, which kept the Germans at bay for three days'. Hopefully, he meant 'part', or did he?

Luckily, for this publisher, it is a rare misprunt that gets pissed their trypesetters.

David Roper

A WEIGHT OFF MY MIND

The other day I caught sight of my naked body in our full-length mirror. Steady, ladies! It appeared to have changed quite a lot since I had last had occasion to inspect my assets. Don't worry, everything was still there, thank goodness — two of everything down the sides and one of everything down the middle. Just like you.

The trouble seemed to be that there was this large lump at the front. I dismissed pregnancy as a possible cause, though I am not on the pill, and concluded it must be my stomach. I looked down and realised to my horror that I had lost sight of my feet. They were still there, otherwise I would have fallen over, but were obscured by this skin-coloured balloon. At that moment a little voice in my head whispered,

"You're digging your grave with your teeth, David Roper."

The voice was right. Since finishing touring with 'An Inspector Calls' in July, I had rather indulged myself in whatever vices are left to a chap on the cusp of sixty - eating, drinking, shouting abuse at the Tele - you know, the usual stuff.

Compounding all that, I had lapsed into lethargy and become allergic to exercise. In short, I was mentally contracting while physically expanding.

"The time has come," the voice then said, "to think of many things:

Of coronary heart disease and what indulgence brings."

So, in this menopausal frame of mind, I decided to reclaim my body before something else allowed medical science to beat me to it.

The jury is still out on the Atkins Diet, although stuffing myself with loads of protein did have its attractions, so I opted instead for moderation in all things - eating, drinking and, most of all, exercise.

An Actor's Life For Me

We have been members of a Health Club for about a year now, but I have been so lax in using it that they have started sending me reminders. However, last Tuesday, I dusted off my membership card, rolled up my trunks in a towel, and set off to unearth that long lost body lurking somewhere inside me.

I had forgotten how huge these places are and how much equipment they have. Running machines, rowing machines, cycling machines, God-knows-what-this-is-for machines stretch out in never-ending lines, like the little white crosses at the end of that film, 'Oh, what a Lovely War'.

I headed for the nearest cycling machine, hopped on and was confronted by a display console that would not have disgraced a light aircraft. I started pedalling, pressed 'start' and was cleared for take-off. Words flashed across the screen. Did I want fat burn, calorie burn, Chinese burn or George and Gracie Burns? I selected fat burn. More questions popped up. Level? Minutes? Age? Inside leg measurement? Mother's maiden name? Fancy a drink when you've finished? It went on and on. Working it out was a workout in itself, and I was out of breath just pushing the buttons.

Eventually I did 10 minutes of fat burn for a 59 year old at level five, until Air Traffic control gave me permission to land. Legs like jelly, I staggered to a rowing machine. Now, I was a rower at school, with the tankards and the thighs to prove it, so I quite enjoyed thrashing up and down and imagining myself skimming along the river (For any aficionado out there, I rowed bow in a clinker four at senior level).

By this time I was pretty knackered. I took one look at the weights department, turned round and went for a swim. As I showered off before entering, I glanced across at the swimming pool. The Club's resident *Captain Webb* was apparently training for his cross-channel swim in lane one, ploughing along at 30 knots, with a flotilla of ill-matched others bobbing up and down in his wake. The main area of the pool was much more sedate, and I really enjoyed splashing around in it for a while.

On my way through the changing room I passed the scales I had weighed myself on when I arrived. Coyly dropping my towel to the floor, I stepped on. The needle went round…and round…and round. I had put on 2lb!

Stuff this for a game of soldiers - where's the nearest chippy!

David Roper

REALITY RULES THE WAVES

"What are you watching, darling?" - "Broad Street, Birmingham, on BBC-CCTV2." "Oh, I caught a bit of that last Tuesday. What's going on today, my little voyeuse?" "The couple with the tattoos are quarrelling outside that Lap-dancing club…again." "She should ditch him!"

"How can she? She's got his name, address and post code emblazoned right across her boobs. Nobody would touch her!"

I have just popped in from our kitchen-cum-TV room after watching a fist fight down West Street on ITV-CCTV3. No serious injuries as yet, but it is well before the nine o'clock 'bloodshed'. 'Kicking-out Time' is a different programme altogether.

You see, today is September 27th, 2038, and Television has come a long way in the last couple of decades. Reality TV is now our TV reality. Starting around the turn of the century with Big Brother and its associated siblings, the crunch came when it dawned on the TV Companies how incredibly cheap reality programmes really were. They embarked on a systematic campaign to cut drama budgets to nil, and within two years the great 'phasing-out' period of the early 21st century began.

'Brookside' was the first casualty, along with 'Casualty'. They were eventually cunningly combined to create 'Celebrity Vasectomy', an interactive programme where viewers voted for an ex-Soap star to undergo the operation, and the studio audience decided which ex-Casualty star would perform it. Unfortunately, with only one 'snip' per star, its run was predictably short.

'Emmerdale' was next to go, giving way to 'Farmyard Deliveries', involving live coverage of the birthing of lambs, calves and piglets by Davina McColl, in elbow-length surgical gloves. The show created somewhat of a cult following among thirty-something rubber fetishists, and peaked at 23 million viewers for its Christmas Special (broadcast from a stable in Bethlehem), for which Davina got her MBE.

'EastEnders' followed the trend, with the last episode featuring 20 bulldozers flattening Albert Square to make way for Ian Beale's grand design for the Walford Safari Park and Eaterie. In the final scene the entire cast of characters was devoured by wild animals, delivered early owing to an administrative cock-up by Ricky Butcher's hastily formed transport firm. Several female cast members were nominated for BAFTA's 'Best actress in a death scene', the award eventually going to Pam St Clement, whose character, Pat Evans, had single-handedly suffocated two lions and a hyena, before succumbing to a fatal squeeze from a boa constrictor hiding in one of her earrings.

'Coronation Street' hung on until the early 30s, partly due to William Roache (Ken Barlow) invoking the clause in his contract about pension rights, but primarily to Prince Edward's gracious (not to say grateful) acceptance of the role of 'West End' Eddie, landlord of The Rover's Return.

Among ITV-CCTV's successes over the years have been: 'In the Chiropodist's Chair', presented by Carole Vorderman; 'Dustbins of the Rich and Famous', presented by Carole Vorderman; and 'Carole Vorderman presents Carole Vorderman', presented by Carole Vorderman, sponsored by the Vorderman Institute for Self-advancement.

BBC-CCTV countered with: 'I'm a Backbencher, get me out of here', in which MPs were voted out of the House of Commons to gain the ultimate prize of a seat in the House of Lords and dinner with Michael Portillo (optional), and 'This is your Wife', in which a celebrity's ex-wife would disclose the sordid details of their divorce and produce all his mistresses to prove it. The programme featuring Robin Cook over-ran by 27 minutes. But BBC-CCTV's greatest achievement came shortly after Her Majesty the Queen abdicated. King Charles III and Queen Kylie allowed CCTV cameras to be installed at Highgrove House, and 'Through the Throne-room Keyhole', presented by Camilla Parker-Bowles, became an instant international hit.

There was inevitably some opposition to all this, principally from the National Association of Independent Voyeurs and Eavesdroppers (NAIVE), but with limited success. NAIVE did manage to have banned the controversial fifth episode of 'Pre-coital Kitchen Capers', involving a tub of low-fat spread, an oven-ready turkey and Ainsley Harriot, but mainly they were ineffective.

David Roper

"Darling, it's starting!"

"Coming!"

I'm off. Can't miss our favourite programme - episode 9 of 'Enema of the People'. Keep watching!

WORK? WHAT'S THAT?

There is no easy way to tell you this, I'm afraid. I have just got to come straight out with it and confess. I will be appearing as Abanazar the Wizard, in 'Aladdin' at the Theatre Royal, Brighton, over Christmas.

Oh no, you won't! Oh yes, I will!

It will be my very first Pantomime, and I am delighted, excited and terrified all at the same time. Delighted to have a job in the first place, excited at the idea of working in my adopted town, sorry - City, and terrified I will look a total prat in the costume and will make a complete dog's breakfast of the whole thing.

Actors' paranoia is alive and whining.

To tell the truth, I haven't even got a script yet, so I have no idea what is expected of me or what I will be wearing. However, because of the nature of the part (baddie), I suspect my job will be to get the kids hissing and booing at every available opportunity, while looking like a cross between Pat Butcher and Yasser Arafat.

I can't wait!

Luckily, I won't have a song to sing - lucky for the audience, that is. I have sort of sung on stage, it is true, and I did once make a passable attempt at singing eight lines of an Operatic Aria, but I have also (with the help of some of Andrea's family, who are equally talented in this department) emptied the top floor of Choy's restaurant by using the Karaoke machine. One poor Brighton couple no doubt still shudder at the thought of the night their romantic Chinese meal for two was ruined by a rendition of

'I'm a Believer', massacred by the combined voices of the Whitehawk Road Male Voice Choir.

David Roper

At the other end of the scale, so to speak, I have also got a job working for BBC Scotland. A new TV series that nobody has heard of yet (apart from the people who are making it of course) is being filmed in Glasgow as I write, and I have a small part in the last episode. A curious thing happens when you work in TV, particularly at the BBC for some unknown reason, and is perhaps most graphically illustrated by the experience of a mate of mine.

He was offered £2000 for four days work on a two-hour episode of a costume drama. You know, the sort of programme that, in accordance with some unwritten law, must be broadcast at 8.00pm on a Sunday. These shows always contain, alongside brand-new costumes authentic in every detail, dozens of pieces of genuine antique furniture from the historical period involved. Maybe I am being picky, but wouldn't the furniture of the time also have been brand-new? I mean, I simply just don't believe that Henry VIII, say, would have been seen dead eating off a chipped and worn 500 year old table. He would have sent Anne Boleyn off to MFI for a new one, surely.

Anyway, my mate thought, 'Great! Two thousand quid? That's five hundred knicker a day.' He bit their hand off. The trouble was the filming was spread over three months, and his four days were evenly distributed throughout that time. The result was: he found himself committed to the Beeb for twelve weeks, was unable to accept any other work during that period and ended up earning only £166.66 pence, recurring, per week - a far cry from the £500 per day it seemed at the start.

No such anomaly arises in the theatre, however. In Aladdin we will be paid for working two performances a day, six days a week and no time off for good behaviour. The problems of working in the Panto will indeed be very different. Will it be worth taking my make-up and costume off between the matinee and evening performances? If not, should I borrow Harry's Action Man lunch-box and take sandwiches to sustain me?

But my biggest problem will be: what kind of reception am I going to get in the playground, when I pick up Harry and Jack after the school's trip to see Aladdin?

Be gentle with me, kids!

OUT OF THE MOUTHS...

To be honest, I only said it to get a bit of peace and quiet. You know what it's like, you have just settled down to do something - in my case to write this very article – when one of the kids starts snapping round your ankles. This time it was Harry.

"Will you play a game, Dad?"

"In a minute."

"Come on, play a game."

"I said – in a minute!"

"OK, I'll time you. One…two…three…"

"Look!"

This is when they make you feel that you are the worst parent in the world, and guilt oozes from your every pore. You must have met it. I tried a different tack.

"Why don't you read a book or write a story or whatever? Go on. Daddy's busy."

I don't even remember saying it, but I must have done.

Anyway, off he trotted, and I returned to the blank piece of paper in front of me. What on earth was I going to write about this week? I've done nothing particularly positive in the past seven days, that's for sure. I didn't mow the lawn, do any paper work or clean Andrea's car. All a bit negative, and not much to write home about.

Oh, I did go up to London for a costume fitting at the BBC, but even that turned out to be negative and depressing, as I had obviously lied through my teeth about my waist measurement. So, what shall I write about?

It was then that it dawned on me. I must have got writer's block! It was bound to happen one day, I suppose - but to one so young? Relax, David. Make yourself a nice hot cup of tea, watch a bit of Kilroy discussing 'I married my niece, now my brother-in-law is my father-in-law, and my ex-wife is my aunty.' and all your problems will seem as nothing in comparison.

It worked. The ideas came flooding into my head. The only trouble was, having spent so much time bemoaning my lack of inspiration, I found myself fast running out of space.

It was at that moment Harry came to my rescue.

"Dad, I've done it."

I had this horrible feeling I was going to have to unblock the downstairs loo yet again. (NB: Exercising his right to copy control, Harry wishes to make it clear that it was Jack who blocked the downstairs loo last time. Jack denies this, so I am going to have a few choice words with Andrea.)

"Done what exactly?"

"I've written a story. You can put it in your writing if you want."

So I have done...

JAMES AND THE BABYNAPPER
BY
HARRY ROPER

There once was a boy called James. He only had a mum, his dad died in a car crash. His mum was going on holiday. She organised for a baby-sitter to come round and look after James. When the day came the baby-sitter was late. When she arrived, she seemed eager for James' mum to leave.

When his mum left, the baby-sitter slammed the door shut and locked it. When James' mum heard the slam, she reversed the car and tried to barge the door open.

It was the Babynapper! She tied James up. (The reason she was a babynapper was because her baby climbed onto the top of the railings and fell off the balcony, and the reason she was late was probably because she was getting her stuff ready to rob).

Suddenly James' mum barged the door open. The baby-sitter pushed James' mum out of the window. She had a broken leg. Then she got her bag out and started robbing.

Then James broke free and kicked her. Then James phoned the police and the ambulance. When they arrived, the police arrested her. James' granddad and grandma looked after him. He went to visit his mum every day at the hospital. From then on James always went on holiday with his mum. They lived happily ever after.

Thanks, Harry, you have saved my life. Now listen, have you got any more ideas for next week...?

David Roper

THE PRICE OF FAME

Once upon a time, when I was working with Sir Peter Hall at The Royal National Theatre (about as high as you can get on the acting scale), somebody said to me,

"Ah well, I expect it will lead to better things."

That simple remark reveals a complex catalogue of attitudes among the public about the nature and status of actors and the acting profession.

In the old days, BT (Before Television), actors were relatively unknown, apart from Film Stars, of course, and you didn't see many of those at the pick-'n-mix in Woolies. Actors would work in weekly Rep., in the West End or on the road touring, and the total audience they could reach would be numbered in the low thousands.

However, in the years AT (After Television), dating realistically from the mid-fifties, actors were exposed to audiences numbering millions, and the public found itself able to recognise an increasing number of 'famous faces', both on and off the box.

This change brought about a fundamental shift in the public's attitude to actors and acting, and created a whole new hierarchy within the profession itself.

From the public's perspective, instead of well-known actors being shady figures from the world of 'legitimate' theatre, there arose a new generation of 'in your face' actors from the world of 'illegitimate' TV. Henceforth, an actor's success would be judged by the frequency of his appearances on the box, rather than by whether he was any good or not. That is not to say that TV actors were/are no good. Not at all. It is just that the public perception of success shifted from quality to quantity, and if an actor was off the screen for a few months it was assumed he was dead, or even worse had emigrated to New Zealand. I can't tell you the number of times people have said to me,

"Haven't seen you on TV recently. Are you still acting?"

The effect of all this exposure was no less profound within the profession itself, and spawned a new being - the celebrity actor. As a result of this elevated status, some actors can demand treatment and wages commensurate with, though sometimes disproportionate to, their new-found 'clout', which is in turn directly proportional to their celebrity status on TV. This situation can often degenerate into the frankly absurd.

There was one famous actress who tried to insist on having her own 'exclusive' car to ferry her around on a TV series. When her agent was told that this was not possible and she would have to share a car, he said,

"Well, she'll agree, under protest. But she has to sit at the front!"

Another result of this 'cult of celebrity' has been the far greater emphasis on billing. You might infer from its name that 'billing' is solely concerned with an actor's position on 'the bill' - the list of performers in order of importance. Not so. These days billing has widened its scope to embrace such decisions as: which dressing room an actor is allocated; the position of his name in the programme (theatre), or in the credits (TV); and, most crucially, the size of his Winnebago. His what?

Winnebago is actually a trade name that, like Hoover, has become synonymous with a particular product - in this case, the luxury motorised caravan used on TV and film sets to house actors. The quality, distribution and size of these 'Winnies' are fought over with a tenacity unheard of since the Battle of the Somme.

The leading actors insist that they each have their own 'detached' Winnie; the second lead actors vie to occupy one that has been divided in two - the 'semi-detached' Winnie; lastly, come those whose accommodation is dished out to them, and which has been split into three or four separate rooms - the 'terraced house' Winnie.

As it happens, I have just got back from Glasgow after filming an episode of BBC Scotland's new TV series - the one I mentioned a couple of weeks back. You won't need me to tell you whereabouts I featured in the pecking order, when I say that I was born in a terraced house and I have ended up in one!

David Roper

ALL THROUGH THE NIGHT

You find me back in one of my favourite cities, Glasgow, gainfully employed filming BBC Scotland's new series, 'Sea of Souls', which I guess will be broadcast in the new year, and in which I have a small part in one episode.

It is really good to be back here, and to rediscover the delights of a great city. What I didn't expect to rediscover, however, was the team of men in Buchanan Street, working behind the notice announcing, 'Caution! Chewing gum removal in progress'.

If you recall - and if not, why not? - when I was here with 'An Inspector Calls' six months ago, I mentioned these lads and their bizarre occupation. I have to report, without a word of a lie, that they are still at it, yet have progressed a mere 120 yards down the road. Whether this bears testimony to the vast quantity of squashed Scottish gum beneath their feet, or to the slowness of their work, is not for me to say, but at that rate Harry and Jack will have passed through puberty before these lads get anywhere near Sauchiehall Street.

I have been up here a couple of times in the past fortnight, and the BBC have splashed out on airline tickets for me. Flying to and from a job always makes me feel rather grand, especially on a scheduled flight with plenty of leg-room, free food and booze, and a car to pick me up at the other end. I feel like a film star - bless!

This week is made up of four consecutive night shoots - the bane of an actor's life. Naturally, I complained to Andrea about this as soon as I got the schedule, and was soundly rebuked for having moaned for two months about being out of work, and here

I was moaning about being in work before I had even started. She has a way of pin-pointing my faults that is, quite frankly, a little disturbing. I must have a word.

You have to admit, though, that kicking off at six o'clock in the evening and finishing, or 'wrapping', at four o'clock the following morning doesn't sound much like a barrel of laughs. Apart from anything else, what it does to your corporeal clock is beyond imagining. Suffice to say that waking at one o'clock in the afternoon, lunching at eight o'clock in the evening and dining at two o'clock in the morning throws your various bodily functions into a violent state of turmoil that it would be indelicate to go into here.

Compounding all that, for me anyway, is the mystery of why the chambermaid felt moved to knock on my door at two o'clock yesterday afternoon to ask if I wanted my room serviced. What part of the 'Please do not disturb' notice didn't she understand, I wonder, and by what telepathic stroke of genius did she manage to time her intrusion to coincide exactly with me plonking myself on the toilet? I shuffled out of my en suite, hoisting my underpants up as quickly as I could, and poked my head round the door.

"Would you like your room serviced, Sir?"

"No, Sir ruddy well would not! Can't you read? Now bog off so I can bog on!"

That is what I felt like saying, but I didn't, of course. Instead I smiled as sweetly as I could, having more pressing things on my mind, and politely declined her generous offer.

The point about that little incident is that it highlights one of the fundamental flaws in British hotel management, and in much of British life in general for that matter. Namely, that organisations, purporting to be run for our benefit are, in fact, run for the benefit of their own internal system(s). For example: the Peter Jones store in Sloane Square used to have toilets on each staircase floor, very convenient (no pun intended). However, one day a notice appeared saying that *For the convenience* (pun probably intended) *of our customers, toilets are now situated on alternate staircase floors.* Great. I have always wanted to chase up two flights of stairs with my legs crossed to get to a loo that I thought was only next door. The thing is, any deviation from their preordained idea of how we should behave throws them into a state of corporate confusion. I was once in a hotel that insisted on...

I don't believe it! As I write, the phone has just trilled irritatingly in my bedroom. It is three o'clock in the afternoon. The hotel housekeeper was on the line.

"Would you like your room serviced, Sir? You see, the chambermaids finish at four."

I rest my case.

WHERE THE NUTS COME FROM

Here is a juicy tit-bit for you. Men who drink coffee are likely to have more vigorous sperm than those who abstain from it, according to a recent report in The Times. This intriguing tendency was unearthed at the University of Sao Paolo in Brazil by a research team headed by Fabio Pasqualotto - may his tribe increase, and it probably will by the sound of it. The secret, it appears, lies in the caffeine.

For reasons best known to himself, and who am I to question his motives, Senor Pasqualotto analysed the semen of the 750 men who had attended the university's clinic for vasectomies. Why so many of Sao Paolo's male population chose to rush headlong, if that's the right word, into such a drastic course of action is not known. However, our friend Fabio, who evidently knows a gift-horse when he sees one, grabbed these Brazilian lads seconds before some scissor-happy surgeon could get 'snipping', and persuaded them to let him evaluate the motility, or swimming ability, of their sperm. A better example of 'shutting the stable door after the horse has bolted', I can't imagine, but there you go. It turns out that the coffee drinkers won hands down, which is presumably how they produced their samples in the first place, but that is not the point.

Brazil, being the world's leading producer, has an understandably vested interest in promoting this revolutionary selling point for its coffee, and must be tickled pink at the unexpected boost to both its world profile and its potentially even greater market share. Coffee barons, from the Tumuc-Humac Mountains to the Lagoa dos Patos, must be grinding their beans with glee at the thought of all the extra revenue heading their way thanks to the spermatazoally challenged, but that is not the point either.

Lest you think me flippant, I must pause here to confess that I am one of those unfortunate creatures, and there are many of us, handicapped by having been found one sperm short of a conception. Whilst I do not take the subject lightly, I do feel justified in approaching it with an insider's sense of irreverence. So there.

But neither is that the point.

The point is, what effect is this striking news going to have on coffee as we know it, and more importantly, on the Advertising Industry's concept of how they would like us to know it? Will the cosy, flirtatious, Gold Blend-type adverts become a thing of the past, to be superceded by the more explicit, hard-hitting 'perk up your prostate' variety? Will 'dark, satisfying aroma' and 'real coffee taste' be consigned to history, to be replaced by the tempting prospect of 'rich, sperm-boosting bouquet' and 'fertilisingly fresh flavour'?

I reckon that if the Advertisers play their cards right and shift their perspective in order to cash in on coffee's new-found sperm-enhancing properties, they could knock a sizeable hole in the alcohol market for a start. Heretofore, the beer and lager-swilling fraternity has maintained a monopoly on its butch image, unchallenged by its gentler tea and coffee-sipping counterparts. Now, as a result of Fabio's inspired initiative, all that may be about to change. Henceforth, downing ten pints of the amber nectar, which only goes to increase desire but decrease performance, may come to be considered deeply un-cool, while sipping ten cups of caffeine-rich, sperm-zapping coffee will become the height of butchness for the lads in the local.

"How much did we get through last night, Kev?"

"Dunno, Brian. I lost count after the eighth cup. Tell you what, though, that bird from Accounts was well impressed at me downing that triple espresso all in one."

"Give over! It was decaffeinated. That's why she blew you out."

"What! That could knacker my sperm count for a week!"

And therein may lie the demise of 'decaff' altogether. Will the European Court of Human Rights insist that all jars of decaffeinated coffee carry a health warning? 'Drinking decaffeinated coffee can seriously damage your sperm. Get help to stop: phone 0800…' It's a thought.

Crikey, I'm running out of space here!

"Andrea, pour us a glass of wine, will you? On second thoughts make that a strong, black coffee. I'm feeling lucky!"

GERREM OFF, GRAN!

Over forty years ago, for light relief from our accountancy studies, Tony, Brian, John and I used to go to The City Varieties in Leeds. Back then, before 'The Good Old Days' arrived and made the place respectable, it was notorious for its strip shows; hence its nickname 'The Leeds Titty Varieties'. By modern standards these stimulating evenings were tame to the point of domesticity. But to a bunch of lads brought up in the 1950s on a diet of magazines such as Health and Efficiency and Spick and Span (ask your granddad), The City Varieties was about as risqué as you could get.

The highlight of the show was the finale - a nude tableau. Because of the Lord Chamberlain's regulations at the time, none of the women were allowed to move, so they just stood there frozen (in more ways than one, by the look of them), flaccid and fifty-something. Nothing against ladies of a certain age, of course, but gravity is no respecter of the passing years, let's face it.

The build-up to this disappointing display was a series of strips by each of these goose-pimpled, grinning grannies. There was one very tall, dark haired woman, I remember, who would always get her knickers caught on the heel of her shoe, and fall over. She did it every time. The audience would roar with laughter, and she would invite us all to…well, 'go forth and multiply' is a rough translation. Classy, or what?

I confess to this misspent part of my youth because yesterday I was standing outside the said City Varieties, recalling those golden moments. I am in Leeds filming 'Heartbeat', and in a few days' time I go up to Goathland, North Yorkshire, where Aidensfield and Ashfordly 'exist', so more of Heartbeat next week.

David Roper

Back in Leeds, I unearthed the marvellous back street boozer that we used to retire to after those sexless strip shows. It was just as I remember it; dimly lit, with marble-topped food counters, and beer hand-pulled from the cellar. Terrific. The notice behind the bar was a bit strange, though.

'These premises will close at 6.00pm today.' I asked why.

"The match," was the reply. "Leeds are playing Manchester United tonight, and all the hard core fans take the day off. They'll be getting drunk as we speak, and later on they'll start chucking ashtrays at barmaids. They're pretty good at it too. So, discretion being the better part of concussion, as they say, we shut up shop. Not a nice place, Leeds, on nights like this. I'd go home, if I were you."

So much for my trolling around tasting the Tetley's. Instead, I opted for a quick 'Saucisse Toulousanne avec puree de pommes de terre' (sausage and mash) at Café Rouge, followed by a strategic withdrawal to cell 504 at the Leeds Novotel. The meal was excellent, the service charming, if over-attentive, and the place mercifully uncrowded. As I was about to tuck in, somewhere above me, in the mezzanine area, the disembodied voice of a mobile phone anorak pierced through the gentle clatter of people eating and drinking and minding their own business. Why do some people find it necessary to shout torrents of useless drivel into these damn things? This particular lad had honed it to an art form.

"I've only just started my main course, so I'll give you a ring when I leave here, and if you give me a ring when you leave there, then I'll ring you back if I get there before you. But if you get there before me, and I haven't given you a ring, you give me a ring, then I'll know you're there, so I can give you a ring when I know when I'm

going to get there, OK?....Cool. Whatever happens meet me in the Frogspawn and Firkin at eight. Cheers."

As I walked back to my hotel, passed the gathering police presence, the bouncers on every pub door, and surrounded by the music of a million mobile phones, I yearned to be back in Leeds's quieter, safer and politically incorrect days, enjoying a peaceful night out and a couple of pints with Tony, Brian and John, and innocently ogling a granny. Happy days.

IT'S A LONG WAY TO...GOATHLAND

Last week I promised more on my stint filming 'Heartbeat' in Yorkshire. So here goes.

'Heartbeat', now in its thirteenth series, is based at an old woollen mill midway between Leeds and Bradford. It is ironic that a building, once dedicated to an industry that was killed off in the sixties by underinvestment and lack of foresight, is now home to a new industry dedicated to recreating that very decade, by shrewd investment and the benefit of hindsight.

The exterior locations are filmed in and around a tiny village, Goathland, on the North Yorkshire moors. To say that Goathland is at the back of beyond is to grossly overestimate its proximity to civilisation. It really is in the middle of nowhere, and to get there makes Sir Ranulph Fiennes' exploits seem like a walk in the park. I had to take a taxi to Brighton station, a Thameslink train to King's Cross, a GNER train to York, where I was met in front of W.H.Smith's and driven the forty-three miles across the North Yorkshire Nature Park to my hotel. It all seemed like a great adventure, and I was quite excited as we drove over Lendel Bridge, under which I used to row as a schoolboy, passed York Minster and out towards the distant and vast expanse of the moors.

As suburban Pickering slipped away behind us, houses were replaced by lonely farms, side roads by dirt tracks, and people by flocks of sheep, which appeared to have a less than adequate grasp of the Highway Code. Braised lamb is a popular local dish up here - I say no more. By the time we arrived at the hotel, The Mallyon Spout, named after a spring at the bottom of the garden, I had been travelling for nearly seven hours. It made Sir Ranulph Fiennes' expeditions look like a Sunday afternoon stroll, and I was in serious need of a lie down and a couple of pints - in reverse order.

Whether it is being set in the laid back sixties, or because cast and crew are thrown together on a kind of television outward-bound course, 'Heartbeat' is an incredibly friendly programme to work on. The days are spent driving around, and filming among, the stunning scenery of Goathland and the North Yorkshire moors, or in the charming fishing village of Whitby. The evenings are spent huddled together in the Hunt Bar of the Mallyon, drinking pints of cold Guinness and eating Whitby Cod served with chips the size of small table legs.

The whole experience is like joining a large, extended family, in which nobody pulls rank, everybody pulls their weight and every five minutes somebody pulls your leg.

My scenes are with two old mates, Peter Benson (Bernie Scripps) and Geoffrey Hughes (Vernon Scripps). Peter and I go back over thirty years, and Geoffrey and I realised yesterday that we go back nearly that long, too. I was the copper who arrested Geoffrey's Coronation Street character, Eddie Yates, for nicking tins of corned beef from the corner shop in 1974, when we both had waistlines and could be contained in a two-shot without the cameraman widening the lens. I hadn't seen either of them for decades, but when we met it was as if we had never been apart.

That happens a lot in the acting profession - for two reasons. Firstly, actors tend to follow other actor's careers, and they often see each other in the theatre or on TV, so they never really feel as though they have completely lost touch. Secondly, the nature of the profession, which necessitates getting on with people instantly, means that even short-lived 'friendships' can get cemented very quickly.

Hello! It looks as though I am about to be called for my last scene. With a bit of luck and a following wind I'll be finished by lunchtime, and will be able to set off on my epic seven hour trek back to Brighton.

Sir Ranulph - eat your heart out!

TYPE CAST? NO WAY.

The world has turned against me!

Andrea refuses to kiss me, and Harry and Jack turn away at my very approach. If I stray within striking distance of them, they turn up their noses and declare,

"Ugh! It's horrible!"

Even my friends have started to look at me in a strange way, and in shops I am given the widest of berths.

The reason for my rejection and isolation is not, as you might suppose, because I stink of drink and garlic, which I confess I often do, nor because I have B.O. of nose-curling proportions, which I hope I don't. No, it is simply the fact that I am in the process of growing a...beard!

Before we go any further, I must tell you this is no mere whim on my part. In fact, I have little choice in the matter. I have been asked to grow this appendage by the director of 'Aladdin', in which I will be appearing as Abanazar, at the Theatre Royal, Brighton, over Christmas. To be fair, it wasn't exactly an order, more a polite request. However, I decided to give it a go, since the alternative of sticking a false one on with glue, and removing it with surgical spirit every night, didn't appeal to me much.

It is now four days since I last shaved, and the fungus on my face is inching its way across my physog, and making me look decidedly scruffy and unkissable, at least according to my nearest and dearest. To be honest, I have never had much success with facial hair in the past. My previous moustaches have looked quite respectable, it's true, but my last attempt at a beard was greeted with derision by all who managed to spot it. All it amounted to was a wisp of bum fluff stuck to the end of my chin.

What a difference a day makes, though. Yesterday, I shaved off the rough edges and those bits creeping down under my collar, so that out of all the grotty growth, emerged an embryonic 'goatee' beard. 'That's more like it,' I said, as I looked at myself in the mirror. 'Not bad at all. Another couple of weeks, and you'll be looking like Errol Flynn as Robin Hood.' Bless! OK, maybe Friar Tuck, then.

Actually, the main effect is to give me a slightly sinister look, which is just the ticket for Abanazar. You see, generally speaking, I tend to get the more amiable, unthreatening kind of parts, and have had to work hard to look...well, 'hard', if you understand me. It is all to do with the shape of the face and the look in the eyes. Every actor - everybody, for that matter - has something about their face and bearing, which tends to put them in a certain category; hard, soft, put-upon, shifty etc. This has nothing necessarily to do with what they are really like, but everything to do with how others, and, in my profession, casting directors, initially see them.

And therein lies the actor's problem. In order to play against 'type', he has to bring out those covert characteristics within himself, which go against the overt impression he gives, and often needs as much help as he can get.

A lot of that help can be in the form of costume and/or make up. I remember once having to play a Nazi Officer, Commandant of Auschwitz Concentration Camp, and finding it very difficult to portray the necessary air of superiority and arrogant certainty, although Andrea did say that she couldn't see my problem. It was only when I put on the costume, and walked around in the way the uniform and jack boots force you to do, that I could find the look and the bearing I needed for the part.

In a similar way, I hope the goatee beard is going to provide me with some help in achieving the 'wicked wizard' effect needed for Abanazar. Besides, and don't you dare tell her this, I think Andrea is rather warming to her new dashing-looking rogue of a husband.

"Hey, Maid Marion! Come over here and give us a kiss!"

GOING DOWN: MIND THE STAIRS

How much earlier can it start? As the sun streaks through Stonehenge to mark the Summer Solstice? On May Day? At Easter? Where will it end, or rather begin?

I speak of the build-up to that triumph of commerce over conscience: Christmas. Be fair, its origins have got somewhat clouded. As the lady in ASDA said, referring to a Christmas card with a church window on it,

"Look at that. They're bringing religion into everything these days."

I know we are nearing the end of November, when you might reasonably expect the shops to be anticipating Christmas, but I seem to recall becoming aware of its imminent arrival shortly after Harry and Jack returned to school in early September, for goodness' sake!

When I was a lad - oh, no, here he goes! - nothing happened until Bonfire Night was a dim memory, and Christmas would only appear on the horizon just before my father's birthday on December 9ᵗʰ. My mother would wheel me the eight miles to the slag heap in my pram, fill it up with Nutty Slack, and we would crawl back on our hands and knees, gnawing at a crust of stale bread, as we passed the glittering display of Bradford's Christmas Lights: Red; red and amber; green; amber; and back to red. Excitement would be thick in the air, and packed into two or three weeks, instead of being thinly spread over two or three months, as it is now.

The problem these days, of course, especially if you have kids, is that long before the clocks go back, TV ads and Catalogues abound, all displaying a mind-boggling quantity of available 'goodies'.

The other day, I wandered into the lounge and found the boys reading and writing, or so I thought. In fact, they were flicking through the Argos catalogue, like two women in search of a new outfit, and composing seemingly endless lists of what they required from Santa on the big day. It was our cue to start shopping.

'And so it came to pass that David and his wife, Andrea, who was heavy with credit, were summoned by Daewoo Lanos to Churchill Square. But there was no room in the car park. "Lo!" quoth David, "Behold! An empty Mother and Baby space. Sod it, let's park there for once."'

We were in search of toys we had never heard of, and it wasn't a good start. Having scoured the shelves in vain, we approached the assistant.

"Excuse me, you know Gooey Louey…"

"Not personally, but that's the one where snot comes down his nose, isn't it?"

"Yes, thank you. Well, there's a similar one, apparently, called Hungry Hughey, I believe, where you stick your fingers down his throat, and he vomits all over you. Have you got one?"

"Sorry, we've sold out. You're the third person to ask that. Hughey's been very popular."

Very popular! I thought our boys had weird tastes, but to think that they are just two among millions, makes me seriously wonder about the future of mankind. Do you know there are toy babies on sale now that not only cry and eat, but also urinate and defecate with astonishing authenticity? You wait, in a couple of years they will be producing dolls that will be sick the moment they are dressed in clean clothes, will start crying at random intervals during the night, and will say 'Oh, God, not that old trout', when picked up by your mother-in-law (no reference to mine, naturally).

As light relief, we wandered into WH Smith's to buy a next year's diary, and go upstairs for a paper. Now, am I the only person to have puzzled over why WH Smith's in Brighton boasts the only escalator that goes down, and not up? You see dozens of the less agile among us, struggling up the staircase, to be greeted by the sight of more sprightly people, merrily stepping onto the escalator that takes them effortlessly down. Lift or no lift, it still doesn't make sense. There may be a perfectly reasonable explanation for this tampering with gravity, and I, for one, would welcome it.

Answers on a postcard, please!

1966 AND ALL THAT

As I write, the England Rugby Union team has just made its triumphant return from Australia aboard 'Sweet Chariot', and I add my voice to the cacophony of congratulations that has greeted them.

From a dramatic point of view, the victory could not have been better if it had been scripted. England proved they could play the game by actually scoring a try, and by beating the host nation and arch rival, Australia. Mind you, they did keep us on the edge of our seats until that last minute, toe-nail biting, drop goal from the star of the show, Jonny Wilkinson. As finales go, it was unsurpassable.

I must here confess to a vested interest in this boost to the game. Not only am I a rugby fan, but I harbour the fervent desire that England's new Rugby World Championship status will finally and mercifully put to rest the ghost of 1966, when we beat Germany in the football World Cup final.

OK, it was a momentous event in our country's sporting history, and we all remember it well. But the point is, as a nation we have been banging on about that dim and distant English victory for over forty years, and I really think it is about time we all grew up and let 1966 lie, to gracefully take its place alongside our other great European achievements - Agincourt, Waterloo and Puppet on a String.

For a start, the vast majority of present day football supporters were not actually alive in 1966, and there are even fans, of bottle throwing age, whose fathers were not yet born then either. Certainly no member of any current England team was even a glint in his dad's eye when,

"They think it's all over. It is now!"

entered the language for good.

It has always struck me as odd that it has never occurred to football commentators that, by going on and on about 'England's greatest moment', they are actually doing inestimable harm to the beautiful game, by continuously drawing attention to the fact that nothing of note has happened in the intervening decades of barren, footballing years. Yes, we might have qualified for subsequent World Cup competitions, and even reached some of the final stages, but second, third and fourth are merely degrees of disaster.

There is another strange question that has always intrigued me. Why does football induce such violence in its fans, but rugby doesn't? There were 50,000 English rugby supporters in Sydney, and, as far as I know, there were no reports of aggro at all, apart from some inevitable Pommy-bashing, and the odd snide remark about Erinsborough and Summer Bay. Imagine what would have happened if 50,000 English football supporters had been in Monchengladbach, say, to watch us play Germany in a World Cup final, instead. You know as well as I do that bars and restaurants, from the Rhine to the Polish border, would have been boarded up or wrecked, and World War III would have broken out.

Searching for an answer to the disparity in the two games' levels of spectator violence is not easy. Has it to do with the tribal nature of football supporters? Maybe, but rugby supporters can be equally partisan. Has it to do with the fact that football attracts young, testosterone-filled lager drinkers? Maybe, but so does rugby.

Perhaps, and this is my personal theory, it has to do with the lack of, or surfeit of violence on the pitch. Footballers are physically repressed, and violence is severely punished. Rugby, on the other hand, has violence written all over it, and, although outright brawling is stamped on, the very nature of the game means that it often seems like organised gang warfare in sweaty designer shirts. Football fans, therefore, have to find their physical release elsewhere, typically on the terraces or after the match, whereas rugby fans are witness to so much physical activity during the game that they have little stomach left for thumping the opposition afterwards.

That is all very well as a theory, David, but, if it's true that spectator violence is inversely proportional to player violence, then I would steer clear of watching snooker if I were you!

ACT BETTER!

'Aladdin' opened two days ago to rapturous applause - I hope, because I'm putting pen to paper last week – if you can fight your way through that timescale. As I write, we are rehearsing up in London at the Old Vic for six days, before descending on Brighton to put the show together. What that means, of course, is commuting every day, at my own expense, and staggering back home in the midst of the rush hour.

However, rehearsing at the Old Vic gives me quite a 'buzz', as it is one of the most famous and prestigious theatres in London. Although it is not actually in the West End (London's Theatreland), it was where Laurence Olivier often performed and where he founded and based the now Royal National Theatre, before it moved to its permanent home on the South Bank of the Thames. Just rehearsing at the Old Vic makes you feel that you are a small part of the history of the theatre in the UK.

Successful rehearsals often depend on the atmosphere created by the director, and can be stressful at times. I worked with one woman director, who treated the whole process as if she were giving birth - from conception of the idea, through the labour of rehearsals, to delivery of the first performance. We were forced to suffer labour pains with her, and the opening night was the dramatic equivalent of a breech birth. Before you ladies have my balls for albondigas, I hasten to add that male directors can also treat rehearsals as an opportunity to work out their emotional inadequacies.

There was one maniac male director who took great delight in 'putting down' actors at every available opportunity. One young lad, after making a tentative entrance and fluffing his lines, was greeted with,

"Yes, thank you, John. I must say, the stage is a little emptier by your presence." To an actor uncertain of his moves, the same director said,

"What on earth do you think you're doing? You're wandering around the stage like Peter Pan looking for a mantelpiece!"

Great lines, if you like that kind of thing, but not designed to instil confidence into a nervous young actor. Neither was the note given to me, actually, during rehearsals early in my career,

"Really not bad, David, but could you, sort of...act better?"

It was John Gielgud, though, so the story goes, who really struck a blow for us actors. He summed it all up when one 'avant-garde' director, having spent rehearsals in unusually inappropriate and irrelevant improvisations, insisted,

"Come on, you lot! I want you all to stand down-stage and frighten me. Really frighten me!"

Gielgud walked to the front of the stage and boomed,

"We open tomorrow!"

In Aladdin, I find myself surrounded by dancers, singers and acrobats, and am feeling a touch inadequate in the talent department. You see, my dancing has been a source of merriment to Andrea for years, my singing has emptied theatres quicker than a bomb scare, and my acrobatic skills have been stretched to their limit by the simple act of changing a light bulb on the landing. Luckily, my role as Abanazar is restricted to standing still, at which I am a past master, while delivering lines in my best 'wicked wizard' voice. No dancing, no singing and absolutely no acrobatics. My main purpose, of course, is to be booed and hissed every time I appear, and to be just this side of frightening to all the kids in the audience.

One of the pitfalls of rehearsing the comedy in a Panto, or in any play for that matter, is the law of diminishing returns. What I mean is: the first time you hear one of the jokes it is hysterical, the second time it is quite funny, but by the umpteenth time it has lost whatever appeal it had, and seems like the unfunniest thing you have ever heard. All you can do is to hang on to that initial reaction, and keep reminding yourself that each audience will be hearing it for the first time.

Oh no! They've just decided to put me in the song and dance finale! Look out for me. I will be the big one on the end with the two left feet and a voice like an elephant in labour. Enjoy!

THE NAME GAME

"As soon as we go up, I'll set your worker OP, so you can change out of your opener, ready for the blinder that goes out after the 'front-cloth', and then you're on. Your walk-down will be set in the prompt side wing change area at the interval. OK?"

What on earth was the wardrobe bloke talking about? Panto-speak is a language all its own, and to me, an illiterate newcomer in this strange linguistic world, it was a complete mystery. I did know that 'go up' = start of the show, 'you're on' = go on stage, and that 'OP' = opposite prompt-side (not that we have a prompter these days, although the name has stuck), but I had never come across 'opener', 'worker', 'blinder', 'front-cloth' or 'walk-down'. What could they all mean?

It didn't take me long to find out.

It appears that my 'opener' was the costume I would wear for my first entrance. After my exit, I would change into my 'worker', which was the costume I would wear throughout the rest of the show. The 'blinder' is a black curtain, behind a gauze, to 'blind' the audience to a pre-set scene. That scene is put there during a 'front-cloth' scene, usually between two actors, and played, of course, in 'front' of the gauze and black curtain. My 'walk-down', as I thought, was the costume I would wear at the end of the show, when we all 'walked down' and took applause, and would be an over-the-top version of my 'worker'. Does all that make sense? Took me a while!

It was amazing, though, when the penny finally dropped! With one rub of the magic lamp of language, the rock of ignorance had rolled aside, revealing an Aladdin's Cave of etymological gems and enriching my vocabulary no end.

The bad news is: I have been diagnosed as having a severe case of the highly infectious 'boo-boom!' syndrome, symptomatic of over-exposure to the Panto joke.

My prognosis is not good, as this most insidious of conditions has already started to manifest itself in my everyday conversation.

"David, what would you say to a pizza after the show?"

"Hello, pizza, did you have a good time?" Boo-boom!

Shakespeare, it ain't, as one member of the cast was heard to say, but I am not so sure that Panto and The Bard are really that far apart in many respects. I reckon the relationship between actors and audience in his day is reflected far more clearly in Panto than in a lot of the stuff you find these days at the Royal Shakespeare Company.

You see, Panto characters have quite specific roles (hero, villain, romantic, comic), demanding a certain response, and have virtually exact parallels in many of Shakespeare's sharply drawn protagonists. For example, it wouldn't surprise me if the first Elizabethans' reaction to Richard III's character, say, wasn't much the same as today's Elizabethans' reaction to my Abanazar - booing, hissing, and revelling in his wickedness and ultimate downfall. It is a sobering thought that today's kids, shouting 'Rubbish!', 'Get off!' and 'Oh no, it isn't!', are echoing their long dead ancestors' equally vociferous version of audience participation.

It is not just the kids either. Many adults really get their rocks off on the freedom to voice their reactions, instead of sitting in polite silence, as is usual in the theatre. They are as inclined as the kids to join in the songs and shout 'He's behind you' or whatever, without very much encouragement, if any. They seem to find a great feeling of release in letting themselves go, as it were.

Maybe that's it! Panto is a form of collective psycho-therapy - the dramatic equivalent of Primal Scream, where you vent your pent-up frustrations by uninhibited shouting, without the constraints and consequences of doing it in real life. Fancy that!

We are not just luvvies in gold lame, then, but thespian therapists out to release an audience's anger, with daily consultations at 2.30 and 7.30. (Interval drinks available).

"Mr. Roper, this is your call."

Must dash. Off with my opener, on with my worker, and enter OP behind the blinder after the front-cloth.

My patients await - oh yes, they do!

IT'S PARTY TIME

How was it for you? Christmas Day, I mean. I expect the turkey has, by now, lost quite a bit of weight, you've put on pretty much an equal amount, and your intestinal tract is having a nervous breakdown. Nevertheless, I hope you had a good time and that Santa came up with the goods.

From our point of view, I can tell you that for us Panto performers Christmas Day is, as always, our one and only day off in the two long weeks leading up to New Year's Eve. But worry not on our behalf, as you sit in the Churchill Square car park queue, waiting to exchange the presents you got but didn't want, while the antacid tablets fight a running battle with the laxatives for control of your system, for sympathy is not what we crave. Not a bit of it. You see, we are happy bunnies, because, and this is my point, working all over the Christmas period is going to make the whole affair that much more enjoyable.

For a start, by having to prance around on stage twice a day, our food and booze intake will be necessarily limited, thus sparing us the customary seasonal liverishness, while working off whatever minor excesses we have allowed ourselves.

On top of that, it is without doubt that every performance, and the whole run, really, is like some fantastic never-ending party. The audience, to a man, or more properly to a child, is sitting out there determined to enjoy every moment, and the cast members are in a similar state of mind, too.

What makes each performance a party, at least for those of us on stage, is that the cast is made up of such a wide variety of performers. There are the principals (often well-known artists), the male and female dancers, the comedians, the acrobats, the romantic leads, the troupe of dancing and singing kids and the old farts like me playing Baron Hard-up or some such a character. Because of all the different ages involved, and their various backgrounds, it makes for an amazing 'party' feeling, perhaps mostly because of the kids and their excitement about it all, which spreads rapidly through the rest of the cast.

However, perhaps more to the point, we will have the pleasure of bringing a little joy and, hopefully, plenty of laughter into lives jaded by all the inevitable Christmas pressures, such as: serving up sprouts that everybody leaves on the side of their plates, like baby Dinosaur droppings; entertaining relatives, who only turn up at Christmas, and that's once a year too many, thank you very much; and being forced to spend days on end cooped up in the house, with the kids bickering, mum working her tights off, and dad regaling us with a feast of festive farting all through the Queen's speech (it is a treasonable offence, did you know, and contravenes the Flatulence (Royal personages, in the presence of) Act, 1522.

The funny thing is, we put ourselves through it all to celebrate the birth of Jesus of Nazareth, who must look down every year and marvel at how his Dad's gift to mankind of a Saviour has been turned into an obscene, over-indulgent commercial event, wholly unrelated to, and unrepresentative of, the message 'Peace on Earth, goodwill to all men.'

Don't get me wrong, I don't dislike Christmas, it's just that all the effort you put into it always seems so disproportionate to the limited pleasure you manage to squeeze out of a measly twenty-four hours. Be honest, how many times have you forced yourself to think, 'I'm going to enjoy this day, if it kills me!', then spent the whole time wishing it were all over and that you could get back to work?

Of course, one of the problems these days is that Christmas means that all activity, apart from emergency services, granted, comes to a grinding halt for about a fortnight. In the olden days, when I was a lad, businesses closed for Christmas Day and Boxing Day, and you prayed that they would come before or after a weekend so you would have four consecutive whole days off.

Talking of Boxing Day, the word that always springs to mind is 'anticlimax' - no, it is not what your uncle's wife experiences during sex – it is the feeling that it is all over far too quickly. OK, maybe aunty has a point. Boo-boom!

You can tell I am still doing Panto, can't you?

RESOLUTION REVOLUTION

I am not exactly over-endowed in a certain department…hang about! I'm going to rephrase that.

I am not exactly endowed with much in the resolve department. That's better. However, putting that aside, and in an effort to be at least a tad more decisive, this New Year I will definitely try to:

1) Lose weight, because I am too mean to throw away my 40 inch waist trousers, and too embarrassed to be seen in High and Mighty buying 46 inch ones. It is not that I am all that High, mind, it is just that I am a touch too Mighty for my own good.

2) Crack the mystery of why, every time I go into Barclays Bank at 9.35, there are only two tellers, out of a possible nine, to serve a queue of thirty-six impatient people.

3) Answer the question, 'What do they do to actors between leaving a Soap and signing a 'golden handshake' TV deal that turns them into miscast and/or pretentious shadows of their former selves?' With the exception of Amanda Burton, naturally.

4) Go to the David Lloyd Torture Centre three times a week, assuming I can summon the desire and the energy, because it really hurts a Yorkshireman not to be getting his money's worth.

5) Be more tolerant of people who are handicapped by being caricatures of themselves - Tony Blair and George Bush will do for starters.

6) Watch a whole episode of any continuing drama that I've never been in, without cursing them for never offering me a part in it. Get over it, David!

7) Figure out why I can't buy just 'a coffee' anymore, but have to fight my way through lists of mochas, frappes, grandes, medios, americanos and lattes, stretching to infinity. It used to be so simple:

"What would you like, sir?"

"Black coffee, please, no sugar."

"Certainly. There you are."

"Thank you."

Mind you, I have to admit that I was chucked out of a cafe in Leeds for asking that very same question. But then, it was the Ceylon Tea Centre, so maybe they had a point.

8) Understand why women weather forecasters invariably sport inane grins and are so relentlessly jolly, or else get shoved outside in the freezing cold to stop them flirting outrageously with the news-reader. Not to mention the fact that they, and their male counterparts too, will insist on standing slap bang in front of Cornwall on the weather map, thus obliterating everywhere west of Truro.

9) Make a citizen's arrest on the next cyclist, over the age of consent, that I see riding on the pavement.

10) Get my brain round one of life's great mysteries: the appeal of Reality TV. Doesn't real life throw enough at us already?

11) Stop throwing the phone at the wall when listening to the mind-numbing catalogue of choices reeled off by the recorded voice of some bird from north of the Wash.

12) Find out which imbecile schedules films that straddle the late News, making them impossible to follow, and ensuring that they finish well past everybody's bedtime.

13) Fathom the pricing structure on the railways, which throws up such amusing little anomalies as: the price range for the journey from Brighton to Manchester - £28.50 to £231.70, or thereabouts, depending on whether you buy your ticket seven years in advance on the third Tuesday in May, travel after 10.00am on a Thursday and return before 6.00pm on a Sunday, but not more than 48 hours later than your 100th birthday, and only if your inside leg measurement is less than 34.

14) Understand why anybody in their right mind would buy a copy of The Sun. I honestly can't see why it exists, save as a relatively expensive masturbation aid, or something to wrap your fish and chips in.

15) Get through a performance of 'Aladdin', or of any other play in which I manage to land a part, without fluffing any lines or giggling.

16) Work out why BBC2 and Channel 4 always manage to show different documentaries on exactly the same subject at precisely the same time on the same day.

17) Squeeze out more money for writing this witty, charming, informative, always delivered on time, just coming up to its first anniversary so it's about time I had a rise - article.

Happy New Year!

David Roper

LOOK BACK IN HUNGER

All actors have a working past, a few have a working present, but it is rare to find an actor so confident of a working future that he dares to put a year planner at the top of his list for Santa. An actor's diary, too, apart from maybe recording his birthday and his Spotlight renewal, tends to be somewhat blank, to say the least. You need only to eavesdrop on a group of us actors chatting, to realise how true that is.

In the present, actors talk little of the future, but will toss the past tense around like nuts on Boxing Day.

"I *did* an episode of that."

"When I *was* at the National…"

"The day war *broke out*…"

You've heard it, no doubt. Much of all that can be put down to name-dropping, which actors are prone to indulge in occasionally, although it can backfire. I remember one actor, who had worked with Laurence Olivier saying,

"I used to call him 'Larry', you know."

"Really? None of this 'Mr. Lamb' nonsense, then?"

What has brought all this on is the end of yet another year and the realisation that, with nothing to look forward to in the coming year, the only direction I can look in, with any real pleasure, is backwards.

You may recall that this time last year I was gazing at the vast, fertile plain of a seven month tour of 'An Inspector Calls' and the harvest of a steady income stretching out before me, ready to be gathered in. This year I peer out of the oasis that is 'Aladdin', which, by the way, ends a week tomorrow, and stare at the endless expanse of the Unemployment Desert, shimmering in the heat of uncertainty, and throwing up mirages of leading roles in long-running series. Hope springs eternal.

Oh crikey, he's feeling sorry for himself again! Not at all. I am just gearing myself up for the inevitable effort I know I am going to have to make to think positive, and to keep reminding myself of what the Patron Saint of unemployed actors, Mr. Macawber, so wisely said,

"Something will turn up."

If - no, be positive, David! *When* that something does turn up, it will be my agent who will ring to give me the good news. As we all know, the phone call from the agent is the single most important thing in any actor's life. To exemplify that there is the apocryphal story of the actor who came home one evening to find his wife in a state of profound distress, and his house ransacked. Supressing panic, he asked,

"What on earth has happened, darling?"

"It was your agent!"

"My agent? What about him?"

"He came round about an hour or so ago. When I opened the door to him, he burst in, ripped off my dress and assaulted me, drank the remains of your single malt, kicked in the tele and then ran off with all the cash and my jewellery!"

"Oh, my God! Did he leave a message?"

I told this to Andrea, who nodded knowingly. At least she has got the message.

In the meantime, I must say that my stint in Aladdin at the Theatre Royal (seats still available) is turning out to be infinitely more rewarding than I ever thought it could be.

Because of the nature of the beast, every performance is like one great family party. I think I touched on this a while ago, but it is, without doubt, absolutely true. You see, the cast is made up of those who, in the real world, may be uncles, aunts, mums, dads, cousins or whatever, but who, in the Panto world, all display their respective and often amazing talents. As for the children, well, our sixteen Babes (two alternating troupes of eight mixed girl and boy dancers) bring a freshness and enthusiasm that is a fantastic antidote to any jaded feeling brought on by the attendant seasonal and inevitably indulgent festivities. It really is a pleasure to go to the theatre knowing that, whatever worries might be playing on your mind, they will be whisked away for two hours or so, while you immerse yourself in the world of Panto.

Do you know, I haven't had so much fun since Michael Portillo lost his seat at a General Election!

WHAT'S IN A NAME?

Indeed, what is in a name? A bizarre mixture of continuity and change, if the latest league tables of the most popular boys' and girls' names are anything to go by.

Continuity, in the sense that the top ten names in both lists are exactly the same as the previous year, albeit in a *changed* order. *Change*, in the sense that names derived from TV do *continue* to pop up with alarming regularity. The result is, it seems, that a Jack, Joshua or Thomas (top three boys) has a far greater chance of ultimately marrying an Emily, Ellie or Chloe (top three girls), than an Alfie (from EastEnders - a new entry at No. 18) has of ultimately getting his leg over a Chardonnay (from Footballers' Wives). Ninety three girls were inexplicably so named. Perhaps Shiraz, Merlot and Cabernet Sauvignon will not be far behind.

Football, too, has its fans in the naming game. Ryan Giggs' parents for one, or two I suppose, have a lot to answer for, if they were indeed responsible for naming him and for creating a whole generation of copycat Ryans in the process.

Royalty, of course, has always had an influence on the popularity of names, although royal 'naming' has been strictly in the mainstream and kept very much to names such as Edward, George, Charles etc. That system seems to work well for them, and does avoid the alarming possibility of us being ruled by, say, King Darren and Queen Deidre. No disrespect to anybody with such a name, of course, it's just that some names, rightly or wrongly, don't seem to sit well in the tally of English royalty.

On the issue of names, Andrea and I appear to be on the side of Royalty, and are firmly in the mainstream. For instance, I called my first son, by a previous marriage, George (No. 16 on the list), and Andrea yelled out 'Harry' (No. 11) and

'Jack' (No. 1) at the very moment of their delivery. Well, not quite, but we decided that 'Oh, my God!' and 'Never again!' were marginally unsuitable as boys' names, though it was a close run thing, I must say.

Of course, that was before the Beckhams christened their son, Brooklyn, and opened up the intriguing possibility of naming children after the location of their conception. We would have had a problem with that, as it happens, because the twins were conceived via IVF, and would have necessarily ended up as 'Harley' and 'Street', or, more properly, 'Test' and 'Tube', I suppose. However, if 'location, location, location' is to become the rallying call to parents agonising over the choice of a name, where will it all end, I wonder? Will future generations of children curse their parents for that one moment of passion in Grimethorpe? Will the world be littered with kids called Bike-shed, Backseat and Broom Cupboard? And pity the poor sod whose parents couldn't keep their hands off each other on that day trip to Wales and Llanfairpwllgwyngyllgogerychwyrndrobwllantysiliogogogoch.

At least a location has the virtue of permanence. Call me conservative, but I think anybody who names a child after some transient TV character is stark raving bonkers - no disrespect to the parents of any Scooby-doos out there, by the way.

That said, I must confess that my maternal grandparents did lay some of the groundwork for those wanting to mark their off-spring as being 'of their time'. Lacking TV, radio and popular culture as a source in 1916, they turned to the biggest event affecting their lives at the time - the First World War - and named my mother after two of its recent battles. No, she is not called Ypres Somme, but goes by the rather romantic-sounding handle, Lille Louvain, and I think they are quite lovely names.

On that basis, perhaps I shouldn't be so sniffy about TV derivatives, and should wish Alfie and Chardonnay all the best in their future life together. Congratulations!

THE END IS NIGH

'Aladdin' finished its five week run last Sunday and I will sadly miss it. Admittedly, trudging into the theatre and facing a six day stint of twelve performances on the trot did sometimes feel like the theatrical equivalent of community service. However, the roar of the crowd, the party atmosphere and the sweet smell of a month's sweat on my costume did wonders for my mid-winter blues, if not for the nostrils of those in the front row of the stalls.

Thinking back over the whole experience, I suppose what amazed me most was how quickly we managed to get such a complicated show on. Sitting in the auditorium and watching this extravaganza it must be hard to believe that within a mere ten working days, all our lines were learned, the dance routines choreographed, the songs perfected, sets erected, music arranged, lighting and sound synchronised and the whole lot put together to create our 'Aladdin'. Truly, it was an amazing feat of dedication, application and sheer hard work by everybody.

On top of that, the whole run has gone so smoothly. But Sod's law is never far away, is it? We have given sixty-one performances without injury, illness or catastrophe - until the very last day!

Arriving at the theatre on that afternoon we were greeted with the news that one member of the cast was stuck on the M25 and wouldn't make the matinee; an acrobat had injured his foot; a dancer was unable to perform because of a twisted ankle...it never rains!

Miraculously, within half an hour; understudies were pressed into service; routines rearranged; everybody doubled their concentration and we got through it by the skin of our teeth.

I must pause here to tell you that, although you are reading this after we have closed, I am actually writing this in my dressing room during the last performance.   I am about to make my final entrance, and I feel a touch emotional.

As with 'An Inspector Calls', if you remember, I am about to say goodbye to my temporary 'family'. It is odd to think that I may never see some of these people ever again: people who I have become so close to.

To be honest, I have never really come to terms with this aspect of the business, and it chokes me every time.

I remember leaving Nottingham Playhouse in floods of tears after the last night of 'Funny Peculiar', perhaps the funniest play I have ever seen or been part of.

However, it isn't really the leaving of the play or the theatre that gets you, it's the leaving of the people, of course, and the thought that 'that's it', 'it's all over', 'bye, bye'. I think that everybody feels the same actually, and it is a bitter-sweet parting that follows.

But back to business.   For the audience, we hope, the show (even this afternoon's blighted matinee) looks so effortless, as we enter and exit, music starts and stops, and sets appear and disappear on cue.

Therein lies the trick, though.   That apparent effortlessness is the result of all the effort that has already been put in.   What is it they say in boxing? 'Train hard – fight easy.' It's the same principle.   Whether you are talking about Audley Harrison winning his title, Beckham flashing in a free kick or Bobby Bennett (our fantastic Dame) working an audience, they are all achieved with an apparent ease, which belies the hours of training and years of experience that have led to that 'golden moment'.

It is all over, though - but leaving the theatre for the last time and turning down North Street, as I do now, I swear I can hear a distant voice shouting, in true Panto fashion, 'It's behind you! It's behind you!' Sad to say, it is.

THE END OF THE ROAD?

I made it! And so did you, dear reader. We have both struggled through two collections of these columns to arrive, breathlessly, at my first anniversary offering - the fifty-third in total on your song sheets.

I must thank you for your fidelity, the publishing house for its faith and Andrea, Harry, and Jack for their fortitude, because the several hundred words I produce every week are but the tip of the iceberg of anguish, toil and panic that is the columnist's lot.

If there is one thing I have learned in the past 12 months, it is that there is nothing more guaranteed to bring on a bout of literary amnesia than sitting down with a pen and a blank piece of paper, and saying,

"No, I can't put the rubbish bin out, I'm writing my column!"

In the early days, I used to worry myself sick over where I would find inspiration. I would trawl the deepest recesses of my brain for ideas, and often come up with an empty net. It was around then that I realised I was approaching the whole business from the wrong end. If I wandered around in my head, all I would come up with were memories, facts and experiences, all very interesting to me, and occasionally useful, but necessarily subjective and in the past tense. What I needed was something of the present, even the future.

It was a revelation. All I had to do (I say 'all' - it's not that easy) was to open my eyes and ears to what was going on around me. So I did. It is amazing the things that occur to you if you simply open yourself up to your surroundings, and, I must say, it has turned my once tedious walks into town into quite wonderful voyages of discovery and taken me through a brave new world of intrigue, wonder and amusement.

For instance, living in Brighton, as I do, I am intrigued by the metamorphic history of Hannington's departmental store, as was. Originally, going by its layout, there must have been a collection of small individual shops, which all eventually amalgamated into one big departmental store and called themselves Hannington's. When Churchill Square (like it or lump it) dragged retail Brighton into the 21st century, Hannington's closed. Almost immediately, in its shell, small individual shops started to spring up, which, presumably, will all eventually amalgamate into one big departmental store, thus proving conclusively that Hannington's should never have closed down in the first place.

Also, you know the toilet that used to be on the Steine, but which is now Frank-in-Steine's coffee bar (and very good it is too)? Don't you wonder, though, about the thinking behind closing down a toilet, and replacing it with an establishment where you fill yourself up with liquid, which makes you want a toilet, which doesn't exist anymore?

But the real laugh is the sign on the Palace Pier proclaiming 'FREE ENTRY'. Now, I know it's true, but you try taking eight year old twins on there, and see just how much it costs you to get out through the EXIT!

Maybe I should stop looking around.

AN ACTOR'S LIFE FOR ME

PART THREE

AN ACTOR SCORED

David Roper

AN 'OFFER' IS ON OFFER

"Hello."

"David, it's Susan."

My agent on the phone at 10am? That's a new one on me.

"Mersey TV in Liverpool want to *offer* you a job."

Silence. You could 'ear an 'h' drop.

"Pardon?"

I must tell you that the word 'offer' is the actor's equivalent of an electable Tory Leader - rare to the point of extinction. Much more common than an actual offer, is the standard procedure of being invited to spend vast quantities of your hard earned cash on trudging up to London for an interview/audition. This will inevitably take place at somewhere like BBC Centre House, which, at the time of writing, is arguably the most inaccessible place on the planet. Once there, having negotiated the intricacies of the rail and underground systems, some pre-pubescent Director will video you while you make a complete hash of reading two or three pages of script, he will tell you how very much his mother admired your work when she was at school, and then decline to give you the part.

Alternatively, you will be told that they definitely need a genuine Northerner, aged around 60, who is quite tall and clean shaven, all of which describes you perfectly. However, when you finally watch the programme, having not got the part, of course, you discover that they cast a bearded Scottish midget in his late twenties. Typical.

If you do manage to be offered the job (in my case about 10% of the time), your feelings of elation, together with the re-writing of your BAFTA acceptance speech to fit the circumstances, usually take somewhat of a knock when your agent calls back to say,

"Well, it's not a big part, just the one scene, but it is pivotal to the story, they say. I think you should do it. Oh, by the way, they're filming it all in a disused Sewage Works just outside Wolverhampton, and the money's crap as well."

But this is 'an offer', which means one of three things: EITHER they think you are the best thing since sliced bread, and no-one else could play the part, OR they offered the part to Peter Davison, who wouldn't touch it with a barge pole, OR they can't be bothered with the expense of auditions, and, anyway, any old fart will do. Vanity and sanity make me opt for the first.

"So, what is it?"

"They're not sure."

"What do you mean 'They're not sure.'?"

"Well, it hasn't got a name yet, and there are no scripts."

"So it doesn't exist."

"Oh yes, they're doing it. It's just that they're wanting input from the actors - sort of Reality TV in a dramatic format. Improvisation, I think was one of the words they used"

"Improvisation, eh? You mean like 'The Office'?" Golden Globe Awards here I come!

"Er…possibly."

"Sounds… very interesting."

"That's what I thought. They'll pay your second class return rail fare from Brighton to Liverpool, and put you up in a hotel for three nights."

"Terrific. What about the money?"

"Ah!"

"What does 'Ah!' mean?"

"Well, the thing is…"

At this point the words 'low' and 'budget' quite often miraculously come together, and succeed in dampening all the fire of euphoria you originally felt. Let's face it, you don't have to be a Shadow Chancellor to work out that 'low budget' is a wholly transparent euphemism for 'cheap'. Curiously, I have never heard of a film or TV programme being 'high budget', at least where I'm involved - funny that.

But never mind! It is a job, it represents money and I will be able to visit a few of my old haunts round Liverpool.

Speak to you soon. Wish me luck.

GUILTY OR NOT GUILTY?

It was way back in 1974 when I got my first break into TV. I played a Police Constable in a couple of episodes of 'Crown Court' for Granada TV in Manchester.

'Crown Court' was something of a unique programme in its time. It was shown over several days at lunchtime, and dealt, of course, with a case in the Crown Court, which involved prosecution and defence barristers cross examining witnesses, and ended with a verdict from the Jury.

What was unique about it, apart from being shot wholly inside a four-sided box set (more of that later) was the fact that the Jury was made up of members of the public, with the Foreman of the Jury being the only actor. Not only that, but the Jury was hearing the evidence for the very first time, and would be sent away towards the end of the programme to discuss the evidence and reach a genuine verdict. In other words, the whole case was dealt with as if it were, to all intents and purposes, for real. That being the case, we actors had to rehearse two different endings, dependent upon whether the verdict was 'guilty' or 'not guilty'. Sometimes those two endings could be violently different.

The box set meant that the viewer saw all four walls of the Court, unusual in a studio-based video production set, which is normally three-sided. To enable the cameras to move in and out of the set, one of the walls would be slid back to allow them to enter and exit. The result was that, during the programme, all four walls would be seen, as if in a real courtroom. Difficult to explain on paper, but I hope that makes sense.

In those days, cameras were the size of Smart Cars, and would glide around the studio floor like Daleks on speed. Not anymore. On my current job, I have just come across the latest in TV technology - cameras about the size of your fist, wall-mounted and operated by remote control. They look just like CCTV cameras, actually. Is this the future?

Way back, you would be confronted by up to four cameramen swinging their lumbering machines around the studio, aiming and firing off shots like rear gunners on a Lancaster Bomber. From now on, it seems, there will be just one of them, huddled miles away, twiddling his little knob like an Air Traffic Controller at Swannick. Wait 'til the Union hears about that!

The point is, TV is becoming so impersonal. In the seventies, actors and cameramen were friends. We would work, rest and play together. In fact, Anne Kirkbride (Deidre in Coronation Street), even went so far as to marry one of them. Assuming I were to be available and so inclined, that will soon be impossible, as actors and crew will rarely meet each other. I think that is sad.

Alongside that, the job I am doing here in Liverpool is so fraught with confidentiality and security that I am sworn to secrecy about any of its content. To be fair, scripts usually mention that you shouldn't give away the story, but it ain't a hanging offence, except in the case of the Soaps, of course, where storylines are even more jealously guarded than the whereabouts of WMD, and besides, they prefer to leak the juicy bits themselves, thank you very much!

But on the front of this script it says:

'Disclosure of any part of this episode will result in instant castration, hanging drawing and quartering, or, in the worst instance, a six month sentence watching Celebrity Fat Club.' Seems a tad redundant to me, as there is virtually no script and anyway actors will be improvising most of the dialogue.

On top of that, security is so tight at the studios that yesterday our taxi was forbidden entry to the complex, and we actors had to walk the last 400 yards in the pouring rain. Curiously, the guard omitted to ask for our identities, which seemed to me to somewhat negate the whole premise of security. But there you go!

I guess all this secrecy is because the company has not yet sold the non-existent programme to the network, and is terrified somebody will hear of it, nick the idea and get in there before them. Paranoia rules, as always.

By the way, it is possible that my episode of 'Sea of Souls' (BBC1) will be broadcast next Monday and Tuesday, although I don't appear until Tuesday, I think – I am not really sure. Sorry if that is so vague as to be laughable, but, by one of those strange coincidences, that very word more or less sums up what one TV critic thought of last week's episode; laughable.

So, for goodness sake, don't tell your friends that I am in it!

David Roper

THE WONDER OF YOU

I have been thinking about women recently. No, not in that sense, although I admit I have never bothered to actually *listen* to any of Beyoncé's songs, but that is my personal problem, so let's not go there.

The women I am talking about are Tracy Cropper (nee Barlow) and Jenny Bond. Last night, as I write, they both graced our screens in different circumstances and on opposite sides of the world.

Tracy (Coronation Street) gave birth to a 6lb 4oz daughter. Nothing world shattering about that, you might think, except that she was delivered of the baby, took a shower and was standing in the hospital corridor, on the phone to Steve Macdonald, all within the space of an hour! Roy Cropper confirmed this later.

Andrea and I sat there, our mouths open in disbelief, Salmon Florentine (ASDA, two for a fiver and really very good) dribbling down our chins, stunned at this remarkable feat of female fortitude. In less than sixty minutes, our Tracy had managed a recovery so rapidly as to make a Friesian cow blush. What an amazing piece of work she is.

But that is not really my point. What I always find so disturbing about TV births is the amount of compulsory screaming and shouting that goes on. OK, OK, OK, I plead guilty and accept that, as a mere male, I am on extremely dodgy ground here. What concerns me, though, is not that such distress happens, and I am sure and sorry that it does, but that, here in the real world, it doesn't *always* happen, and is avoidable. Like me, don't you feel desperately sorry for any young girls watching, who must be horrified to think that, when they give birth, they will obviously and necessarily have to go through the same apparently appalling pain. It is enough to put them off for life. TV-land doesn't seem to have heard of epidurals, TENS, pethidine, gas and air or even natural childbirth which, although ruddy painful no doubt, is not always the gynaecological equivalent of having your finger nails ripped out. Once again, OK, OK, OK! I am certain that I will inevitably, and justifiably no doubt, come in for a load of flack from all those on the receiving end of the birthing process, since I am only a man and, therefore, arguably partly responsible for the situation in the first place. But girls, take heart and don't swallow all that you see.

Which brings me to the phenomenon whose name is Bond, Jenny Bond (BBC Royal correspondent). Bond was in Australia and she did swallow all she could see. Namely: stick insects like jumbo twiglets, fish eyes the size of gobstoppers, and grubs as fat and juicy as Lincolnshire sausages, among others. I just about managed to watch this further incredible feat of female fortitude, before elbowing my bag of M&M'S and diving behind the sofa.

Needless to say, it was all in the name of 'I'm a Celebrity, get me out of here', a programme filmed in Australia, and which I have never watched before, and am unlikely to watch again. I had heard that the programme took several celebrities into an antipodean forest, asked them to consume examples of the surrounding wild life so that they could win 'ordinary' meals for themselves and the rest of the chosen few.

I stumbled upon Bond, gobbling these delicacies as if they were petit fours at a Royal Garden Party and with hardly a flicker, whilst I was doing my own flicking between channels, and I must say, regardless of my initial reaction, she did impress me no end. Whether or not that kind of edible horror is the typical Australian's idea of picnic food, I have no idea.

Neither have I any idea what Bond's fee was, but they would have to add several noughts to it before they could persuade me to crunch my way through a beetle bigger than a Shih Tzu dog. How about you?

On reflection, though, it may be that Jenny Bond has an advantage over all of us, having spent the last decade or so eating in the BBC canteen. Who knows?

David Roper

LIGHTS, CAMERA...FUN!

I am pretty sure that it was Gore Vidal, the American writer and intellectual, who was quoted as saying,

"I stopped going to the theatre, when I realised that the actors were having more fun than I was."

Difficult to say whether he meant that as an indictment of the play or of the performances, but speaking as an actor, I think that either way he had a point. We actors do enjoy ourselves. Gore, as he is known to his friends, I guess, could equally well have applied that small snippet of his undoubted wit to watching a filmed episode on TV, I suppose.

You see, filming, either for the big screen or for TV, is about the most fun an actor can have without actually forming a relationship, although it can be totally disproportionate to screen-time produced and intrinsic audience 'fun factor'. For example, a scene lasting less than two minutes on screen (and how much fun can there be in that for the viewer?) could represent a whole fun-filled day for actors and crew.

Take 'Sea of Souls' that I appeared in last week. When I was due to start filming, I collected my airline ticket at Gatwick, a chauffeur driven car picked me up at Glasgow airport, and I was whisked away to my hotel, where I found an en suite bedroom, a Leisure Centre, a swimming pool - the lot. There was a bar, too, but more of that later. Being treated like royalty inevitably starts you wondering what it must be like for those who have to put up with it every day. Poor things.

The following morning, another chauffeur driven car, with me comfortably ensconced in the leather seats at the back, sped me to the location. Once there, I was served breakfast in my own caravan, or Winnebago, as the trade name has it.

Actually, the size and internal fittings of a Winnebago can sometimes give rise to contractual disputes that rival the most hard-hitting negotiations. Some actors, mainly Americans, in my experience, no offence, insist on the 'Winne', as it is known in the trade, travelling with them wherever they go, even if only down the road to the location. English actors, on the other hand, being inevitably impressed that the 'Winne' is only for them, are just happy to say au revoir to it and wander along to the location unaided.

So, having settled myself in, it was time for my own make-up girl to repair the ravages of the previous night in the bar, for the wardrobe guy to lay out my costume and for me to be supplied with a constant stream of very good coffee. Compared to touring in the theatre with 'An Inspector Calls', when I had to find my own transport, digs, make-up and coffee, it was like working in Hollywood! That's where the Americans get it from!

The location for that day was an up-market housing estate in the suburbs. It was sort of 'Footballers' Wives' territory - large, detached houses with immaculate lawns, landscaped gardens and the compulsory BMW in the drive. You half expected the entire Earls Park first team to come jogging round the corner, which, let's face it, would be a welcome change from the horizontal jogging that makes up their usual training schedule.

We spent the whole morning outside, filming a scene where I was mowing the lawn (not that it needed it), and greeting a guest. It took that long because one of the unwritten laws of film-making states that 'The location for any filming will always be directly beneath an airport flight path.' The planes were so low we could hear the in-flight announcements.

Lunch was provided from a mobile kitchen. Believe it or not, two blokes, inside a converted lorry, had prepared a choice of four main courses, three puddings, cheese and biscuits, tea and coffee for *seventy-five* of us, and it was absolutely delicious.

Thus, a sleepy afternoon was spent filming inside in the lounge and kitchen, and at 6.00pm we knocked off and retired, exhausted, to the hotel bar. It's a hard life.

In the final broadcast, my 'mowing the lawn' scene was cut completely, and the interior shots were pared down to less than 90 seconds. I have no idea how much fun the audience got out of it, but we had one hell of a time.

Maybe Gore Vidal really did have a point!

David Roper

STAND AND DELIVER!

When Angela Rippon burst out from behind that news desk on the 'Morecambe and Wise Show', and revealed to an incredulous world that she actually had legs, she had no idea what she had started. Up until that point, and I accept that revealing her limbs was part of a comedy/musical item, news readers would remain firmly ensconced behind a desk of some sort. However, Angela's routine showed the rest of the world what a peripatetic news reader could look like.

Over twenty years later, though, they are all at it, have you noticed? Apart from Moira Stewart and Anna Ford, who may be legless for all I know, and if they are, I unreservedly apologise, every news reader on every channel seems compelled to strut around these days, as if someone on high has decided that Angela Rippon had a point and, anyway, current affairs and news are so dull they need animating.

Why? What is so wrong with reporting news from a sedentary position? Did we not get through the Falklands war, the fall of Maggie and the climax of Big Brother without the benefit of peripatetic news presenters? Why do we now need the likes of an upright Sophie Rayworth in black trousers, however fetching that might be, to guide us through the latest breaking news? Frankly, if you are that way inclined, and I am not, I hasten to add, it was possibly much more exciting to imagine that she was wearing a mini-skirt, or nothing at all, beneath her cool, sub-Sloane Ranger exterior.

And why is this approach to news broadcasting now universal? An EU directive? Or does it come from the same producers, who have encouraged Fred Dinenage, Sally Taylor and any number of other news persons, to engage in jolly little bouts of banter with the weather person over the closing credits? And doesn't that get up your nose? What are they talking about, for Heaven's sake, and why won't they let us in on it?

I think it is bloody rude, actually! I mean, you sit there for half an hour, dutifully listening to them droning on about depressing local, national and international issues, only for them to suddenly perk up at the appearance of the weather person, start tossing around some hilarious in-joke and then end up cutting you dead. It is just not on.

Quite honestly, I think we have a right to know what Karl Tyler, or any weather man for that matter, and the news 'anchor' are creasing themselves up about. For all we know, what is being said is,

"What a load of crap that forecast was. It's going to sling it down all week! I wouldn't go out on Tuesday without a brolly, if I were you!"

Lip readers must have a field day, as they must be the only people who get any kind of fun at all out of these exchanges. Must learn to do it asap.

Talking of weather persons, don't you get fascinated by that little button thing they keep pressing to change the picture? I just can't take my eyes off Michael Fish's right thumb, as he flicks us from the 'overall satellite picture' to those pretty little cumulus nimbus clouds, or whatever they are called, plonking precipitation all over East Anglia and the Isle of Sheppey.

Let's face it, we all know that weather persons are standing in front of a blank screen (the picture is superimposed or something) so, if you're anything like me, you also get transfixed by trying to spot them periodically sneaking the odd look at the off-screen monitor to make sure that their left index finger really is pointing at the Great Glen, wherever that is, and is not poking provocatively up the Bristol Channel's nether regions.

It must really hack you off, though, if you live somewhere west of Bodwin Moor and/or down to Land's End in Cornwall. Forgive me if I have said it before, it is one of my hobby horses, I'm afraid, but it appears to be a fact of TV weather reporting that weather persons always stand screen left (another EU directive?), and have a tendency to block out everywhere from, say, Truro to the Isles of Scilly. Why don't they stand screen right and block out Belgium and The Netherlands instead?

On second thoughts, that would probably contravene an EU directive on the Meteorological Rights of the Low Countries!

SYNCHING IS A CINCH

There is not usually much scope for topicality in this column, but today is different. True, I am writing this on Monday, but can comment on what will happen on your tomorrow, Sunday, if you get me. My episode of 'Heartbeat' will be broadcast then, and I thought I would explain a bit about it, without giving away the plot, of course. Heaven forbid.

Filming 'Heartbeat' is a bit like the apocryphal painting of the Forth Bridge - no sooner has one series finished, than another starts. I am in episode 13 of series 13, which sounds ominously unlucky to me, but you must be the judge of the final product.

The other intriguing part of filming 'Heartbeat' is the journey to get to the main location in the first place. The base camp, as it were, is a converted warehouse on the outskirts of Leeds, where the inside of the police station, the pub and other sets are built. However, all the outside shots of the pub, police station, garage, the village in general and all locations, have their base at the main location in the village of Goathland, which nestles in a dip somewhere on the North Yorkshire moors.

Now, getting to the 'base camp' near Leeds was easy, but getting to Goathland was a tad more complicated. I was sent an itinerary that said, without a word of a lie:

'From King's Cross Station take the train to Edinburgh.

'Get off at York and walk over the bridge and down towards the exit.

'When you get to the W.H. Smith store, wait outside it.

'A man will approach you and take you to his car.

This was sounding more bizarre by the minute, believe me.

'He will drive you to Goathland.

All that did indeed happen, although I nearly got arrested for winking at various men who wandered past while I was waiting outside W.H. Smith's. But all was well.

We filmed the episode last autumn, mostly at Newby Hall in North Yorkshire. However, although what you will *see* of me happened six months ago, what you will *hear* of me was only recorded four weeks ago in Leeds. This is because a certain amount of 'post synching' was necessary. Post synching, or post synchronisation to give it its proper name, occurs when circumstances make sound recording at the time of filming difficult or impossible, so it has to be done days, weeks, or as in this case, months later.

The reasons for having to resort to post synching are many and various. For example, there might be so much unavoidable peripheral noise that your voice is drowned out - if you were driving a tractor, say, or if you were in a street with noisy traffic passing. It could also be that you are at a great distance from sound equipment and the camera, or be walking away from it. In those cases your voice would be recorded separately in a studio, and synchronised to the action afterwards, during post production - hence, 'post synching'.

When a scene is indeed composed of middle/long distance shots, post synching is relatively easy, and the sound engineer can 'tweak' the dialogue to correspond to the action. Unfortunately, in my case, 'tweaking' was out of the question, as I was plunged into the altogether different world of 'lip synching'. That meant the shots of me were so close up that I had to synchronise the dialogue with my own lip movements, as there was a lot of peripheral noise. Honestly, it was a ruddy nightmare.

There I was, in a sound studio at Yorkshire TV in Leeds, one eye on the script, the other on a monitor showing the scene, and with no recollection whatsoever of the lines I had said all those months ago. You might think it would be relatively easy. After all it was my face, my lips moving, and the words I had once said. Could I get it right? Could I heckerslike! It is amazing how many tiny pauses, elongated vowels and explosive consonants you can pack into one sentence, and all of them have to be replicated in the smallest detail.

To be fair, I didn't do it that badly. The difficult part was one four-line speech. In the end I re-learned it and regurgitated it, while staring intently at myself on the screen. Eventually, they were satisfied and released me just in time to catch the 15.05 train to King's Cross.

I realise, of course, that I have made a rod for my own back, because those of you who watch the episode will, no doubt, be glued to my lips tomorrow night. What a strangely intimate thought!

IT'S THERE IN BLACK AND WHITE

Shortly after I left the Bristol Old Vic Theatre School in 1971, I played Lodovico, 'a vision in gold' according to the director, in Shakespeare's 'Othello' at the Bristol Old Vic Theatre itself. A professional part in a professional production. Great.

My role, small though it was, meant that I would enter upstage, see Othello and Desdemona, both lying dead on their bed, say the immortal line,

"Who is this rash and most unfortunate man?" and cross to downstage right.

All went well, until one night I said my line, turned to face the deceased couple in silence and farted loudly. Whether the audience heard the resultant explosion, I have no idea, but Othello and Desdemona certainly did, and proceeded to giggle their dead hearts out on the marital bed.

Isla Blair played Desdemona, and Paul Rogers, a white actor, took the eponymous lead role of Othello. Paul had to 'black-up', because Othello, 'the Moor of Venice', was, of course, black.

Nowadays, that just would not happen. Along with The Black and White Minstrels, white actors blacking-up has long been regarded as unacceptable in a racially integrated society. The last time I came across it was when Ilkley Amateur Dramatic Society also put on 'Othello' nearly thirty years ago. I remember that production well, not so much because of the blacking-up, but because of the local newspaper's headline to its review: 'Ilkley Moor a winner!' I love that.

But back to the point. Quite when the shift away from what many saw as the offensive practice of blacking-up came, I am not sure, but for many years now black characters on stage have been played by black actors.

However, acknowledging that we were moving towards a multi-cultural and multi-coloured society had a different effect on TV. During the seventies there was increasing pressure on TV drama producers to reflect the changing social scene. This particularly applied to so-called soap operas, which professed to be a 'slice of life'.

The problem for many, though, lay not in suppressing any inherent prejudice in TV producers, even if it existed, but in exposing the inherent prejudice in existing soap opera characters themselves. It dawned on the TV companies, with increasing horror, that by introducing Afro-Caribbean or Asian families (under the generic term 'black') into a white working class soap opera community and, if the programmes were to accurately reflect at least some parts of life in the real world, many of the established 'lovable' residents would have to be exposed as being potentially racist.

The problem was solved by simply ignoring it, and for many years, characters under that generic term 'black' either never appeared or were so peripheral as to never raise the central issue. It is interesting to note that soap opera 'corner shops', which in the areas portrayed, and in reality, would probably have been run by an Asian family (and why not?), were only handed over to an ethnic minority group, on screen, once the outside world had matured, accepted and dealt with the initial racist reaction to the real thing.

Even today, in our allegedly more enlightened culture, the true natures of many of the most popular of our TV characters is studiously avoided, so as not to alienate an audience, which, if truth were told, probably harbours many of the same prejudices.

In other words, however much we, as a society, would like to think that we are liberal and open minded, racism is not yet dead and buried, either on TV or in real life. It is just that, a lot of the time, the cracks have simply been papered over. One of those cracks appeared, in the most moronic denial of racism that I have ever heard, when some idiot said to me, in all seriousness,

"I'm not a racialist (sic). I like curry!"

God help him - and all of us.

DEARLY BELOVED...

As if we did not have enough on our plates, the question of gay marriage has entered from the U.K. political wings, and is vying for centre stage. Best of luck with that, lads. No, honestly, I do not mean that disparagingly. In fact, while the world in general is in turmoil, what better time for the gay community to push for legislation to raise the standing of its members, if you understand me correctly?

Coincidentally, President Bush, taking time out from policing the world, has also woken up to what is going on in his own gay back yard. He has discovered that certain States of the Union have already sanctioned 'marriage' between lesbian and/or homosexual couples, and he is intent on a Constitutional amendment to outlaw the practice. Funnily enough, it appears that the lads who penned the Constitution of the United States, and who emphasised in it the need for Liberty, did not, apparently, explicitly exclude the rights of homosexuals and lesbians to marry. Otherwise, why would Bush feel the need for an amendment to outlaw it? Presumably, he cares little for the Pink Vote, a fact he may regret in the run-up to the Presidential elections.

Back home, the Tory Party is taking the opposite view. Desperate for any votes (red, yellow or sky blue pink with yellow dots on), the Tory leader, who always appears to be talking with his tongue in somebody else's cheek, seems broadly behind the Government's proposed Civil Partnership Bill. If the Bill is passed through the Commons and becomes an Act, it would give State recognition to gay couples as a partnership, and endow them, should they wish to take advantage of it, with similar rights and responsibilities as heterosexual married couples (inheritance provisions, hospital visits as a relative, the right to a mother-in-law etc.).

It has not gone so far as to be outright Tory policy, but there have been indications of support for a free vote in the Commons. In other words, the Party will be able to take credit for supporting the Bill, if it gets through, or take credit for allowing the Commons to democratically decide for itself, if it doesn't. It has also been proposed that the Tory Party, if ever elected again, should be committed to calling a Gay Summit (Ben Nevis, presumably), and to providing gay mentors in schools, and we all know that that will end in tears, don't we? Do I hear the word 'bandwagon'?

The Government itself is keeping a stiff upper lip, above its loose flabby jaw, presumably in the hope that the Pink Vote will swing its way, and nobody will notice that a Prime Minister is once again sticking to a policy of doing the right thing for all the wrong reasons. Well, it's a job!

The good news for the gay community is that their claim to actual 'married' status is even more likely to be legitimised, if only as a result of the Pink Vote being useful as a political football. Both major political parties are bending over backwards, if you know what I mean (oh, leave it out, David!), to score with the gay community, and are so paranoid about giving away an own goal that the resultant drawn game (politically) will inevitably mean promotion to the Premier Division for many a gay team, and give a whole new meaning to Man United. End of my convoluted football analogy!

However, there is an intriguing paradox in all the recent to-ing and fro-ing over the question of gay rights, and the arguments for and against legislating for civil partnership and/or marriage in the homosexual community.

The paradox involves the heterosexual community, its opinion on marriage in general, which it embraces as its own, and its attitude to marriage within the homosexual community. The point is that that same heterosexual community, which considers marriage to be its natural right, has in fact largely turned its back on it, whilst at the same time objecting to the 'unnatural' nature of marriage within the lesbian and homosexual community, which, in its turn, cannot get enough of it.

However, you have all the balls in your court, lads. Go for it!

TIME ON MY HANDS

"Resting, are you?"

"Yes, I'm afraid so."

"Anything in the pipeline?"

"Only a large blockage, that's all."

Yes, folks, it is that time of year yet again. The Vernal Equinox is behind us, the clocks have leapt an hour in front of us, and here I am in the middle with no job. But will I let it get me down? Probably. Well, to be fair, I wouldn't have done, except that it has been one of those weeks when nothing seemed to go right. You know the kind of thing: nobody returns your phone calls; bills drop on your door mat like parachutists at Arnhem; the Archbishop of Canterbury slags off Footballers' Wives; and when the kids are not driving you mad, they are huddled together in a corner humming the theme tune from The Great Escape, 'Dit dee di-dit dee.'

Talking of which, were you as gutted as I was to discover that The Great Escape scene in which Steve McQueen tries to leap over those barbed wire border fences on a motorbike was total fiction? Why did they have to tell us that? I recognise that truth is stranger than fiction, and in this case a damn sight more tragic, so wasn't it great to think that somebody had almost pulled off a stunt like that for real? I know this is going to sound daft, but every time I watch that bit, I always involuntarily shout out,

"Go on, my son! You're going to make it this time!"

Funnily enough, in the real escape, a friend of my father's was next in line in the tunnel for his turn to leg it, when that German sentry spotted them running off. Considering what happened to most of the escapees, that must go down as a massive stroke of luck, although he didn't think so at the time.

Meanwhile, back in the 21st century, I have to admit that one of the ways I escape from these periods of unemployment is by writing this column. You see, finding some form of escape from the rigours of reality is an eternal problem for actors, and there are as many ways of dealing with it as there are Equity members. Sir John Gielgud, I understand, used to read a lot, on the grounds that, 'It stops you thinking.' I reckon he got it about right. It is not just unemployment, though, that needs a coping strategy. An actor on tour needs help, too.

Perhaps the guy who had the best solution to the touring conundrum was a theatre director friend of mine, who simply said to me,

"You must give yourself something to do."

He was absolutely right. An actor on tour, who has no discernible purpose, will almost undoubtedly be seen clutching a plastic bag, while walking the streets of some provincial town. The plastic bag is peculiar to the acting fraternity, goodness knows why, and usually contains a bottle or two of cheap white wine.

However, give that actor a purpose, and his life can miraculously turn into something full and fulfilling. That purpose need not be anything world shattering or particularly expensive, in fact it could be doing anything at all: exploring the town's history; losing weight; writing letters, or a novel; playing squash; finding the best restaurant in town; anything to keep the mind ticking over and the body out of the pub until theatre time.

I have said it before: actors are self-obsessed, paranoid schizophrenics, who think far too much about their plight, and who need a kick up the bum from time to time. My own personal bum-kicker is Andrea, who refuses to tolerate my self-indulgent ramblings, and is living proof that behind every great man is an even greater bum just waiting to be kicked by a woman.

And so it is that every week I get off my aching backside, and find my own escape from reality by tunnelling out of the prison of my problems, and letting my imagination leg it over the fence.

Trouble is, like Steve, I never quite make it.

WHO'S WHO?

"Hello."

"Hello. May I speak to David Roper, please?"

"Certainly. Who's calling?"

"David Roper."

"Yes, I know who you want to speak to, but who's calling?"

"David Roper. May I speak to David Roper?"

"You want to speak to David Roper?"

"Yes. David Roper."

"Right."

That bizarre conversation took place quite a few years ago, when I was at The Royal National Theatre, but I will explain exactly what it was all about a little later. The root of it lies in the fact that throughout my life I have been dogged by being mistaken for somebody else of the same name, David Roper.

I first encountered this strange set of circumstances when I was in my late teens. In Bradford, where I was born, a certain David Roper (not me, of course) was goalkeeper for Bradford City Football Club. We were of a similar age, similar height and, from a distance, yes, you've guessed it, we looked quite similar. One Sunday lunchtime, in my local boozer, I was mystified by a series of derogatory remarks about my ball-handling skills, emanating from a group of, what turned out to be ardent but disgruntled, Bradford City football fans. Eventually, they all wandered over to me, and I discovered to my amazement that I stood accused of being instrumental in ensuring the team's relegation to a lower division by letting in three goals in the previous day's match.

"What?" I protested.

It took me over half an hour, having enlisted the help of the pub landlord, to persuade the gathering lynch mob that I was a useless goalkeeper (a fact they heartily endorsed), but more to the point, and the landlord swore to this, that I had spent the previous afternoon propping up the very bar at which we were standing. I got away with a rather half-hearted apology from the group, and the offer of a pint to make amends for their mistake. Phew!

The somewhat distressing culmination to that particular case of mistaken identity came when our next door neighbour offered me her condolences, after reading in the local paper of the sudden death of David Roper's paternal grandmother two days before. I was sad to hear of what was evidently my goalkeeping namesake's loss, but it was news to me, as I had seen Grandma Roper sitting in her favourite armchair less than an hour before. Admittedly, she was a bit quiet, but I could have sworn she was still breathing when I left her.

I was also nominally mistaken for a David Roper, who was musical director of a play I was rehearsing. Now, taking me for a footballer is one thing, but entertaining the idea that I am in any way musical, is about as credible as confusing Saddam Hussein with Santa Claus. However, David (the other one) graciously changed his surname in the programme, thus sparing me the embarrassment of having to admit to all and sundry that I was no musical director, and that I didn't know a quaver from a Quaver.

The Royal National Theatre (RNT) incident that I mentioned above was altogether more hairy. I was metaphorically, indeed almost literally, 'put up against the wall' by the RNT's casting director, with the accusation:

"It was you, wasn't it? You had better have a good explanation!"

Again, I protested,

"What are you talking about?"

It transpired that yet another David Roper, who was a theatre critic with the magazine, Plays and Players, had given all the current RNT productions unbelievably lousy reviews. This blow to the thespian art had reached the ears of Sir Peter Hall, who ran the place, and he was furious that one of his actors was, apparently, not only moonlighting as a critic, but was biting the hand that fed it.

Hence the strange phone call. When we finally sorted out who was talking to whom, David Roper, the theatre critic, was most apologetic to David Roper, the actor, and promised that he, David Roper, the theatre critic, would make it clear to the RNT that it was not David Roper, the actor, who was slagging off the RNT's productions, but that it was, in fact, David Roper, the theatre critic.

Well, thank goodness I got that cleared up!

VOICING MY OPINION

In the vast catalogue of world shattering disasters, it is hard to identify which has had the greatest impact on humanity. From earthquakes to forest fires; from flash floods to volcanic eruptions; from World Wars to the second series of Crossroads; it has been impossible to determine which one qualifies as the most tragic - until now.

One event has emerged head and shoulders above all others, and has plunged morale to an all time low in the Roper household, and in much of the English speaking world, I shouldn't wonder. It is hard to imagine anything more likely to strike terror into the hearts of parents, from Timbuktu to Telscombe Cliffs. Andrea and I can hardly comprehend its enormity, and the only light in the darkness is that the kids have been temporarily struck dumb by this monumental tragedy.

You see, the voice-over artists on 'The Simpsons' are on strike, and the next series is in serious jeopardy! What could be worse?

The argument, inevitably, is about money. The actors who provide the voices for Homer, Marge, Bart etc. want their £25,000 per episode fee trebled, to bring them more into line with the fees dished out to others in American Light Entertainment. Setting aside the global implications of a protracted dispute (not to mention the crucial fact that 'The Simpsons' keeps the kids quiet through dinner), the whole business throws into sharp relief the disparity in voice-over fees, and actors' fees in general, on either side of the Atlantic.

Being paid £25,000 as a voice-over in one half hour episode on UK TV would not just be highly unlikely, but would be so far beyond imagining as to be in the realms of deranged fantasy. You see, your average UK actor would bite your hand off for £500, leave alone £25,000, and would quite willingly sign a contract, and forego a year's repeat fees, for a flat £1,000, OK £750, plus VAT, if you twist my arm.

As far as I know, actors' fees for actually appearing in films and/or TV programmes exhibit a similar disparity on the two sides of 'the pond'. Taking it as a vague rule of thumb, I estimate that any given fee for a UK TV actor would have to be multiplied by at least 10 in order to get anywhere near a USA TV actor's fee, and I wouldn't be surprised if that was one heck of an under estimate. I did hear a rumour that Peter Falk (Columbo) gets £185,000 for every episode repeated on UK TV, and that is only for one foreign TV showing. Maybe that is way out, (sorry, Peter), but if it is anything like true, goodness knows what he coined in for making each original episode in the USA.

All these thoughts about actors' money were brought to mind recently, when I tried to revive my own flagging voice-over career. At one time I was 'the voice of ASDA', and was earning a decent whack, although I have to say I have since paid back the money several times over at their check-outs down the ASDA at Brighton Marina.

Believe it or not, I was also the voice that kicked off the Cadbury/Coronation Street campaign, and could be heard at the beginning and end of each programme - except when I was appearing in it, of course, because the powers that be didn't like the idea that one of the Corrie characters might sound as though they were endorsing any particular product. To get round that, Granada TV, in its infinite wisdom, cleverly replaced me with someone who sounded just like me. It seemed to escape their notice that their cunning plan rather defeated the objective of not having a character being identifiable as a product voice-over, but that's TV executives for you.

Somewhere along the line, though, the work dwindled away, and it is over a year since I have been anywhere near a sound studio. The effect on the old wallet has been dramatic, I can tell you.

So, this is in the nature of a plea to anybody in the Brighton and Hove area who needs an experienced, professional voice-over artist with a wife and twin boys to support.

I don't come cheap, mind, but if the repeat fees are reasonable, I am open to offers.

SOUNDS GOOD TO ME

It was a close run thing, I must say, and there was a moment in the middle of last week when I was convinced that it would never happen. But it did. Yes, after writing to several of them, with only one of them replying, by the way, I finally managed to get myself a new voice-over agent. So you find me sitting back and waiting for the work to roll in.

It is almost impossible to stress too highly the advantages of voice-overs, and to express how dear they are to an actor's wallet. You see, in the same way as being, say, 10th or more in line to the throne, voice-overs take up very little time and pay large sums of money, but perhaps their greatest advantage is that they invariably involve a trip to the West End. For me, at any rate, that always presents the rare and delightful opportunity to grab a quick Mozzarella and Tomato Salad (£4.25 as a starter, £7.25 as a main course) at the Pizza Express branch in Dean Street.

I first embarked on a voice-over career over twenty years ago. I had no idea that I would be any good at it, and it came as somewhat of a surprise when a bloke I just happened to be talking to in a Soho pub said to me,

"You've got the right type of voice, you know. Ever thought of getting a voice-over agent? You would do really well. I'll take you on, if you fancy it."

I hadn't a clue that he was a voice-over agent, but I certainly did fancy it, so I agreed then and there, went on his books and started my voice-over career almost immediately. He was absolutely right, and I took to it like a duck to an orange. Before long I was doing a couple of voice-overs every week and was coining it in.

In those days, in order that your agent could contact you, we all had 'bleepers' sticking out of our top pockets. We would either congregate in the John Snow pub in Soho, lined up like tarts in a brothel waiting to be 'picked', or else would prowl the West End streets like Consultant Surgeons on call. If you were lucky, your bleeper would go off in the pub, everybody would turn, stare and go green with envy, as you immediately trotted off to the nearest pay phone to call your agent for news of the next job. The mobile phone, of course, has inevitably changed that rather leisurely life style beyond recognition. Nowadays, proximity to a pay phone is irrelevant, and we can all be reached instantaneously wherever we are.

Studio technology has also advanced leaps and bounds. In a computer-driven age, when sound recordings can be speeded up, slowed down and generally shunted around at the touch of a button, it is hard to believe that not so long ago the two most important pieces of equipment for any Sound Engineer were a razor blade and a roll of sticky tape. These would be used to slice out a section of recording tape, and then to stick the two ends back together again. Antiquated or what? It is like comparing the London to Brighton Vintage Car race with the Monaco Grand Prix.

The other advantage of voice-overs is that they can be quite easily fitted in around an existing job. I remember that when I was playing Albert the Horse (fantastic part, by the way) in 'The Wind in the Willows' at The Old Vic, I used to nip across to the West End between shows, and earn more from half an hour in a sound studio than I did all week in the theatre. Those were the days.

However, my new voice-over agent has well and truly put me on the road to kick starting my career. I have done quite a few already, including voicing a new ASDA Christmas campaign.

The curious thing, though, is that the skill required of a 'voice' is not necessarily proportionate to acting ability. You might have a mantelpiece heaving with Oscars, BAFTAs, or loofahs for that matter, but still be unable to say 'That's ASDA price!' with any degree of conviction. I once had to re-record an entire commercial for a very famous actor, because his version was, not to put too fine a point on it, a load of crap. Don't tell anybody, except those you can trust, but his name was…damn, I've run out of space.

THE BIG SCREEN BECKONS

If you have been taking notes after reading my previous articles - and if not, why not? - you will by now have compiled quite a detailed dossier on my life and times. That being the case, here is an extra little nugget of biographical knowledge for you to add to your collection.

Here goes: as well as being a star of stage, screen and wedding reception, I have also graced your local cinema - once, at least, at the time of writing. I was reminded of this, and delighted, of course, when I discovered that my first contribution to the cinematic art had been released recently on DVD.

The film was called 'Downtime', and although it had limited distribution success, it sold rather well on video, and will hopefully do the same on DVD. Lest you should think that my film career has fuelled a lavish Hollywood lifestyle, I must pause here to tell you that actors do not get paid a single penny extra for cinema showings, and only cop for a modest tickle from video and DVD sales. All of which goes to explain why I am writing this in the peace and quiet of Joe's Café in Saltdean (coffee, tea and all day breakfasts available), rather than in the middle of the hustle and bustle of Sunset Boulevard.

Nevertheless, I must drag you back to the point and into to the glamorous world of my film star status.

My one and only feature film, so far, 'Downtime', is set in Newcastle, so naturally we filmed it all in Liverpool. Don't ask. But if you insist, as far as I could make out, it had something to do with the Merseyside Film Corporation and Channel 4, I think, hence being filmed in Liverpool, together with the fact that the story was written involving very much north-eastern characters, hence being set in Newcastle. Such is the convoluted world of cinema production.

The central story involved four people trapped in a tower block lift, which was moving up and down erratically, due to a fire caused by some kids at the top of the shaft. The four people were: an ex-police psychologist with a psychological problem; a young mum, who the psychologist had just talked out of a suicide attempt; her traumatised seven year old son; and the grandfather of the family, who eventually fell to his death. Think: Debenhams' top floor to Churchill Square car park (level 2) in Brighton on a bad day, and you have almost visualised the drop. It has probably occurred to you by now that we are not talking hilarious comedy here, although, it has to be said, there were a couple of mildly amusing moments.

It was my job to play the detective friend of the shrink, and act as the cavalry, for want of a better analogy, galloping in at every appropriate moment to save the day.

The opening scene, over the introductory credits, was a real cracker, and it was at the climax of that scene that I staked my claim as the all-purpose saviour. The mum, clutching her son, was threatening to jump from the outside of a twenty-second floor balcony. The psychologist had persuaded her to hand over the boy, and she was just climbing back herself, when she slipped and fell. A uniformed copper grabbed her sweaty hand and managed to hang on to her for just about long enough to give my character time to rush to the floor below and catch her as she plunged earthwards. Easy-peasy on paper, but at 230 feet above the ground on a wet Wednesday night in Everton, it was brown trousers all round, I can tell you.

I was anchored to the balcony by a thin wire embedded into concrete, and had to lean out, from the waist up, and grab the stunt woman, who was dangling in mid-air on another thin wire - and I thought I had problems. Add to that a balcony covered in pigeon poo, a torrential downpour and a hired police helicopter hovering twenty feet away, blowing the stunt woman in all directions, and you will appreciate just how glamorous a film star's life can be. It was enough to make me join in with the pigeons, I can tell you.

I think I'll stick to voice-overs.

BIG SISTER IS WATCHING YOU

Standing naked before her, she turned and stared straight at me. The look in her limpid eyes told me it was over and she had to leave. She ran her tongue provocatively across those lips, whose work I had watched with wonder, and I knew she would be back. She couldn't get enough of it, so that made two of us.

A bead of sweat ran over my well-toned pectorals and made its way down my exhausted body. Her eyes seemed to follow it downwards. The corners of her mouth rose into a Giaconda smile, but her meaning was clear. Yes, she would return.

"I'll be back. Same time tomorrow," she murmured and then she was gone.

No, I don't always get involved in such provocative autobiographical scenarios, but on this occasion the 'Trisha' programme happened to be on TV in the changing room at the David Lloyd Leisure Centre the other day, as I was getting dressed. A fellow nude viewer - there's a lot of it about down there - glanced at the screen and asked,

"Why don't you write an article about all that reality rubbish and stuff that's always on the TV these days?"

"Well, I would," I replied, "except that, as I spend half my life desperate for a part in virtually anything on TV, 'reality rubbish and stuff' included, it might be construed as a bit thick to go around slagging it all off."

"Yeh, since you're in that business as well, I suppose you've got a point. Shame, though, it might have been quite interesting."

By the same token, I realised that he had a point as well, and it got me thinking. Funnily enough, not so much about the relative merits of TV programmes and whether or not any of them were any good, but rather about what we were actually doing there i.e. having a nude conversation in a Leisure

Centre changing room. Now there's an idea for a reality TV show! It would be an instant hit, and would capture the hearts, and other parts of the anatomy, of all the voyeurs from John O'Groats to Land's End. What's the betting Sky have already commissioned a pilot episode. My money's on them calling it 'Bare Essentials'.

Meanwhile, back to my point. Although I am not privy to how often you chat away starkers, but whenever you do, have you noticed that eye contact is studiously maintained in those circumstances? I mean, when fully clothed, your eyes will flit all over the place. You might well notice a man's tie, his shirt or even his trousers, everything and anywhere is permitted, but woe betide any furtive flitting when eye ball to eye ball, as it were, with a naked body. It is just not allowed and there is no etiquette that covers it.

Trouble is, it is tantamount irresistible, isn't it? Because you know it is strictly taboo to venture a quick butcher's at another chap's nether regions, don't you find it almost, I stress *almost*, impossible not to sneak a quick one, even if only to establish his religion? So, to combat this childish urge, you fix each other with an unnatural gaze, and stare each other out like two arm wrestlers. Only when the underpants (Yves St. Laurent or Marks and Sparks, it matters not) are safely on, can you both relax, have a civilised conversation and admire each other's choice of boxer shorts with impunity.

Harry and Jack, being eight-year-olds, naturally have no such inhibitions. Changing, after swimming, they are necessarily confronted with a bird's eye view of a range of genitalia, which fascinates them beyond belief.

"Dad, look at that one. You said…"

"Shut up, Harry. You'll get me arrested!"

It was ever thus, I suppose, and marks us out as the animals that we are. Monkeys clean each other, dogs sniff each other and…well, boys will be boys. The only difference is that we grown-up humans have Trisha in the corner to keep an eye on us!

THE JOY OF HUMAN CONTACT

"Good morning. Thank you for calling the Couldn't Care a Cuss Company Limited. Your call is important to us. Unfortunately, our intensely irritating automatic answering service is out of commission at the moment. This is a human being speaking. My name is Joy. How may I help you?"

It wasn't exactly like that, granted, but the other day I phoned a multinational company, with whom I have an account, in order to order, if that is not tautological, a small part for a dishwasher, and I was miraculously put straight through to a real person. Yes, a *real person*! An actual human being. You must have met one or two in your time. Anyway, enough of all that.

Naturally, this threw me to such an extent that I completely forgot what I was calling about. Like the rest of you out there - and don't tell me you have never come across it - I had been poised, digit at the ready, waiting for the inevitable:

"If you wish to place an order, please press 1.

If you wish to pay your account by credit card, please press 2.

If you wish to complain, please piss off, as we're all on a tea break.

For any other enquiry, please hold, and we will play you one of Vivaldi's Four Seasons until your children have passed through puberty, or until you die of boredom, whichever is the sooner."

But there was none of that for me. Oh, no. For I had fortuitously stumbled on the fragrant Joy; a living, breathing, talking (if slightly mechanical in her questions) member of our species. Nevertheless, I still had to run the gauntlet of security questions to establish my identity. You know the sort of thing:

"Could you confirm your date of birth?

Mother's maiden name?

Inside leg measurement?

Capital of Peru?

How many times did you have sex (excluding one night stands) before the outbreak of the Korean War?"

Yes, you know exactly the sort of thing. Having established that I was me, and not some illegal immigrant, who had risked life and limb to make it to the West in order to illicitly obtain a dishwasher part for his aunty in Bratislava, a lady who had been washing up by hand since her Hotpoint conked out in 1994, I was then asked for the dishwasher model number.

"And where would that be, Joy?"

"I'll just check….it's on a metal plate, underneath, at the back."

"This model number is essential, is it?"

"It has to be quoted in all communications."

"I don't want to quibble, Joy, but wouldn't it have made more sense to put it at the front, where we could all could see it?"

"It's always underneath at the back. Company policy."

"I see. So what you're saying is that the genius who designed this essential piece of domestic equipment decided, in his wisdom, to position the model number, which has to be quoted in all communications, in such a place that it is impossible to see without sliding the machine out, uncoupling it from the water supply, turning it upside down, and sustaining a hernia?"

"Yes."

"I'll get back to you.'

In the end I discovered that the part I wanted (a round piece of plastic no bigger than your average sphincter muscle) would end up costing me £36.99, excluding VAT and delivery.

"Andrea! Where's the washing up liquid?"

WIN SOME, LOSE SOME

Last night, as part of the Brighton Argus Newspaper Achievement Awards, hosted by that well known newsreader, Nicholas Owen, and held at the Hilton Metropole Hotel, Brighton, I was privileged to be asked to present the Parent of the Year award.

When I told our twins, Harry and Jack, about this honour, it took me several attempts to assure them that I was not *receiving* the award as Parent of the Year, but simply *presenting* it. I must say I detected a twinge of disappointment in their response, although I was rather flattered that they obviously considered me to be deserving of such an award. Thanks, lads.

All I can say about being a parent is that it is one of the hardest jobs going, and that the eventual winner was someone who had gone above and beyond the call of duty in the role of parent, and who thoroughly deserved to be Parent of the Year.

Congratulations.

You see, the difficulty with being a parent is that you are thrown into the job with little or, more than likely, no training or experience whatsoever. One day you are pregnant, cushioned by medical professionals, the next day you are on your own with responsibility for a helpless bundle of humanity (and that's just your husband), as well as being the parent of a creature that is a loud noise at one end, and no sense of responsibility at the other. As it happens, in our case we were blessed with two of the little bast…boys. (cheap joke, David, stop it)

What happens is that, over the years, without any previous knowledge, you are called upon to be; doctor, nurse, friend, teacher, playmate, disciplinarian, psychologist, toy assembler, bicycle mechanic, bum wiper, snot remover and general dogsbody.

On top of that, you find yourself suffering from that most insidious, debilitating and mysterious condition known as Parental Paranoia. Everybody you see or meet appears to be on top of the job - except you. Their kids are always immaculately turned out and well behaved, and are taken to Legoland, Disneyland and Switzerland ("He's really good off-piste, you know!") at disturbingly regular intervals. Your kids, on the other hand, always wear their breakfasts like campaign medals across their chests, are constantly bickering, and you are forever saying,

"No, we can't! Anyway, Switzerland is closed today. Go watch The Simpsons, it's on in five minutes."

All of which makes you feel like the worst parent in the world.

Paranoia turns to downright worry, though, when you install the dreaded baby alarm. You set it up to transmit what goes on in the baby's room, and you sit downstairs, or wherever, listening avidly while trying to concentrate on eating dinner and/or watching 'Coronation Street'.

One of two things then occurs. Either, you hear the baby crying, worry that he/she is ill, hungry or upset and rush upstairs, or, you *don't* hear the baby crying, worry that he/she is not breathing or has fallen out of bed, and still rush upstairs. Whatever happens, you become a nail-biting slave to this stress-inducing machine, which is supposed to make your life stress-free, for the rest of your baby's infant life.

But that is as nothing compared to the gut-churning wrench (or do I mean gut-wrenching churn) of 'the first day at school'. And that is a day to remember, if ever there was one. You stand, overlooking the playground, heart in mouth, stomach in turmoil, as some stranger, no older than your teenage nephew, takes your child away. You stare after them until they disappear, and then wait, convinced you will never see your baby again. Later on you will say you wish this were true - jokingly, of course, but that is when the guilt sets in. You feel guilty about bringing into this world another human being, who you fail miserably, shout at seemingly incessantly, and who drives you to distraction.

Then, when you have rushed to the school for kicking out time, it happens. The paranoia, worry and guilt vaporise, as your child rushes over, hugs you, kisses you and shouts out,

"I love you."

That is when you realise that there is only one 'Parent of the Year', and every child is heir to it: you.

GOT IT ALL SEWN UP

You find me in a state of excitement and anticipation this week. No, I haven't won the Lottery, nor found a parking space on Bond Street, and neither have I persuaded the twins to call a Bank Holiday ceasefire.

The source of my mood lies in getting a part in Doctors, the daytime medical soap. More to the point, though, I will be working with Diane Keen, one of the regulars in Doctors and an old sparring partner of mine from way back in the 1970's, when we appeared, along with Lewis Collins, in The Cuckoo Waltz. I haven't seen her for yonks, and it will be great to compare notes on our respective adventures over the years.

Although we played husband and wife, Chris and Fliss Hawthorne, in The Cuckoo Waltz, and spent many a happy on-screen hour in bed together, in real life we were actually more like brother and sister. Indeed, it may well have been just because we had no hidden agenda that we managed to portray a very much in love, married couple with such apparent success.

I have no idea how many people, if any at all, fancied me in those days, but it is without question that Diane was very much the dish of the day, and I was envied by millions for being paid to snog her in bed. Little did I realise, though, how deep and disturbing this was to vast numbers of the UK male population. That aspect of our relationship reared its ugly head, if you get me, when I was giving a talk at a Rotary Club lunch some years later. I wittered on, as I am prone to do, about acting and stuff, told a few of my old jokes, and then threw myself open to questions. The first bloke got up on his hind legs and, without a word of a lie, asked me,

"When you were in bed with Diane Keen, how did you manage with the old, you know, erection business…that is, what did you do with it when you got one?"

The rest of the assembled diners craned forward, all ears, ready to hang on my every word of explanation as to 'what I did with it when I got one'.

"What did I do with it when…?" I think that told us more about him than about me, but I did give an answer of sorts,

"The thing is, I have no idea what turns you on, or in your case, sir, I think I do, but believe me, lying in bed (even with a beautiful woman by your side), surrounded by cameramen, sound men and countless others, and confronted by an audience of 400 or more members of the public, is in no way conducive to any form of arousal whatsoever, least of all sexual."

In order to satisfy their obvious lust for tit-bits of titillation to enliven their lunch, I said I would, as a favour, reveal to them an intimate trade secret, but it was for their ears only, so their lips must be sealed. I paraphrase, as follows:

Whenever Diane and I hopped into bed together, Vera, our smashing wardrobe mistress, always used to sew up the fly on my pyjama bottoms. This was not, as you might suppose, I told the randy Rotarians, to avoid any unscheduled appearance on prime time TV of a certain flaccid part of my anatomy (it doesn't have an Equity card, anyway), but the idea was to stop some eagle-eyed viewer in Wolverhampton, or wherever, writing to complain that he/she had spotted David Roper's underpants peeping out from inside his jim-jams, which proved conclusively that realism on TV was dead. The Rotarians nodded in appreciation at this State Secret.

I am really looking forward to getting the script for Doctors and to finding out how many scenes, if any, Diane and I will be appearing in. The programme is made in Birmingham, by the way, and has its base in a collection of old stone-built buildings, set in rather attractive gardens, on the outskirts of the City. I will be driving up the night before my first call, as wardrobe need to fit me out with a costume (no pyjamas, as far as I know).

Talking of which, it is highly unlikely that Diane and I will be in bed together in this episode of Doctors, but I am packing a needle and thread just in case.

ALL ABOARD!

My parents and I would make only one train journey per year - to Scarborough, as like as not, for our holidays. My feelings of excited anticipation, as a magnificent steam train would chuff its way out of Bradford Exchange Station, were equalled only by my feelings on Christmas Eve. I would stare out of the window at the Ridings of Yorkshire flying past, until eventually the train would come to a steam-blowing halt at Scarborough station. As we walked along the platform, my parents would insist that I said 'Thank you' to the driver, who always seemed pleased to be so appreciated.

Outside the station, we would wait in line for one of the Scarborough school boys, with his 'guider', to wheel our luggage round to our chosen digs. This was in the days when to take a taxi was a luxury my Dad couldn't, or wouldn't, afford. The 'guider', by the way, was usually made of a large wooden box on four wheels, and was pulled along by a boy no older that 10 or 11. Dad would give him half a crown (12.5p), a lot in those days, and the boy would leg it back to the station to grab another 'fare'. I found the whole journey really exciting, especially the steam train.

How times have changed, though. Last week I had two long distance train journeys to make - one to Manchester to audition for Sky TV's 'Dream Team', and the other to Leeds for 'Fat Friends' (no comments, thank you very much) - and I viewed both trips with nervous trepidation, rather than excited anticipation.

You see, all those childhood feelings have long gone, to be replaced by confusion over ticket pricing, worry about getting a seat and exasperation at arrival times. In fact, instead of being a magical dream of a journey to a world of wonder, rail travel now seems more like a stress-laden nightmare of a slog through a catalogue of catastrophes.

For a start, from a train window you only see the backsides of houses, and the worst of the backside of towns and cities. Amazing, isn't it, the amount of rubbish accumulated by the side of railway lines - how do those supermarket trolleys get there? - and who in their right mind builds a conservatory ten feet from the West Coast Main Line, with Virgins whizzing by every twenty minutes?

Then there is the whole business of eating and drinking. In a fit of un-Yorkshire-like extravagance I treated myself to a vodka and tonic. After recovering from the shock of the price, I staggered back to my seat, clipping the heads of several passengers with my elbows as I was thrown from side to side, and settled down for a shot of the old 37.5% proof. Unfortunately, the tonic had been shaking on the shelf since Stockport, so when I opened it I sprayed seats 47 to 55, like a Formula 1 racing driver celebrating his top podium position. I then proceeded to miss the plastic glass and pour the remaining tonic into my lap, due to the driver, amusingly, deciding to practise his emergency stop technique. Neat vodka might be OK with just ice, but no joy there, I'm afraid, as they had run out of the stuff just south of Macclesfield.

To be fair, there have been improvements to trains over the years. They are cleaner, smoother, and I think this is rather sweet, they like to pretend to be aeroplanes, which themselves, of course, started off by pretending to be ships. You must have noticed the shift from ships to planes and into rail language:

'The 14.20 to Manchester Piccadilly is now ready for *boarding.*'

'Your *on-board crew*, today, *Karen and Darren*, will be passing along the *central aisle* to offer you refreshments from the *on-board trolley*.'

The *Chief Steward* (guard) will inform you, 'Our estimated time of arrival is 13.17 at Leeds, where the temperature is only marginally greater than that in Reykjavik.'

And the Train *Captain* (driver) will tell you, 'We will be cruising at an altitude of 18 inches, our air speed will vary from 125mph to dead slow and, when we get to that long straight stretch just north of Peterborough, will Karen please pop along to the cockpit for the usual?'

They also, somewhat surprisingly, provide plugs for lap-tops and mobile phones, and what's the betting that the next time we travel Andrea brings the Hoover just to keep her hand in?

DON'T CALL US...

It doesn't look too promising, I must say. A while ago, if you recall, I auditioned for Sky TV's 'Dream Team' and YTV's 'Fat Friends', and I have not heard a dickie bird from either of them since. Apart from the obvious disappointment at not getting a part, it adds insult to injury when you are obviously so insignificant that they can't be arsed to drag themselves to the phone. Even if they bothered to call and say,

"You were rubbish. Ever thought of a career in plumbing?"

at least it would mean that they had kept your phone number.

(I must interject, at this point, to apologise and add that I did, in fact, get the part in 'Dream Team'. I had to wait another week before they offered me it, but ne'er mind!)

But back to the point. That point being: it is a buyer's market. All an actor can do is opt for the sales technique of the tarts on the Reeperbahn in Hamburg, and sit in the window (or in Spotlight, the actors' directory), hoping to catch the eye of some passing TV producer, who likes the look of you and has money to burn. Not an unreasonable analogy, I think. I mean, let's face it, we all sell our bodies in one form or another, don't we?

The difference between a tart and an actor, though, apart from the fact that a tart earns more money (in cash) and doesn't have NHI stamps deducted, is that a tart is not daft enough to give away free samples. You see, an actor will voluntarily perform at an audition and bare his all, without payment or any guarantee that what he is dishing out, gratis, will turn anybody on in the first place. There is a school of thought, by the way, that holds that the decision to hire you, or not, is made within the first 20 seconds after you step into the room. There is a grain of truth in that, I think.

Alternatively, some producers and/or directors can't even be bothered to turn up. Instead, a video of your reading of the script is made by the casting department, and is later shown to the producer at his leisure - the thespian equivalent of a high-tech escort agency, I suppose. I do like to squeeze the most out of an analogy, don't I? Collections of these audition tapes exist, no doubt, and are scattered around the various TV companies, to be dragged out for a bit of light entertainment and to lift morale, when bidding for the next franchise gets tough. You can guess the sort of thing,

"Stick that video on of David Roper doing his dreadful Birmingham accent, Verity, I could do with a good laugh".

You may think that it is a cruel way to conduct business, but, unfortunately, it goes with the territory. Every actor knows, or soon discovers, that an Equity card comes with 'disappointment' written all over it. You just have to learn to cope with it, and after years of being rejected, you do become somewhat immune to the feelings of hurt and inadequacy that you felt in the beginning. If only you had known about it all those years ago, life might have been a tad less stressful.

That being the case, perhaps Drama Schools should offer classes in how to deal with it. Alongside learning the techniques of voice production, verse speaking and improvisation, maybe there should be classes in rejection acceptance, coping with humiliation and 'How to live with the fact that David Jason never stops working.' Nothing against David himself, of course, good luck to him, but most of us would give our right arm to be earning the VAT on his repeat fees alone.

So, why on earth do we put ourselves through it? If an actor's life is really so bad, why don't we stop whingeing, pack away our dreams of fame and fortune (or, in my case, the fading hope that I will be the next James Bond) and get a proper job? The answer is simple. Most of us don't want the fame, or even a great fortune. We simply want to do the job we love.

The trouble is that for most actors work is like middle-age sex - you hang around for months waiting for it, and if you get it, it is over before you've even noticed, and all you are left with is another long wait until your next performance.

I wonder what a one-way ticket to Hamburg costs.

MANY HAPPY RETURNS

If you see me on the Tele or in the street, take a good look at my face. What does it tell you? Is it the face of a cruel man, a kindly man, or simply the face of a pompous old fart? (I knew it was a mistake letting Andrea have copy control).

Whatever impression you might get from my face, there is one thing about it that you would not be able to tell - at 09.02 tomorrow morning that face will have been staring at the world for exactly sixty years. I can't believe it either. It seems impossible that I am sliding gracefully (hopefully) into my seventh decade, especially when I feel as though I am still that vital, vibrant twenty-something that burst onto the unsuspecting world of British theatre in September, 1971.

But to go back to the very beginning: not long after British, Commonwealth and American troops had landed on the beaches of Normandy and had started to push back the German lines during June 1944, my mother was doing her own pushing for the war effort at St. Luke's Hospital, Bradford. From what she tells me, the final push to Berlin, and the end of World War II, was a piece of cake compared to ejecting me into a world on the brink of peace.

Apart from me growing somewhat bigger, older and self-opinionated, of course, a lot has happened in the intervening six decades. Winston Churchill surprisingly lost the General Election of 1945, and a Labour Government was swept into power. The old *pre-war pessimism* was gone, and the nation looked forward to a brave new world of social justice, equality and the NHS.

Sixty years later, with another Labour Government in power, the old *post-war optimism* had gone, and the nation looked back, as it still does, and wondered what the hell happened to social justice, equality and the NHS.

It is not so much that things have come full circle, but rather that somehow we wandered down a political cul-de-sac, the subsequent U-turn leaving us looking longingly at a past that we thought would be our future. Such is politics today.

In many ways the world now is unrecognisable, compared to the world I emerged into sixty years ago tomorrow. Virtually everything we take for granted today was either in its infancy, like me, or had never been thought of, unlike me, I hope.

Motor cars were for the rich and famous, mass air travel was unheard of and the telephone was confined mostly to those big red boxes on street corners. The actual telephones inside were rather bulky and black, and to work them involved sticking four old pennies into a slot, dialling your desired number and then pressing button 'A' to speak, or button 'B' to get your money back. Some of them do still exist, although most of them have been sold to middle class 'yuppies', and turned into trendy shower cubicles. What they press instead of buttons 'A' and 'B' is their affair.

Radio was spreading nationwide (we got ours in 1949, I think), but TV, although it had been invented, and some sets produced before the war, was light years away from being the principal conduit of news and entertainment that it is today. What would many of us do without it?

Now here's a funny thing - if TV had been invented first, so we all had one, and then somebody had had the revolutionary idea of broadcasting only sound, maybe radio would have been hailed as the great communication medium of our time. Perhaps we would all have been singing its praises by proclaiming,

"Radio? It's great. You can cook, clean and potter round the house, and still hear it. You don't have to sit in one place and give it your undivided attention like that stupid old fashioned TV!"

Who knows? It might have caught on.

What it all adds up to, of course, is the Technological Revolution. Travel, business, entertainment and communication have advanced beyond recognition, and at breath-taking speed. Who's to say what the consequences of such varied and rapid change will be?

All we can do is ponder that old chestnut of a Social Science question:

'What have been the effects of The Industrial Revolution on the 21st century?'

And recall the answer:

'It is too soon to tell.'

WHOSE IDEA WAS IT?

'A little learning is a dangerous thing. Drink deep, or taste not the Pyrean spring.' Thus wrote Alexander Pope, and the kiddie had it just about right.

I suppose he was warning us of barrack-room lawyers and the like, including those travellers of limited nous, who avidly advise the A30, not the A303, when heading for the West Country. Those are the same lads, by the way, who slip into their leather driving gloves (who needs driving gloves these days, for goodness sake?), and insist that you take a short cut,

"Just to the west of Sodom Hall, turn left at the Unfrocked Vicar pub, and if you fancy a pint, try the Curate's Finger. You won't be disappointed, believe me."

By the way, Pope (Alexander, that is, not the bloke in the Vatican) is often misquoted as having written, 'A little *knowledge* is a dangerous thing,' which isn't quite the same thing as 'a little *learning*', when you come to think about it, but seems near enough for most people.

Funnily enough, that oft-misquoted quote popped into my mind the other day, when I was admiring my ageing Daewoo Nexia motor car. Where they get these names from beats me. Who knows, perhaps Nexia is the Japanese God of spark plugs.

Anyway, apparently my car has twin cams and sixteen valves, all of which means absolutely nothing to me, but did set me thinking about how many things exist in this world, of whose invention and/or construction I have absolutely no knowledge whatsoever.

From Jumbo Jets to jockstraps, from Brighton rock to brassieres, from TV sets to tickling sticks, the extent of my ignorance is vast. Even the pen I am writing with now is a mystery of manufacture to me. How do they make all these things, and who thought of them and designed them in the first place?

I read somewhere that the last man who knew as much as there was to know in his time was Leonardo da Vinci. Well, I am here to tell you that old Leo, bless him, would be hard pushed to claim that these days.

I am on a railway train at the moment, and it is amazing to think that everything around me - seats, windows, upholstery, the wedding ring on the bloke opposite, who is picking his nose, by the way ('when you get to the bridge, give us a wave'), in other words, the lot - has been designed and made by people with a knowledge that I have no knowledge of, if you get me.

And how, and why, do people land up opting for a career in all these weird and unfathomable jobs? What primeval urge, for instance, drives a man to decide to become a false teeth maker? Was he untimely ripped from his mother's breast, and never quite got over the toothless trauma of it? Did something unmentionably catastrophic happen to the lad who ended up as a suppository designer, or a Preparation H preparer? Whatever it was, somebody ends up doing those jobs.

And what about food? Someone, somewhere, sometime must have looked at a pig and thought,

"Cor, blimey! That looks tasty. Why don't we kill it, skin it, cut it up into bits, then we can burn it to a crisp, hang about until HP sauce gets invented, and we'll have a bacon sarnie to die for?"

Difficult to imagine that happening, but it must have done, and I'm glad it did.

Hang about, what if pigs (sheep and cows, too, for that matter) had not taken that certain someone's eye? What if it had been dogs and cats and other animals or birds that had got the taste buds tingling? Would we now be confronted with a whole new lexicon of a menu down your local Ho Lee Fuk Chinese take-away? Yes, one with that name does exist. Right at the far end of the King's Road, for your information.

And what about the offerings at the ubiquitous Italian Trattoria?

"Hey, signor, why donna you trya da Labrador Lasagne? Is very fresh. I take him fora da walk dis morning."

"No thanks, I had a Shia Tsu sandwich for lunch. I think I'll go for the Braised Budgie, followed by your Pussy Supreme."

Actually, given a choice, I reckon Chihuahua Chow Mein would take the biscuit. What do you think?

OUT FOR THE COUNT

Using a mobile phone can seriously damage your sperm count. Did you know that? So says The Times, reporting on recent research by a Dr. Imre Fejes of the University of Szeged in Hungary. He studied 221 men over a period of 13 months, and found that men who used their phones consistently had a markedly lower sperm count and sperm motility (swimming ability) than men who did not have a phone at all. Why Hungary should be so hungry for that information, I don't know, but male infertility was certainly an important issue in the Roper household for many years.

Whether my mobile phone influenced my sperm count is uncertain, but my debut on the sperm sample stage was definitely not promising. You see, masturbation has always been a bit of a ticklish subject, so, with a mixture of embarrassment, pride and genuine physical relief, I presented Andrea with my very first sample. We both thought I would fill the bottle, but I had barely managed to cover the bottom of the ruddy thing. By the way, why are sample bottles so disproportionate to the size of your average dick? Have the people who designed them ever tried to ejaculate into one? If you want to experience what it is like, try squirting Tomato Puree into a thimble, while jogging up and down.

Back in the real world, the idea was that I should get my sperm sample down to Pathology, which is where they test these things, keeping it warm on the way. Not difficult, eh?

Wrong.

In my wisdom, I decided to stick the sample bottle under my armpit. OK as far as warmth was concerned, but it meant hunching my left shoulder, making me look as though I had some terrible spinal problem, or else was auditioning for 'Quasimodo'.

So, when I put the hand brake on in the hospital car park, my arm went out and all our potential children ended up rolling around somewhere under the back seat. There is a middle-aged woman from Brighton, who probably still tells the story of the morning she saw a madman scrambling around in the back of his car, muttering something about lost kids.

Outside the entrance to the Pathology Department building, there was a small cardboard tray, the sort that yoghurts sit on in supermarkets. It had a hand-written sign on it, saying 'Specimen bottles here, please'. I was about to oblige, when a woman came along, punched numbers into the security lock and I followed her in.

"Excuse me. I'm looking for Pathology," I said.

"Sperm?" she asked, eyeing my hunched shoulder. "Top of the stairs, on the left."

I made my way up, feeling a bit like a trespasser, and went along the corridor towards Pathology. Now, I am no expert on Laboratory etiquette, so I had no idea whether I should knock on the door and wait, or just knock and walk in. In the event, the door was open, so I just wandered in.

"Hello!" I called.

A disembodied voice floated in from the next room,

"If it's Sperm, write your name and time of production on it, and I'll be out."

Time of production? I hadn't got a clue, but since I'd had to turn off Terry Wogan in order to concentrate (no offence, Tel), I guessed it must have been just after half past eight. A few seconds later 'Jim' appeared. I didn't know his name at the time, of course, but over the years I became such a regular customer there was even talk of me being invited to the Pathology Laboratory Christmas Party. I never did go, but I have often wondered what a group of Path. Lab. Technicians get up to over the warm white wine and twiglets. Do they talk 'shop', comparing gripping tales of gigantic sperm counts, or talk football, making lewd jokes about David 'Semen' and positive ball-handling? I will never know.

'Jim' was great. He had obviously been through it all a thousand times before, and put me at my ease by treating the whole business as if I had just dropped in to buy some of fags. I retrieved the sample bottle from my moist armpit, and handed it over.

"If you've got five minutes, you could hang about and have a look," he said.

"At what?"

"At the stuff you've brought in. I'll do yours first, if you like."

The idea of being invited 'backstage' in a Pathology Lab. was irresistible. So I hung around while he did the business, and then he called me over.

"Have a butcher's at that lot."

He offered me the microscope, and I nervously peered into it. What I saw quite took my breath away. I counted 25 wiggling sperm. Trouble was, Jim said I needed millions to have even half a chance of conception.

Oh, well, back to the drawing board.

David Roper

SPLASHING OUT

So, how did I celebrate my 60th birthday? Admit it, you're itching to know.

A star-studded surprise party at Stringfellows? A luxury holiday in Barbados? A World Cruise? Of course not, what do you take me for? I'm no cheapskate. Naturally, I went the whole hog and spent an arm and a leg on a family weekend break to Bournemouth.

You can scoff! Have you any idea of the prices they charge at UK hotels these days? I could have had a fortnight's self-catering on Lesbos for the cost of two night's dinner, bed and breakfast on the West Cliff.

Originally, we were intent on going to Eastbourne, but my 87 year old mother warned us off, saying,

"You wouldn't get me there. It's too full of old people."

She had a point. It probably explains the road sign I once saw on the way to the Channel Tunnel. 'Folkestone for the Continent' it said, and underneath someone had written, 'Eastbourne for the In-Continent.' Harsh, perhaps, but with a disturbingly amusing grain of truth in it.

However, it is true that Eastbourne does have more than its fair share of people old enough to remember Cliff releasing his first single. It also has a thriving, subsidised Assisted Conception Unit, and it strikes me that these two facts, at opposing ends of the genetic scale, may not be totally unrelated. With a disproportionate number of its population shuffling off at an alarming rate, and Funeral Directors cashing in by offering 'Two for the price of One', what better way to 'reforest' Eastbourne's fading population than by ensuring a regular supply of replacements? It is just a thought.

Back in Bournemouth, we had a really peaceful, relaxing time. It is a fine place. There is mile upon mile of beautiful sandy beach, unlike the marine equivalent of a building site that is Brighton beach, covered in what looks and feels like hard core, and with a panoramic view of a derelict pier. Why has no local authority ever thought of demolishing Brighton's West Pier and putting it, along with the rest of us, out of its misery? I have heard that it has something to do with it being a listed building. A what? A rusted building, yes, but listed? Perhaps they really mean a *listing* building. Its only use appears to be as an embarrassing backdrop to every TV report from whichever Party Conference happens to have chosen Brighton as its venue.

Bournemouth also has spectacular cliff walks, backed by leafy glades, teeming with squirrels, and dotted with courting couples enjoying a spot of al fresco anatomical research.

The hotel was great and the staff helpful, if uniformly pre-pubescent, being possessed of an endearing lack of knowledge about how to serve a drink. I generously gave the barmaid a good two minutes, before sympathetically pointing out the inadvisability of trying to open a bottle of wine with a beer-bottle opener. She took it rather well, giggled and fetched the manager, who proceeded to give her a lengthy lesson in the physics involved in the operation of a corkscrew.

My 'big' present this year was to be a gas barbecue, but being too bulky to fit in a suitcase and to cart all the way to Bournemouth and back, it was not until yesterday that we dragged ourselves to the Garden Centre to buy one. I chose a Mayfair model from the Outback range, which looked splendid on display, but now looks terrifying, laid out on the dining room floor, waiting to be assembled.

There must be nigh on a hundred different screws, washers, nuts and bolts, not to mention the structural elements of the damned thing. Why couldn't they have put it together before they delivered it, and saved yet another poor sod from a nervous breakdown? It seems to be a worrying trend these days that nothing comes fully erected, if you get me? That's modern life for you, though.

So you must excuse me, while I refer to the 'destructions'. What does it say? 'Take rear right hand leg (B3), turn upside down and insert into rear leg support slot (B4). Secure with countersunk screws (D2).'

Andrea!

David Roper

SMACKS OF ABUSE

So, it is official. The Government has made the limits crystal clear to all of us.

I am talking, of course, about how far we parents will be allowed to go in beating our children, or smacking them, or chastising them - take your pick of the punishing euphemisms. You see, it appears that the Government has stopped short of an outright ban on...okay let's compromise and call it, arbitrarily, ...hitting a child over two years of age, leaving the way free for a spot of legitimate, light violence in the cause of discipline.

The argument goes that if the law against hitting a child were to be brought into line with the law against hitting an adult, then the Courts would be swamped with litigious kids bringing cases against parents, who had, in the Government's view, used wholly justifiable violence against them. Underpinning that is the Government's reluctance to outlaw the right of parents to 'reasonable chastisement', whatever that means, and wheresoever it ends.

The result seems to be that we can officially hit them, but only up to a point. What that point is appears to be somewhat vague, and could still constitute assault, in law, in exactly the same way as if I gently smacked the traffic warden instead of laying him out flat.

"Milud, my client admits to smacking the warden, but, in accordance with Government guidelines, claims it was reasonable chastisement."

No, it just wouldn't wash.

The rather disturbing point is that in not outlawing, outright, the hitting of a child the Government is in danger, ipso facto, of endowing that act of

184

chastisement with a certain legitimacy. Many parents may well take that as an official stamp of approval on their chosen method of discipline.

But what about the others who have chosen the non-violent method? Will they take legitimacy to mean obligation, and join the ranks of the smackers? Will the Government find that saying, 'You may.' will be construed as, 'You should.'? That remains to be seen, but the whole question has left me in somewhat of a quandary.

I have never laid a finger on my kids, but I am now feeling unbelievably guilty that I haven't. What am I saying? You see, the Government is telling me it is okay to 'smack 'em about a wee bit', as it were, while Shrinks are telling me that shouting (generally speaking, my chosen method of discipline, rightly or wrongly) can amount to psychological abuse, causing as much long term damage as the short, sharp shock of physical abuse. You can't win, can you!

So what are parents to do? On a more personal level, what am I to do? Do I carry on apparently psychologically abusing my children, if in fact I am, or do I take the Government's 'hint' and start physically abusing them instead, or perhaps as well? All I can do, I suppose, is take on board the opinions of the 'experts', and make a considered choice on the basis of the evidence before me.

To be honest, I can't really believe that trying to instil the discipline that our society requires of children has got to necessarily involve any kind of abuse. On the other hand, who knows, maybe it has. In which case, do physical and/or psychological methods of instilling that required level of desired discipline equally necessarily amount to 'abuse'? Of course, labelling as 'abuse' any method of forcing/persuading children to behave in a certain way does imply that that method is somehow wrong.

However, assuming that any 'moderate' method of discipline, physical or psychological, does not indeed amount to wrongful abuse, perhaps the real point is determining the question of degree and/or definition? Are we all, in a strangely similar way, like the woman in the apocryphal story, where a man asked her,

"Would you sleep with me for £10 million?"

"£10 million! Of course I would," she replied.

"Would you sleep with me for 10 pence?" he asked.

"Certainly not! What do you think I am?"

"Madam, we've established *what* you are. We're just haggling about your *price*."

David Roper

IT'S ALL IN THE GAME

England's defeat at the hands of Portugal (and that Swiss referee), Tim Henman's customary exit from Wimbledon, failures at cricket and rugby - in fact, all tragic sporting losses throughout the years pale into insignificance when compared to Harry's second place in the 80 yards bat and ball balancing race at last week's Saltdean Primary School sports day (years 3 and 4). This is a sporting occasion to rouse all our spirits, and it does.

Talking of which, it is a well-known fact that parents, particularly fathers, can turn into shouting, screaming monsters whenever their offspring is engaged in any form of sporting activity. This is particularly true wherever football is involved, in my experience. Believe it or not, I have witnessed men, otherwise usually quiet and civilised, transformed into beings capable of vicious and vociferous violence, after a referee's perfectly justified decision against their precious child. Not only that, but some fathers have been known to yell out disturbingly loudly from the touch line, encouraging their little darling to inflict all kinds of horrendous torture on the opposing winger, who is innocently dribbling the ball towards the goal.

No such goings on here, thank goodness, although, as the crowd cheered on Fenton to his victory, the cold chill of defeat joined the icy wind, whipping across the playing field, and froze me to the marrow. We are talking July here, by the way.

We brave band of parents, we unhappy few, dressed up more for a bonfire night bash than a summer sports day, were huddled together for warmth like penguins in an Antarctic winter, and wished that the PTA had been on hand to flog us coffee, soup and sandwiches - they would have cleaned up.

186

Early indications were that Ben would turn out to be a kind of Michael Schumacher, winning everything, which he more or less did, but other stars also shone. Louis, an Energiser battery on legs, gave us his impersonation of an Exocet missile, proving conclusively that all good things come in small parcels. How he could get his little legs to move at such an amazing pace, beats me.

The obstacle race, which I propose should immediately be embraced as an Olympic event, hinged principally on who could don a jacket, before climbing through a hoop and dashing to the line in a frantic bat and ball balancing reprise of a finish – an ideal climax to any Olympic Games, you must agree.

Controversy, of course, is never far away in sport, and here was no exception. The howls of protest from officials and parents alike were heard as far away as Deep Sea Den, I understand, as competitors in the 'balancing a bean bag on the bonce' races resolutely refused to keep their hands away from their heads (a serious breach of the rules), and there were several ignominious disqualifications. I think Miss Goodman, the headmistress, should seriously consider employing a sports psychologist to counteract this gross breach of sporting ethics.

The Green team (anchorman: our Jack) romped home in the 4 x 80 yards relay, to an epic first place, but was no match in the end for the Blue team, who, after the final scores were collated, ended up at the top of the podium, shaking bottles of fizzy drink and spraying the crowd in celebration. Most of us ended up freezing and covered in a light coating of frozen Tango. Formula 1 motor racing has a heck of a lot to answer for.

But all in all it was a most successful morning. The children threw themselves into each event with a will, obviously enjoying themselves enormously, and the cases of frostbite among the parents have now been successfully treated without the need for any amputations. I was one of the lucky ones, actually, as it only took three cups of coffee, two bacon sandwiches and an hour in a warm room to regain the feeling in my toes, although I do now have a tendency to limp slightly when the wind veers northeast.

As we trudged away from the bleakness of the sporting arena, a light, freezing drizzle threatened, and there was talk among us of trying for sponsorship at next year's event - Damart won hands down.

David Roper

BROWNED OFF

From May to September, Andrea hates my guts. Not the size of them, you understand, although goodness knows there is room for improvement there, but the colour of them and, more to the point, the colour of me in general.

You see, I harbour a highly responsive supply of melanin. No, not the latest designer drug, nor some chemical in UPVC windows, but the pigment responsible for suntans. The result is that hardly have I finished unbuttoning my shirt, than my stomach is already turning that nicely tanned look associated with a week on the Med.

It drives Andrea potty. She could actually spend a week on the Med and still end up looking like a highly embarrassed, anaemic lobster. Not her fault, of course, nor mine, but simply nature's cruel trick, dividing the bronzed from the barbequed.

There have been holidays when she has prostrated herself daily on a lounger, soaking up the sun, apparently, and ended up a rather fetching shade of pink, with patches of prickly heat rash, somewhat reminiscent of a map of South East Asia. I, on the other hand, would have spent most of the time languishing in the shade, reading my book, only to end up the overall colour of what Dulux would classify as 'Moroccan brown'. I can't help it, or her.

All that might change, though, with the development of a new drug, Melanotan-1 (MT-1), a synthetic version of the hormone that stimulates release of the much sought after melanin, and which would mean off-the-peg tans for all. Armed with MT-1, Andrea would at last be able to compete on a level playing field, and match her bronzed Adonis of a husband (sorry about that) in the all-important dermatological browning department.

What the breakthrough also means, of course, is that if MT-1 is put on general release, tanning salons and sun creams would become redundant, those girls in Boots' make up department would no longer be obliged to cake themselves in their product to hide their pallor, and 'getting away to the sun' would lose much of its draw for millions of us sun-starved Brits.

After all, it seems that for many people, most people actually, one of the main purposes of a holiday is to return with the requisite tan, a symbol of not only having been away, but of having had enough dosh to have been away 'to the sun'. Let's face it, the worst thing you can possibly say to a newly-returned, bronzed-ish, British holidaymaker is,

"We've had wall-to-wall sunshine here, mate. What was it like in Benidorm? Cloudy, was it? I got my tan in Bognor."

So important is this colour-coded snobbery to us (and you must have noticed this) that anybody back from a winter sun holiday will invariably wear white or yellow, and in extreme cases shorts, in mid-January, just to accentuate and show off their colour. Is there any other country in the world where people care so much about the relevance of the post-holiday colour of their skin that they do this?

But what will happen to our quaint, peculiarly Anglo-Saxon game of 'My tan cost more than your tan', if MT-1 hits us right between the eyes, and everywhere else on our anatomies, for that matter? Will all those little white bums, and the big ones too, that are ostentatiously flashed around down the David Lloyd Leisure Centre, no longer be the ultimate status symbol? For rest assured, MT-I will act indiscriminately on bums, rich and poor, and we will all be uniformly brown from head to toe, whether or not we have holidayed in Barbados or Bridlington.

There will be no physical way to show off about the sun-soaked resort from where you have just returned, since everybody you see will look as if they have been away to a similar resort, too. As the Gilbert and Sullivan lyrics say,

"When everyone is somebody, then no-one's anybody!"

It might be all for the best, though, as melanin protects against the sun's rays, and guards against skin cancer. So, all in all, I am in favour of it. Roll on MT-1, I say, not least because it will herald my return to domestic bliss from May to September.

OFFICIAL RETURNS

What does Her Majesty the Queen have in common with our twins, Harry and Jack? Is it that none of them carries money and is chauffeur driven everywhere they go? Or is it that they each rule over an inherited sovereign territory, have a tendency to host impromptu Garden Parties at our expense, and never do the washing up?

Nothing so common. What uniquely connects them is that they all have Official Birthdays. The Queen's real birthday is 21st April, but her Official Birthday falls on the second Saturday in June. The boys' real birthday falls slap bang in the middle of the summer holidays, making a party difficult to organise, as their friends are always swanning around Europe somewhere. So, they have an 'Official Birthday' in early September, when everybody has returned, suntanned and available.

The venue, however, is the subject of much argument during the weeks leading up to the end of term in July, because everybody needs an invitation before trotting off to Tuscany or wherever.

Believe me, Her Majesty has got it made - a quick drive along The Mall (or a clop, if she's feeling up to it), a couple of hours reviewing a few troops, a sly adjustment of the gaffer tape on Phil's mouth, then it's back to Buck House for a late lunch and Countdown, with the inevitable,

"We would like a consonant, Carole."

However, being unqualified to use the royal plural (pluralis maiestatis), I am reduced to using the plebeian singular (singularis plebeis - possibly), when I tell you of my options.

Deep Sea Den (nee Wacky Warehouse):

Basically an embryonic SAS assault course with multi-coloured Slush Puppies thrown in, often literally.

Bowlplex:
A rare opportunity to test the physics of bouncing large cannon balls off a flat surface. Nelson and Barnes Wallis were early exponents.

Megazone:
Mini war game in which participants are 'killed' by laser guns. Good training for the 2020s, when the West will, no doubt, still be invading largely defenceless countries on the basis of dodgy intelligence, seized upon to support preconceived ideas about a non-existent threat.

Cinema:
Limited choice this year - Garfield, Spiderman 2 or Shrek 2. Trouble is you have to take your own food, as the cost of drinks and popcorn for a dozen kids is only marginally short of the price of a Nissan Micra (3-door). On a personal note, I thought Fiona in Shrek 2 was quite attractive. Must be my age.

Party at home:
Avoid at all costs. 'Costs' being the operative word. It always sounds like such a good idea to start with, but then so did Johnny Vaughan's career at the BBC, and look what's happened to that. You see, by the time you have hired the kids' entertainer, bought a ridiculous amount of salad and scotch eggs that no-one eats, and shelled out for goody bags containing the mandatory Faberge egg, Rolex watch and two return tickets to New York, you are skint.

Cash or Cheque:
This option is usually brought up once the kids have realised that the amount of money they could cop for in hard cash would almost certainly be more than the cost of some toy or other, which they would get tired of before the week was out anyway. Call me cynical if you like, but believe me, the moment kids smell money you can kiss goodbye to what you were saving up for to pay for your lavish Coop funeral. Opening a bank account for them is the kiss of death, too. Kids have an in-built calculator, in case you didn't know, that enables them to tot up all the cheques you have deposited in their account, add on interest and come up with an amazingly accurate total that they are saving until they have enough to buy outright a Kawasaki motorbike. So, steer clear of this, as long as you can.

In the end we got bullied into the Megazone. Well, it is for the kids, although because of the military connection I understand Her Majesty intends to give it a go when her Official Birthday comes around. Copycat!

David Roper

AN ACTOR'S LIFE FOR ME

PART FOUR

AN ACTOR ADORED

David Roper

THIS OTHER EDEN

'God made man to plough, plant and water, and to watch as his seed grows in size,

'But whatever it says on the packet, the ruddy thing still always dies.' (Anon)

From the Garden of Eden, via the Garden of Gethsemane, to the Garden Centre on the A23, something always seems to go horribly awry whenever man enters the mysterious world of horticulture.

For example, in Lister Park, Bradford, there was a garden (it may still exist), which was planted with particularly heavily-scented flowers and shrubs for a special reason. On the entrance gate was a notice that said:

'This garden is for the use of blind people only. Please do not enter.'

For ages, I wondered why the garden was always empty, then I read the notice carefully again (because I could, of course) and realised why nobody was in there!

Now, crunching on a Granny Smith's may not be the world shattering event it was in Adam and Eve's day, but the fall out from that single, innocent bite still resounds down the ages.

The modern day Holy of Holies, being Garden make-over programmes on TV, exhorts us to examine our own miserable plots, while devilish Garden Centres tempt us to spend our worldly goods with the promise of a flowering paradise, and Alan Titchmarsh brings down his commandments like a modern day Moses.

Evidently, I am not a devoted disciple of those who have put the cult into cultivation, but I have to admit that I do like a tidy, colourful garden. Even more attractive to me than that, is the sight of an exquisitely mown billiard table lawn. Passing one of those can turn my head far more excitedly than even the sight a pair of oscillating Lycra-clad buttocks down the old David Lloyd Leisure Centre, however tight and firm they may…oh, give it a rest, David, for goodness' sake. It's pathetic.

The result of the assault on us by the plethora of Garden Centres is that we are being subliminally driven to the point of obsession and guilt by the barrage of information on how and why we should create our own mini-Edens in our pathetic, weed-infested back yards. TV throws Latin names for plants at us like confetti (and I bet that word has got a Latin root, too), Evergreen Complete is compulsory weeding for any self-respecting lawn owner, and we bulk-buy slug pellets as if in response to some Government warning of an impending attack by suicidal, terrorist snails.

Perhaps the only way out of our lemming-like rush to the Wyevale Garden Centre (10% off for the over 60s every Tuesday, and I should know) is to go back to basics. Funnily enough, I was up the old Wyevale the other week to buy turf. When the assistant said,

"Trouble is, if it doesn't get laid by Saturday, it's no good to anyone,"

I found myself involuntarily replying,

"I think that applies to most of us, love."

But back to basics, as I said. My Yorkshire neighbour, Clifford, whose wit and wisdom I promised more of, used to say,

"You've got to treat a garden like a woman, lad. Give it the odd poke every now and again, if you must, but you've got to know when to keep your hands to yourself."

You see, Clifford was the fount of all knowledge, and I have to say I did admire the complete and utter certainty he had when talking a load of complete and utter bollocks.

"So, what do I do with my garden now the summer's nearly over, Clifford?"

"Have you learnt nothing, lad? Treat it like a woman! Give her a new winter coat, a last, quick cut and blow dry for the lawn, and don't go near her until the clocks go on in March."

On second thoughts, maybe Clifford could have taught Alan Titchmarsh a trick or two, given the chance. He certainly had the whole business of planting and transplanting, potting and re-potting all sewn up. Even the little poem that he penned, and that I quoted earlier, seemed to beautifully sum up the curse of the modern garden. I make no excuse for reminding you of it here.

'God gave us the trees and the flowers,
And all things that truly have worth.

But you're nearer to a hernia in a garden
Than anywhere else on Earth.'
Thanks, Clifford. You always made my day.

David Roper

THE GREAT DOUBLE ACT

I have never been a foster parent, but I admire enormously those who give up their homes and lives by inviting others to share them. I don't know how they do it.

Last week, though, we got the vaguest sense of what it feels like, when we had the builders in. For five days we played surrogate parents to two lads, who ate us out of biscuits, coffee and sugar, played music on a portable radio, which builders seem to be umbilically attached to, and created enough dust to impress even the most cynical survivor of Pompeii.

My point is not that foster children behave like that - perish the thought - but that sharing your home and life with other people does dislocate the old domestic routine.

Our builders, Kevin and Gordon, for it is they of whom I speak, arrived last Tuesday week. Not unreasonably, I thought they would look like…well, builders - pencil behind the ear, Caterpillar boots, packet of Rizlas sticking out of the crack of their ar…chitypal builders, if you know what I mean.

So, it was a jolt to my stereotyping to be confronted with what looked like two tourists fresh back from Torremolinos - all Bermuda shorts, tanned legs and beaming, healthy smiles. This holiday mood persisted for the length of their stay, and they made the whole business of demolishing a substantial proportion of the house seem to be an act of Samaritan-like kindness.

They were also really great with the kids, who naturally shared their interest in demolition, were tolerant of my total ignorance of construction, and were completely unphased by our dog Poppy's fascination with sniffing the contents

An Actor's Life For Me

of their Bermudas. Only when they lapsed into their native tongue, 'builder-speak', did we temporarily lose them.

"Got the calcs on the steel, Kev?"

"Yeh. Regs say 8-inch return. Is it a 7 by 4?"

"You got it. Should eat this job. When you off to Spain again?"

Pinky and Perky, as we affectionately came to know them, also had their own unique and fascinating concept of time. If they arrived early, they would leave late. If they arrived late, they would leave early. I never delved into the origins of this logic (probably something to do with the illusive Building Regulations), but since they did the work on time and were eternally jolly, who am I to question it.

They covered everything, including Poppy, our dog, when necessary, with dust-sheeting, demolished a wall as if it were Lego, and in the garage their erection (steady!) of a set of stairs is something to behold. They hoovered up behind them, washed up, and, in what must be a Construction Industry first - they even made *me* cups of tea. I bet that is not in the Building Regs. (notice my clever little touch of builder-speak there?)

But, above all, their most endearing quality, which marks them out as lads of impeccable taste, was that they actually laughed at my jokes. In short, they were a pleasure to have around, and worked with the minimum of disruption and the maximum of humour.

Thanks, Pinky and Perky, we will foster you anytime.

And indeed we did - in a sense.

Later that year, I was asked to tour Australia for 3 months, performing in 'An Inspector Calls', the play that kick started these articles in the first place. Andrea point blank refused to let me swan off to a land full of surf, sand and se...Sheilas. No, I tell a lie. We agreed that I would ask the touring company if I could bring along my family (Andrea, Harry and Jack, of course, but no Poppy, who would be fostered herself).

Amazingly, the company agreed, at a reasonable price, so we all packed up and went. Because I would be earning more than enough to keep us 'down under', and with the help of a bank loan, we got Kevin and Gordon to convert the roof area of our house into a couple of bedrooms and a shower room, while we were away. We had full confidence in them to get the work done, and they could come and go as they pleased. Having said that, it is a fact of life that it will usually kick you in the teeth.

Not this time. Pinky and Perky proved it wrong. Thanks, lads.

199

David Roper

TENTS, TOADS AND TIDES

I have done my fair share of camping over the years. Not professionally, you understand, but the tented variety in a field outside of the tiny village of Treen, Cornwall.

Every August would find me motoring west along the A30, across Bodmin Moor, bypassing Truro and Penzance and along that last toe of England, leading towards Land's End. A left fork in the road would lead past St. Buryan and on to Treen. Stopping at the local Farm Shop to register a camping spot, and to open a shopping account for the week, would be followed by the rather laborious task of putting up the tent on the campsite, which is really nothing more than a farmer's field at the end of the road, but what more do you need?

The Treen Farm Campsite, although somewhat grandly named, is mercifully flat and is well-appointed with toilets and running water. It is to be found, after passing The Logan Rock Inn and the Farm Shop, perched high above the fantastic sweep of Pedn Vounder beach. This beautiful bay is only accessible after a particularly precarious climb down the cliffs: an exciting descent, true, but definitely not for the faint hearted.

For reasons lost in the mists of time, the far end of this idyllic sandy beach has been commandeered as the unofficial nudist section. Here everybody, man, woman and child, would spontaneously strip off, and then either flop down on a towel to brown all the bits usually hidden from view, or else wander to the water's edge and stick a toe in.

Perhaps it is being stripped of all socio-economic indicators, but paddling naked in the company of others seems to create an instant camaraderie.

"Morning."

"Morning."

"Come far?"

"Yorkshire."

"Crikey! You've got a long one."

"Pardon!"

"Journey home. It'll be a long one."

"Oh, yes. Right."

And off we would shuffle into the icy waters of the English Channel, emerging later, our respective genitalia reduced to the size and consistency of two almonds and a walnut, and our nipples sticking out like chapel hat pegs.

Along the coast lies the Minack Open Air Theatre. Always a natural amphitheatre, it has tiers of grassy seats and a stage fashioned from the rocks. A beautiful setting. Unfortunately, when I went to watch a matinee of South Pacific by the Truro Operatic and Dramatic Society (the TOADS, as they are known locally from their initial letters) it was quite windy and showery. Twenty of us braved the elements and, as we settled down to be transported to sunnier climes, the producer appeared on the stage. Through the wind and rain, and a loud-hailer, he made this virtually inaudible announcement:

"Ladies and Gentlemen, thank you so much for turning out this afternoon. As a result of your attendance, it has been decided that we will indeed perform this afternoon, but as we hired the costumes at great expense from a London Costumiers, and as we don't want to get them wet, the cast will all be wearing plastic macs."

South Pacific in plastic macs? This I had to see. The opening scene, featuring those two young kids in their swimming costumes, and singing 'Dites-Moi', lost something, I must say, as they struggled to keep their macs buttoned, but I persevered. You see, I was transfixed by the thought of the inevitable entrance of 'Bloody Mary'. When she finally appeared, it was clear that, despite the inclement weather, the actress had indeed blacked up (couldn't do it nowadays, of course). Unfortunately, during the second chorus of her rendering of 'Bali Hi', her pac-a-mac popped open, her make up ran and she looked for all the world like an animated, singing Zebra Crossing. Unable to take any more, I chickened out and legged it back to the Logan Rock Inn to dry off and to toast 'Bloody Mary' in, yes, you guessed it, several Bloody Marys.

All this talk of camping has arisen because Harry and Jack have got a tent. I only recently finished putting it up (after three hours and even more expletives), and it is rather magnificent, if I do say so myself. I promised I would sleep in it with them, and on two occasions I have trudged across the lawn and zipped us in, only to be driven back to my bed by the thunder and lightning. I was OK, though, the boys held my hand.

Tonight will be the third attempt, and I am sitting in the tent as I write, after checking for wood lice and spiders.

Hang about! My fly-sheet is flapping. I am off out to fix it. Such is my lot.

THROUGH THE TRANSFER WINDOW

"Good morning, Arsenal Football Club. How may I help you?"

"Arsene about?"

"Absolutely not, sir. This really is Arsenal Football Club. How may I help you?"

"Ah, right. Sorry. What I mean is: is Arsene…about, as in…available?"

"I'm afraid not, sir. Mr. Wenger is unavailable at the moment. As a matter of fact, he's at the dry cleaners collecting his suit. And before you say it, yes, that means he's out getting his 'Arsene gear'. Don't you worry, sunshine, we've heard every hilarious take on his name over the years."

The reason for that rather convoluted, albeit explanatory, phone conversation was that Harry and Jack were about to miss the transfer window for the current football season. Although, as their manager, my cunning policy of brinkmanship had pushed their joint fee up to £35 million, the basic problem was that our contract with Saltdean United (under tens) was about to run out. Compounding that, the boardroom wranglings at Saltdean had left the team without a manager, making Bill Kenwright's troubles at Everton seem like a mere bagatelle.

So, with Real Madrid financially stretched after Michael Owen's move from Liverpool, and even the sainted Manchester United having to dig deep in their quest to secure Wayne Rooney, the only realistic choice left to me was between Leeds, Chelsea and Arsenal.

Leeds was out of the running, of course, on the grounds that they were down to petty cash, and, in any case, the boys request for a weekly supply of Coke might well have been misconstrued. Needless to say, Claudio Ranieri at Chelsea categorically refused to make a bid for two players so manifestly English.

Arsenal it would have to be then, hence my call to their virtually eponymous manager. After his trip to Sketchley's, I finally got through to the great Arsene as he was trying on his freshly laundered tuxedo, but he was not much help, quite frankly.   The £35 million was no problem, obviously, nor were the £25,000 per week each in wages and the MacDonald's Happy Meals at half time. The deal-breaker was the boys' insistence on having every Saturday afternoon off to go to their drama class. I did point out to them that the chances of there being a football match roundabout three o'clock on a Saturday were marginally greater than 50/50, but unfortunately that landed on deaf ears.   Much the same response greeted Andrea's refusal to let them play any UEFA Cup away games against the likes of Parathaniakos without a generous layer of sun cream and a hat each. Little did I know that on such seemingly insignificant demands football contract negotiations are wont to succeed or fail. The end result was that I inevitably found myself languishing way back in square one.

Weird, though, how it can so often dawn on you that the solution to a problem has been staring you in the face all along. It was Sven, son of Erik, who put me on to it. I caught him in bed, who hasn't, and when I put my dilemma to him he shouted, 'Ah! Eureka!', or was it, 'Ah! Ulrika!'?, I couldn't be sure, but at least it made me realise that whatever he might be depositing on his own door step, the answer to my problem lay firmly on mine. It was so blindingly obvious that I couldn't believe I had missed spotting it.

So it is that Harry and Jack will be signing with Rottingdean Football Club (under tens) at the very moment you are reading this. Admittedly, the transfer fee falls somewhat short of the boys' market value, but what the hell, what we lose in wages we will make up in decreased travelling expenses and bulk purchases of CocaCola.

More to the point, Rottingdean Football Club rents its pitches from Rottingdean Cricket Club, which, in turn, boasts a clubhouse capable of providing bags of chips and bacon sandwiches on those cold, freezing Sunday mornings that form such an essential part of the season.

A bit of a result, don't you think?

OF DOGS, CATS & PIGS

"A dog will look up to you; a cat will look down on you; only a pig will look you straight in the eye."

So would say a Devon farmer I once knew and worked with. Whether it strikes you that he had a high opinion of pigs or a low opinion of his fellowman, depends, I suppose, on personal experience and how long ago it is since you read Animal Farm. However, I do think he had a point, and it says a heck of a lot about humans in particular, I must say.

Consequently, perhaps it is as well that we don't have a pig to look us in the eye as an equal, nor a cat to look down on us with disdain, but we do have a dog, Poppy, who manages to look up to us with wonder and rule our lives, both at the same time. How do dogs do that? She is a Cavalier King Charles Spaniel and has captured all our hearts since she graciously agreed to come and live with us just before last Christmas. Because of her colouring, chestnut and white, Poppy is classified as a Blenheim: the name being derived from the 1st Duke of Marlborough's estate, which was named Blenheim after his victory at the Battle of - would you believe - Blenheim! He kept the breed for hunting, and he is noted as recording their ability to 'keep up with a trotting horse'. How relevant that was, I don't know. Only the deceased Duke could tell you.

By the way, there is a myth that King Charles II issued a special decree granting King Charles Spaniels permission to enter any establishment in the UK, overriding 'no dogs except guide dogs' rules. A variant of this myth is sometimes instead applied to Cavalier King Charles Spaniels, relating specifically to the Houses of Parliament. However, the UK Parliament website states that extensive research has failed to track down any such decree made by King Charles.

Nevertheless, Poppy, wherever she is allowed to wander unhindered, does look beautiful (and knows it), barks rarely, needs but moderate exercise and defecates with a delicacy wholly befitting her regal connection.

On that last, and somewhat delicate subject, I must pause here to declare that we never go out without at least one 'poop' bag, and are fastidious in clearing up behind her. Unfortunately, there are some among you, and you know who you are, who seem to think that allowing a pooch to leave 'messages' all over the place is some kind of joke. It isn't. Stop it at once.

Now, what has been amazing about Poppy is the way she has so radically changed our lives. Not only do we get out more, but for the first time in our lives we have ventured into that last, long and lonely area in ASDA - the Pet Food aisle - and have discovered a whole new lexicon to add to our shopping list: Cesar (sic), Small Bite Mixers, Milky Bones etc. etc. It is a whole new world down there.

We have also experienced that unconditional love and affection which animals (barring humans, naturally) so often exhibit. The first time I came home after being away for a couple of days, Poppy fell on me, snuffling and licking, as if she hadn't seen or smelt me for months. It was infinitely touching, and from that moment I was totally hooked. Incidentally, I have tried to persuade Andrea to adopt this disarming kind of greeting, curiously without success, although I know, deep down, there is the same love and affection invested into it every time she says,

"What time do you call this?"

Another of Poppy's endearing features is her affinity with Nature, in that they both abhor a vacuum. Rise from your seat, your bed or your garden lounger, and before you can say, 'Meaty chunks with vegetables.' she has filled the bum-warmed spot you have just vacated.

Our only problem, if problem it be, is that she moults unceasingly. In the nine months since Poppy arrived, Andrea has hoovered up enough hair to knit jumpers for the whole of Year 5 at Saltdean Primary. Oops! Better go. She's just left a little 'message' for me on the lawn - Poppy, that is, not Andrea.

THE STUFF OF LIFE

There are certain fundamental necessities of life without which we simply could not survive: air to breathe life into us, food and water to sustain us and the sun to maintain the Earth on which we live.

But, delving deeper, life in the Roper household would be intolerable, unsupportable and ultimately inconceivable without those two even more fundamental necessities of life: the vacuum cleaner and the dishwasher.

Considering the world that so many of us live in today (AD - after dishwashers), it is often difficult to imagine what the world was like that we lived in not so long ago (BC - before cleaners). On the downside, if you cast your mind back, one poor sod would be saddled with the job of washing all the crockery and cutlery by hand, and another poor sod would have the unenviable task of drying it all with an increasingly sodden tea towel. On the upside, it has to be said, the whole process did give a husband and wife (for it was usually they that did the work) at least the chance to engage in some intimate personal chat, like it or not.

On the other hand, as far as most types of floor cleaning is concerned, the vacuum has, of course, revolutionised the whole business of keeping your carpet free of dust, crumbs, dog hairs etc. In the old days, most of us would have relied on the good old Ewbank carpet sweeper, which was quite efficient in its way, but did involve one of you having to spend time and energy pushing the damn thing forwards and backwards for what seemed like hours on end.

For us, though, the vacuum and the dishwasher are so essential to our very existence that, when the former was under-performing and the latter had yet to be delivered to our new home (we moved in a few months ago), life took on a decidedly Dickensian aura of deprivation and despair.

You see, our Dyson vacuum cleaner (generic name: Hoover) was not sucking like it should, you know the feeling, and instead of plucking up dog hairs, ten to the dozen, it was rolling them into small balls that were clinging to the carpet with the tenacity of super-strength Velcro. Thus, there was I, on my hands and knees (a grown man, I ask you!), teasing Poppy's tonsorial rejects off the old Axminster, and popping them into the Dyson's upturned nozzle, whence they were somewhat half-heartedly sucked off to oblivion. Quite frankly, the kids have exerted more suction on a strand of Donatellos' spaghetti.

Knowing, as you do, of Andrea's love affair with the vacuum cleaner (*hooverphilia nervosa*, for those of you of a medical bent), it will come as no surprise to find that this tragic situation was tantamount to a bereavement, and necessitated drastic action. Consequently, I was dispatched, hot-foot, in search of the Freeman's catalogue. I found it on her bedside table where she had left it the night before after a spot of light bedtime reading. She prefers Freeman's to Catherine Cookson: not much plot, of course, but the cast of purchasable characters is virtually endless.

And so it was that we ordered the old stalwart, a Henry, on a 'buy now, pay 2045' deal, which was a bit optimistic on their part, I thought, as I will be over 100 by then, but that's their problem.

The next day the sainted dishwasher arrived. Now, I don't want to over dramatise this, but if you can imagine the scenes of tearful joy on Cilla's 'Surprise, Surprise' programme, when some long-divided family is reunited, you will get a flavour of how Andrea and I greeted this prodigal product of the Hotpoint factory. Kisses and hugs were exchanged, and when we switched it on for its inaugural cycle, I swear there were tears welling in our eyes. We stood there, like proud new parents, gazing in awe at our baby's first tentative steps in what we hoped would be a lifetime of faithful service.

Those of you without experience of a dishwasher, or a hoover, God forbid, will consider all that just so much self-indulgent claptrap, but those of you who are dishwasher and vacuum devotees will understand the depth of feeling these machines can evoke.

So, while Andrea nervously awaits the blessed Henry's arrival, I must down tools and feed our new baby. 'Come to Daddy!'

OPEN WIDE

When I was in EastEnders, Wendy Richard, who played Pauline Fowler, gave each of our new born twins, Harry and Jack, a small silver casket, in which to place the first of their redundant milk teeth. It was a really lovely thought, and she gave them to me while we were filming some episodes in Scotland, when I was about to leave the programme.

Since that time, needless to say, we have had to regularly shell out money: to date, over thirty quid and counting, all on behalf of the tooth fairy. We don't begrudge the kids their £1 per tooth, of course, it's just that if I look back to my own childhood, when I got sixpence (in old money), if I was lucky, it appears that the current money grabbing tooth fairy is working on a cumulative inflation figure of 4,000% (APR 86.7%, terms and conditions apply).

Mind you, if you think about it, and setting the tooth fairy to one side, the whole business of dentistry and dental health has changed beyond recognition over the past fifty years.

I remember going with my mother, who was terrified, and who can blame her, when she had all her teeth out…yes, *all*…the complete gobful. There was nothing wrong with them, but it was standard practice in the 1950s to yank the whole lot out. If you got to forty with a full set of gnashers you got an O.B.E. Why dentists were such fans of extraction (or extractor fans, if you like) I have no idea, but I wish my dad had bought shares in Steradent. Neither have I any idea when the penny finally dropped with the dental fraternity, but there obviously came a time when one of them had a brain wave and revolutionised the whole profession's attitude to what to do with everybody's teeth. It was simple really, and the rest of them, the - whatever is the collective noun for dentists: an Amalgam? - must have thought,

"Why didn't I think of that?"

The stunning realisation was this: instead of extracting everybody's teeth all at one go, leaving dentists with no further work to do, and therefore no further income, why not simply refuse to extract teeth, but keep on repairing them until extraction became inevitable. Thus, at a stroke, they would be creating a constant supply of necessary work and, of course, income. Genius! That virtually self-perpetuating cycle of work and income is what keeps the dental profession in the manner it has become accustomed to up to the present day.

However, looking back, it is true to say that dental hygiene was totally unknown in our house, and in many others, I imagine. It seems unbelievable now, but I didn't brush my teeth until I was seven years old. As a result, I had to have one of them extracted ('ripped out' would be a better description) at the local Dental Ripping Out Clinic in Westgate, Bradford.

In those days they knocked you out with gas. Terrific. I woke up early, unfortunately, to be faced with some pimply student, who had his left knee on the arm of the chair, his right hand in my mouth, and was holding what looked like a pair of pliers. He finally ripped out *half* the offending molar, and I went off to swill gallons of blood down the sink, alongside the rest of the morning's victims.

The worst thing about using gas, though, is that, while it may have rendered you temporarily unconscious, it had about as much anaesthetic effect as sucking a Werther's Original. Consequently, even if the extraction had been successfully completed, you were left feeling as if your jaw had been hit with a sledge hammer. In my case this was compounded by the nerve-end of my semi-extracted molar being left hanging free, and I couldn't eat or sleep for a week.

Eventually, my parents dragged me to see a proper dentist, who fished out the remainder of the tooth, and later tore a strip off the clinic's director, a certain Dr. Mengele, for allowing students to experiment on defenceless children.

That story always stirs up the pathological fear of dentists I was left with, and which is made even worse today, as I have an appointment for a filling tomorrow.

Oh, God. Why did I have to choose this week to mention dentists?

AISLE BE BLOWED

If I were ever a contestant on Mastermind, my specialist subject would have to be: 'Foods and their location on the shelves at ASDA, Brighton Marina.' I have never consciously studied this fascinating topic, but I have come to realise that my knowledge of it is encyclopaedic.

This fact dawned on me the other day when I strayed, inadvertently, into Sainsbury's at Newhaven. I had been to B&Q and was on a secondary mission for Andrea to find a lemon, a fistful of shell-on prawns and a gateaux,

"Fresh or frozen, but steer clear of anything with Black or Forest on the packet. Got it?" she had demanded.

Had I been in ASDA, I could have found these things with my eyes closed, naturally, but in the alien environment of Sainsbury's I was well and truly in the dark. To tell the truth, the lemon was a doddle to find, as it is 'rule one, page one' of the Great Superstore Handbook that the first thing you see on entering any supermarket is the fruit and veg. This piece of retail psychology is based, presumably, on the idea that if your first impression is of fresh, wholesome and, therefore, by implication healthy food then you will be well disposed towards all the crap on the rest of the shelves. I never said that!

However, as far as I can work out, and I could be wrong, of course, other little gems of retail psychology are to be found scattered everywhere in the aisles of your average supermarket. For instance, the placing of cheap 'own brand' items next to more expensive 'branded' items (both of which are actually the same thing, but in different packaging) is, in fact, a cunning ploy to exploit your average shopper's obsession with a bargain and/or the desire to buy something 'a cut above'. The theory is, I guess, that some shoppers will go for the cheaper 'own brand' version, on the basis of saving money, as against others who will opt for the more expensive 'branded' version, on the grounds that they must be getting something better. The point of the exercise being that the joint sales of the product will invariably increase. That is because some shoppers will think that they have 'discovered' the cheaper 'own brand' item, while others will think that they have 'identified' the apparent superior quality of the relatively expensive 'branded' item. In reality, of course, they are both buying the same product that, in all probability, neither of them came in to buy, or even wanted in the first place. We have all fallen for it at one time or another. Clever, eh?

Anyway, with a lemon rolling around in my wire basket, and with the determination not to fall for any retail psychology tricks, I set off in search of the prawns. With that innate intelligence given to only the few, I first headed for the sign saying 'Fish', but immediately fell foul of 'rule two, page two' of the Great Superstore Handbook i.e. Sod's Supermarket Law, which categorically states: 'Whichever product you want, they will have run out of.'

Thus I was consigned to the ready-weighed fish cabinet, being careful to note the use-by date on the plastic pre-packed packet of prawns...Peter Piper picked.

Andrea, by the way, is shi...red-hot when it comes to these use-by dates, and has been known to rise at midnight in order to bin any unsuspecting packet of food that has gone a minute over its designated final day.

Far be it from me (and it usually is), but I would have thought that Sainsbury's just might have had more than one chocolate cake on offer. As it was, I settled for the last remaining one in the freezer compartment, headed for the check-out, and as I waited in line, my thoughts turned idly to Magnus Magnusson and Mastermind...

"Your name, please."

"David Roper."

"Occupation?"

"Unemployed actor and underpaid freelance writer."

"David Roper, you have two minutes on your specialist subject:
'Foods and their location on the shelves at ASDA, Brighton Marina.' Your time starts...now. From which two word title is the name ASDA derived?"

"Associated Dairies."

"Correct."

"Which *white* wine, of Australian origin, sold as a 'case deal' from the bottom of the *red* wine shelf, is 12.5% proof?"

"Mighty Murray White."

"Correct."

"Why does ASDA…(Beep! Beep! Beep!.)…I've started so I'll finish…why does ASDA keep changing the shelf location of its products?"

"To piss me off."

"Correct. Mr. Roper, you had no pis…passes and scored 15 points!"

Who's a clever boy, then?

David Roper

IS THAT THE TIME?

That time of year has come round yet again, as it is wont to do, with its inevitably depressing regularity. It is at this time in the calendar that I start to wish I were a tortoise and could grab a Tupperware bowl full of lettuce and hibernate until the early spring.

You see, the autumn winds are gradually picking up, and the evenings are beginning to envelope us in darkness earlier and earlier, as we find ourselves heading, with that habitual inevitability, towards the year's end. Christmas decorations are sprouting on supermarket shelves like weeds in a garden, and have been since late August, I might add, and we're all wondering which Morecombe and Wise or Only Fools and Horses Special the BBC will be dusting off this year.

The key moment for me, though, will be the end of British Summer Time, when I will find myself, along with millions of others, no doubt, having to switch the living room lights on half way through the Countdown conundrum. That is as good a marker as any, I find, and will finally signal our descent into the pot hole of winter, only to emerge, blinking into the light of day, when the clocks go on in March. Talking of clocks going on, and back for that matter, why is it that, apart from Portugal & the Canary Islands, we perpetuate the myth that we are somehow forced to lag behind the rest of Europe by an hour? It really doesn't make sense. Not to mention the fact that it means all UK citizens have to adjust their watches by an hour, one way or another, on journeys to and from mainland Europe, as do all those Continental Europeans, of course, when they travel to the UK.

Instead of having to cope with all the time changes and encroaching darkness, how much better it would be if we could just curl up on the sofa, and spend those dismal months in a semi-coma, waking periodically to stuff ourselves with our favourite food and glug away at a bottle of our chosen tipple. In my case, that would be: foie gras sandwiches and plums, washed down with a nice Beaujolais Nouveau.

It would be bliss. Think of all the things we wouldn't have to endure:

No bonfire night, with dad singeing his eyebrows on a Roman Candle.

No going to work in the dark before dawn, and coming home from work in the dark after dusk.

No more anxious moments worrying about whether the kids will notice Santa's nicotine stained fingers and that lingering whiff of Jameson's on his breath, when they are taken to see him, at enormous expense, in the nearest shopping mall.

No trying to work out which is the biggest problem: the indigestion on Christmas Day, the constipation on Boxing Day, or what to do with all those ruddy nuts that nobody ever eats, even if they can crack them open in the first place.

No having to endure repeats of Police Academy II and yesterday's turkey, or is that one and the same thing?

No wondering just how hard life must be on a three month cricket tour of New Zealand in the middle of a Southern Hemisphere summer, all expenses paid. Poor things.

No worrying about how tough it gets driving around the Balmoral estate in a Land Rover, waiting for dinner to be announced.

No New Year's Day hangover, wondering who you insulted the night before, compounded by agonising over how it is that the Scots manage to wangle two days off, when we only get one.

No trip to M&S in January to cash in on that tasteless piece of tat your auntie gave you, and then bumping into her in the refunds queue. Ooops!

No interminable snooker on the box, which always seems to involve the same half dozen players, complete with evening wear. Come to think of it, why do they dress like that? Surely a track suit, or better still a pair of loose fitting pyjamas, would be much more comfortable, and would avoid the seam-stretching tension to the old trousers that occurs whenever one of the lads leans over the table and attempts a long pot into the green pocket.

No... Aww. All this is making me want to nod off. Do us a favour. Wake me up in March.

David Roper

NEVER TO BE FORGOTTEN

I belong to a little known elite group of actors: an exclusive club that guards a dark and mysterious secret within its thespian ranks.

No, we are not all Fulham or Arsenal supporters living in either Chelsea or Highbury and Islington, nor have we succumbed to liposuction, and neither have we voluntarily sat in the audience of 'An evening with Paul Daniels'.

More shameful than even all that, if it were possible, what binds us together is the embarrassing fact that none of us has ever appeared in an episode of the BBC's continuing A&E hospital drama: 'Casualty'. I kid you not. Exact figures are not to hand, but I gather that there are in existence some lucky actors who have graced the medic-soap on more than one occasion, playing different characters, of course. Not so the neglected members of our apparently undeserving band, it has to be said.

However, and here I must confess, it is with a tinge of regret, only a tinge, though, I must say, that I have been forced to resign from this unique company and hand in my: 'I'd give my right arm to be in 'Casualty' badge.

Yes! You guessed it. I have finally landed a part in the damn thing.

On top of the fact that I shall be finally coming in from the wilderness, there are two other reasons why I am thrilled about this job.

Firstly, and as I write, 'Casualty' is filmed in Bristol, where I was at Drama School for two years and where I lived for a total of five. Old haunts already beckon:

The Coronation Tap, a pub that sells Scrumpy cider strong enough, I was told on my first visit, that it can transmogrify the most unprepossessing barmaid into

216

a Miss World contestant after a mere two pints: it never worked for me, I hastily add, which is perhaps just as well in this age of political and sexual correctness.

The Clifton Suspension Bridge, apparently so tempting as a suicide leap that it used to be closed during Finals week at Bristol University, possibly still is. Incidentally, the only person to survive this drastic action tried it over 100 years ago - she was wearing a crinoline dress that acted as a parachute.

My second reason for welcoming a part in 'Casualty' is that Derek Thompson, who plays its mainstay, Charlie Fairhead, is an old friend. We were together in what is now The Royal National Theatre's production of 'The Mysteries' at the converted Lyceum ballroom in The Strand many years ago. I played one of the soldiers who crucified Christ, and Derek was the Angel Gabriel. What that tells us about type casting is open to debate, but it will be good to see him again.

In that same play, God was played by the much missed Brian Glover, a native of Barnsley in South Yorkshire, which is not a million miles from where my mother was born and bred. When mum and dad came to see the play, I asked my mother what she thought of it. She said, in all seriousness,

"It was quite good, I suppose, but that Brian Glover was all wrong."

"What do you mean 'all wrong', mum?"

"Well, I don't think God was a Barnsley man,"

I told that to Brian the following evening, and he roared with laughter. I miss him.

My most fond memory of Bristol, though, comes, not particularly from spending so much time there, but from a TV sports report I once caught. Bristol City and Bristol Rovers, the city's two football teams, were playing each other in a match to decide a relegation place in one of the Football Leagues. The sports reporter, with a totally straight face, announced,

"This crucial game will decide which of the two Bristols drops down."

Having relinquished my membership of the non-Casualty club (gratefully I must admit), I am honour bound to confess that there is still one secret society to which I belong. Indeed, it may well be that I am its only member. I refer, of course, to that brotherhood of actors, rare to the point of extinction, who have never appeared in 'The Bill'. I have auditioned on numerous occasions, but so far...

Hang about, the phones ringing. It couldn't be...could it?

217

David Roper

BACK TO BASICS

The sun is shining and a family of swans are gliding majestically past my gently rocking boat. The water is calm and the view from where I am sitting is nothing short of idyllic. All in all, the perfect setting for a drink and a spot of light lunch.   Unfortunately, at least for those of a romantic and Continental imagination, this is not some place nestling along the Dordogne valley in France, nor is it the Loire, overlooked as it is by chateau after chateau, neither is it the relatively vast expanse of Lake Como in northern Italy.

This is, in fact, Bristol, my favourite English city, and I am on one of the many floating bar/restaurants dotted along the inland harbour.

Thirty five years ago, I began the two-year acting course here at the Bristol Old Vic Theatre School, which is based in a couple of converted houses on the edge of the downs, and I have been in love with the whole place ever since.

Two years later, along with Jill Baker, I made up the compliment of two graduates of the school who were invited to join the Bristol Old Vic (BOV) Company itself, and thus I became a professional actor. My very first job for the BOV was touring around schools with a version of 'The Mystery' plays. I can tell you, you learn a heck of a lot when you have to perform in front of 30-odd school kids at 10.30 on a wet Monday in Bedminster.

Looking back over half a lifetime of working in the theatre and TV, however, it is hard to recall any moment to match the excitement of reading the letter of acceptance that I had opened with trembling hands. My first day at the school did come close, true, but that first job at the BOV, I must admit, did pretty much top them all.

An Actor's Life For Me

There have been other highlights, of course: EastEnders, the National Theatre, Abanazar in 'Aladdin', but there was something about the thrill of that first step on the ladder that will never leave me.

Now, of course, I am back here, trawling through my memories and pondering on how long in the tooth I am (and how short of them I am, come to that), because I have started work on my episode of 'Casualty'. No big deal, maybe, but these 'continuing dramas', as they are known in the trade, are bread and butter to many a jobbing actor.

You see, with today's drama output squeezed into an ever-decreasing number of slots by Reality TV and its siblings, work for actors on the box is at a premium. Gone are the days when you could pick up a 'Comedy Playhouse' here, or a BBC costume drama there. These days you get what you are given and are grateful.

Having said that, if you do get a job like 'Casualty', you are treated extremely well: chauffeur-driven cars (BBC-speak for taxis, but there you go); excellent location catering; and a many-starred hotel to kip in.

I am at the Marriot and it is pretty posh. You know a hotel is posh when they give you a plastic card instead of a key, the night porter is called the 'concierge' and everybody knows your name. I find that last one a touch disturbing. No doubt it is supposed to make you feel special, but it always makes me feel that I am under constant surveillance, which inhibits my perfectly natural kleptomania vis a vis those little bottles of shampoo in the en suite that we all find irresistible. Bet you have!

However, the whole 'Marriot experience', as they insist on calling it, is actually very pleasant. The only problem is that the mini-bar in my room works on a sensor system - you pick up your chosen poison, tripping the sensor, and it is automatically added to your bill. Fine, except that these sensors are so finely tuned that if you fart within five feet of them you get charged for a double vodka and tonic. So it is that you find me silently tip-toeing passed the damn thing, buttocks clenched, on my way out for the first day's filming.

I only hope bean casserole isn't on the location menu, 'cos if it is, my mini-bar bill will be blown sky high.

David Roper

FOR OLD TIMES' SAKE

What is the difference between Brighton and Bristol? Alphabetically, not a lot: geographically, a fair way, say, 157 miles by car, but in terms of global positioning they are 2 degrees 36 minutes apart. How bloody fascinating, David, I hear you yawn. So what?

Well, this is 'what', mate: come with me up Small Street, Bristol, the city where I am still gainfully employed on 'Casualty', and I will attempt to explain the curious result of this comparatively tiny longitudinal difference. At the top end of Small Street, if you care to turn left and stroll along Corn Street, you will find, no more than a few yards along, that on your right and stuck on the Corn Exchange, is a large clock. It is much like any other clock you might expect to find on a public building, except that it has two minute hands, which are exactly 11 minutes apart.

You see, before English time was standardised across the country in 1880, cities had different ideas as to what time it was at any given moment. The Meridian line of longitude (zero degrees), which passes through Greenwich and Peacehaven, by the way, hence the Meridian Centre, determined London time. So, when the sun was directly overhead it was midday in London and Brighton. However, because Bristol is situated 2 degrees 36 minutes west of the Meridian, the sun was directly overhead there 11 minutes later. Therefore, midday was also determined to be 11 minutes later. Good, eh?

Now, this didn't really matter very much until June,1841, when the first trains began travelling between Bristol and London and back, and Isambard Kingdom Brunel's Great Western Railway Company decided, in its corporate wisdom, that all the new passenger carrying chuffer trains would run on London time, thus causing the 11 minute time difference to rear its ugly head.

You see, the midday train to London would leave Bristol at 12 o'clock midday, *London time*, which meant that it actually left at 11.49, *Bristol time*, leaving a crowd of pissed off commuters standing on platform 1 at Bristol Temple Meads station with nowhere to go. You see, all those poor souls would have arrived, say, five minutes early, at 11.55, to catch the 12 o'clock midday train to London, only to find that they had missed that 'midday' train by a good six minutes, because it had already left at 11.49, *Bristol time* (12 o'clock *London time*). This bizarre state of affairs created a problem that the good burghers of Bristol struggled with for quite some time. Hopefully, you have not had the same problem, and I have made the dilemma quite clear…hopefully.

Eventually, someone had the brilliant, if rather convoluted, idea of installing the now famous Corn Exchange clock, which showed both Bristol and London times simultaneously, but 11 minutes apart, of course, hence the two minute hands that you can see to this day. Quite how useful, or confusing, the twin minute hands were, is not known. What is known is that it was not until 1852, when everybody had apparently had their fill of running for non-existent trains, that Bristol eventually brought itself into line with London, and station staff at Temple Meads were spared the bizarre sight of passengers arriving both five minutes early and six minutes late for the same train.

The two minute hands remain, as I said, and as I stand before them they are still exactly 11 minutes apart, which is why, if you want a straight answer, you should never ask anybody the time in Bristol.

By the way, in the shifting world of time, don't forget to put your clocks back tonight and, as you turn over for an extra 60 minute snooze in the morning, spare a thought for me in Bristol. If the bloke in charge of the Corn Exchange clock forgets to put one of the minute hands back, then Bristol will be behind both London and Brighton time, all trains from the West Country will be 49 minutes late and I will never get home in time to take the boys to football training. Help!

David Roper

DO I HEAR VOICES?

Before I get down to business, forgive me for a moment if I harp back to the previous article about the Corn Exchange clock in Bristol.

You see, apart from that clock's curious two minute hands, the Corn Exchange is host to another set of curiosities. In the street outside, there are located four bronze tables, probably modelled after mobile tables which were taken to trade fairs and markets. Before the Corn Exchange was built in the 18th century, the tables - called *nails* - were located in the Tolzey Walk, a covered area along the south wall of All Saints Church.

These bronze nails, with their flat tops and raised edges, which prevent coins from tumbling onto the pavement, were made as convenient tables at which merchants could carry out their business. The oldest pillar is undated, but may well be late Elizabethan. The second oldest was given by Bristol merchant Robert Kitchen, who died in 1594. The two remaining nails are dated 1625 and 1631.[6]

The four nails were indeed made at different times, as this is reflected in their varying designs. Along the rim of one of the nails is the name John Barker, a wealthy merchant who owned houses and storehouses on the Quay. He was mayor during the reign of Charles I and represented Bristol in the 1623 Parliament.[6]

Deals could be closed by payment on the nails - the popularly supposed origin of the saying 'pay on the nail' or 'cash on the nail'.

Just thought you might be interested in all that. However, back to business:

"We regret to announce that the 09.00 Thameslink service to Bedford and the 09.20 Virgin Trains' service to Manchester have both been cancelled."

Typical!

222

"Passengers are advised to join the 09.17 service to London Victoria, change at East Croydon for stations via London Bridge, or leap off the train at Gatwick, on a wing and a prayer, for the service to Manchester. We apologise for any dislocation this may cause."

Too right, mate! Cancelling one train is unfortunate, cancelling two within twenty minutes looks like carelessness. That sounds familiar!

Andrea, Harry, Jack and I were on our way to London for the day, and we were looking forward to a peaceful, picturesque, old fashioned train journey through the rolling Sussex countryside on board the 09.17 to Victoria (trolley service unavailable).

After that disembodied and fateful announcement, though, the whole immobile crowd on the concourse at Brighton station surged forward, as one, in a spontaneous re-enactment of The Charge of the Light Brigade. We were swept along platform six on a tide of grunting, sweating, elbowing humanity, as the driver looked on resignedly, like Lord Raglan at Balaclava.

"Into the 09.17 up to London rode the six hundred."

The purpose of our visit to the capital was so that the boys could each make a voice-over tape in a small studio belonging to my agent. The idea for them to take up a career in voice-overs was not, as you might cynically suppose, some cunning plan to enable them to keep Andrea and me in our old age, although now I come to think of it…! It was, in fact, my agent's idea, having met the boys a few months previously, and having declared them to be a couple of likely lads fit for life in a sound studio.

And they were, indeed, brilliant. Harry adopted a laid-back attitude, looking and sounding totally at home, as he lounged in the sound-proof booth with a set of cans (earphones, to you) stuck to his head. Jack, on the other hand, became somewhat over-excited, but what he lacked in quiet application, he more than made up for in loud and boundless enthusiasm.

Perhaps the most encouraging result was not so much their ability to speak the lines, but their obvious talent for 'sight-reading' them in the first place. Sight-reading is not a gift visited on all of us, and involves reading out aloud text, which you have never seen before, and making sense of it. Although not a necessary tool for an actor, it is essential in the 'instant performance' world of voice-overs.

To celebrate this successful recording session we had the Full Monty of a lunch at PizzaExpress in St. Martin's Lane, and I was persuaded to go against nature and splash out on a taxi back to Victoria station. As we stared at the departure board, a strangely familiar disembodied voice rang out across the vast concourse,

"We regret to announce that…"

That bloke must never stop working…now there's an idea for the boys' first job!

BASIL FAULTY?

Just when you think it is safe to go back into the water, why does another dorsal fin always seem to glide ominously in your direction? This particular dorsal fin was heading my way when I awoke the other day to the alarming news that Professor Francesco Sala, of the Umberto Veronesi Foundation in Italy, had made a discovery that was destined to strike at the very foundations of one of my greatest pleasures.

Has he discovered that a certain episode of Only Fools and Horses, the one in which David Jason falls through the bar, is never to be screened again? No, I can safely continue to laugh every time I see it.

Has he discovered that watching too much Six Nations and Tri-nations Rugby can seriously damage your sex life? No, my autumn is secure.

Has he discovered that Destiny's Child are, in fact, an expertly made up group of ex sheet metal workers from Sheffield and are all fellas? No, that would be the real killer.

The truth is that Professor Sala's revelation concerns the unlikely, not to mention rather worrying, subject of the chemical constituent parts of young basil leaves. Apparently, he has discovered that the leaves contain a carcinogenic agent (methyl-eugenol), which increases the probability of anyone who ingests it developing a tumour. Scary, or what? The background to this unnerving research by the eminent Prof is that the chemical agent's principal purpose is to protect the infant basil from insect attack. However, as far as we are concerned, the most important of its side effects is that it is also responsible for its appetising taste to humans.

As the basil matures, the methyl disappears, eliminating its carcinogenic effect and, unfortunately, most of its taste. Hence the preference for using young basil leaves in cooking. Fine, but the trouble is: where does that leave you, me and all other devotees of the popular and fragrant herb? In two minds about ever touching it again, I guess.

On the wider culinary stage and more to the point, perhaps, the result is that a black cloud now hangs over the production of Genovese sauce: generic name - pesto, so named from it being made by crushing its ingredients, as in 'pestle and mortar', and whose principal ingredient is basil. Pesto, particularly the version made in the Ligurian region around Genoa - ergo, Genovese sauce, is one of Italy's favourite ingredients, and many of us feel the same way about it. So, what's to do?

Well, while Italy is up in arms (if that is not an alleged contradiction in terms - nice legal get out there, eh?) over this slur to its culinary good name, and Signor Berlusconi is frantically off-loading a large proportion of his share portfolio and heading for the hills of Tuscany, I am faced with an agonising dilemma. Do I, or do I not, order Mozzarella and Tomato salad, with fresh *basil*, on my next visit to PizzaExpress?

The trouble is that researchers and so-called experts, apologies to Professor Sala, have cried 'wolf' so often in the past that it is hard to take anything they say seriously. According to the sum total of their nutritional knowledge, the only safe daily diet, as I understand it, is half a kilo of organic carrots (uncooked) and five litres of Buxton Spring water - and if you can get through that lot in a day you are a better man than I am, Gunga Din. You would also, of necessity, have to spend quite a time in the loo, but let's not go into that, if you know what I mean.

The point is, if so many foods are bad for us, and many, like basil, are potentially lethal, why hasn't the government insisted on health warnings being displayed on them, as on tobacco products?

If they ever did, I can see the headlines now:

'Hamburgers harmful to health!'

'Roast beef and Yorkshire puddings lethal!'

'Basil faulty!'

All this is a deeply depressing prospect. I don't know about you, but I am legging it to the nearest PizzaExpress.

"Mozzarella and Tomato salad, please, and go heavy on the basil, there's a love."

FANCY A DONOR?

'Couples will be able to choose donated eggs and sperm to create their designer child, under proposals published by the fertility watchdog.'

Looks suspiciously like the thin end of a rather strange and worrying wedge, if you ask me. I know that to make an omelette you have to crack eggs, but to make a child?

Where will it end, I wonder? Does what follows here give us a disturbing glimpse into the not too distant future of off-the-peg pregnancies?

\------------------------

Our NEXT (NEO-NATAL) catalogue finally arrived by courier last Tuesday.

"We're bound to find a nice, healthy, middle class one out of all this lot, surely,"

said the wife, flicking the pages and taking a sip from her glass. I didn't comment on the irony of her choice of drink - Babycham - it might have been misconstrued, given the circumstances.

You see, we have been searching for our ideal designer baby for over six months now, and the strain is beginning to tell. Other couples, I realise, just snap up the first fertilisable egg that comes their way, and good luck to them. However, call us picky, if you like, but we are a wee bit more discerning when it comes to the old egg & sperm race. Let's face it, and sadly we all have to these days, you can never be too careful in the maze that is the modern day bespoke embryo market. For starters, we found that it was no help to discover that 'caveat emptor' was stamped on every egg, just below its sell-by date, as a rule. You can appreciate our surprise and shock, but nevertheless we soldiered on.

Our first big disappointment was at Argos. Their free foetal delivery service had appealed, but after punching in the catalogue number, 241/2874 (blonde, tall, strong right foot, should make the England team by age 17), all we got was 'This item is out of stock'. Damn! We had to kiss goodbye to dreams of a comfortable middle age, swanning around Europe watching our talented lad scoring amazing goals in a series of UEFA Cup matches. Oh, well, never mind, I have always been a closet cricket fan at heart anyway.

The Freeman's catalogue looked more promising, however, and with their 'Buy now, pay at puberty' offer, we would not need to shell out a penny until well into the next decade. Their choice of babies was pretty extensive, too, ranging from, 'Tall, dark, handsome and intelligent' all the way down to, 'Small, blonde, ugly and thick as a brick'. Unfortunately, they had run out of top quality sperm and eggs that week, so all that was left was a rather disappointing, 'Medium height, weighty, congenital limp, wouldn't touch it with a barge pole'.

This was not going to be as easy as we had thought, although we did very nearly succumb to a bargain at Littlewoods a few weeks later. They had a sale of discontinued embryos, and when we saw, 'Above average height/intelligence, mother a concert pianist, father an Oxbridge graduate, family medical history: first class.', we were on the phone quicker than you could say, 'Ovarian transplant'.

Sod's law is never far away in the designer baby game, though, and it turned out that this particular embryo would be a red-head, which would have clashed disastrously with the colour scheme we had already chosen for the nursery.

"This one sounds interesting." Back to reality. The wife was already on page 23.

"Which one is that, my sweet?"

"It says, 'Good physical shape, blonde, mentally stable, family history includes world-ranked snooker player.' I like snooker, it's so soothing, and we could always go see your aunty when the lad's playing at the Crucible in Sheffield. What do you think?"

"Sounds good to me. I haven't seen Auntie Ada for yonks,"

I said, dialling the number and handing her the phone.

"Hello. Baby ordering service?...Do you deliver?...Silly question, of course, sorry. That would be down to me, wouldn't it?...Ha, ha!...Yes, I'd like to place an order for number 772/4801...Oh, good. There's just one thing. Have you got it in a brunette?"

AT ANY RATE - I'M WORKING

I have discovered that if you were to draw a graph of the ups and downs of my acting career over the past thirty-odd years, it would pretty much coincide with the rise and fall in interest rates over the same period.

There was a steady rise in the seventies, a heady rise in the late eighties and early nineties, and a long slow decline as we eased into the new millennium, culminating in the recent modest rise, which seems to have stalled somewhat of late. All of which goes to exemplify the roller-coaster nature of the professional lives of investors and actors alike - well, of this actor at least.

Whether there is, in fact, a coefficient of linear correlation (i.e. a direct causal link), tying my career to the Monetary Policy Committee's decisions on interest rates, I don't know. All I do know is that every time there is a change in the one, there is an equal change in the other.

Over the last several months, as all of you (save the unmortgaged) will know, there has been a small rise in interest rates. Lo and behold, there has also been a small rise in my career. Nothing world shattering, you understand, but at least in the right direction, and in an area where you might fancy keeping an eye open, or to be strictly correct, an ear open.

I refer, of course, to the elusive world of the voice-over. Yes, I have actually recorded one at long last. By the time you read this you may well have heard a strangely familiar voice advertising Danone Danocol - 'A natural way to reduce cholesterol.' And that'll be £25 for extra exposure, thank you very much.

Voice-overs are unlike any other area of acting work, if indeed they are part of what you would normally consider to be acting work in the first place. It is a well-known fact, at least in the arcane world of the voice-over artist, that being a good actor does not necessarily endow that actor with the ability to be a good voice-over artist, and vice versa, come to that. The point being that the two skills/talents/abilities, whatever you want to call them, are certainly not mutually exclusive, true, but neither are they automatically one and the same. A great and talented actor could well make a lousy voice-over artist, while a fantastically talented voice-over artist could equally well make a rotten actor. However, when the two talents are present together, and they can be, of course, then the artist in question stands astride the acting world as both a lucky and sought after member of the profession.

The fundamental difference between working as an actor and working as a voice-over artist lies, not only in the actual work itself, but initially in the path that has to be trod before you ever get the job in the first place.

You see, normally, to secure an acting job, you would study and read aloud a section of script at an audition, be offered the job, moan about the money (standard practice before accepting), rehearse, learn the lines and then perform. The whole process taking weeks, if not months.

Not so in the unique world of the voice-over. In this particular case of mine, true, the producer had been sent a tape of my voice, which, I suppose, amounts to an 'audition' in its literal sense, but there the similarity ended.

The only two things I was certain of, as I entered the studio in Dean Street, Soho, last week, were the name of the product and the time of my train home. I was presented with a script, seated in a sound booth and charged with sight reading the lines, while timing their delivery to the pictures on a TV monitor in front of me. If you want to get a sense of what this kind of activity does to the brain, try stirring a cup of tea with one hand, while simultaneously writing a letter to your aunty in Bolton with the other.

After about a dozen 'takes', everything finally coincided and I staggered off to the Coach and Horses in Greek Street for a pint. As I sipped my extra cold Guinness and idly flicked through The Times, a headline caught my eye:

'Interest rates on hold for the foreseeable future!'

Ah, well, it had been nice while it lasted.

SPEECH! SPEECH!

Believe it or not, I ran into the Queen and Prince Philip the other day, or should I say, they very nearly ran into me.

Walking to the West End from Victoria railway station, along my habitual route via Buckingham Palace, I was confronted by a massive road block, manned by what appeared to be the entire Metropolitan Police Force. Obviously, something big had happened or maybe was about to. Either some wayward politician was about to launch a coup, as a desperate stab at power, or else the mains water supply to Buck House was having a nervous breakdown. In the event, neither of those wild guesses of mine was anywhere near the truth.

I had, in fact, stumbled upon the security arrangements surrounding the State Opening of Parliament. Specifically, the Queen's journey from Buckingham Palace to The Palace of Westminster (The Houses of Parliament), where she was to deliver the aptly, albeit euphemistically, named Queen's Speech. It is, of course, not her speech at all, but has been written by the Prime Minister. Basically, Her Majesty is simply 'sight-reading' what she has been told to say by the incumbent Government.

You see, the Queen's Speech is the occasion upon which our monarch gets dolled up in full state regalia, pops a pair of Specsavers' varifocals over the royal lugholes, and delivers a kind of Government mini-manifesto, laying out before the people of the UK all the wonderful things it has in store for them in the coming session of Parliament. Promises, promises.

To listen to the aforementioned speech, the members of both Houses of Parliament, The Lords and The Commons, assemble in the chamber of the Upper House (The House of Lords). At every State Opening of Parliament, one of the most well-known images is that of the duty performed by the Gentleman (or Lady) Usher of the Black Rod, a senior officer of the House of Lords responsible for controlling access to, and maintaining order within, the House and its precincts.

Black Rod is sent from the Lords Chamber to the Commons Chamber to summon MPs to hear the Queen's Speech. Traditionally the door of the Commons is slammed in Black Rod's face to symbolise the Commons' independence.

He or she bangs three times on the door with the rod. The door to the Commons Chamber is then opened and all the MPs - talking loudly about what they did at the weekend, as a rule - follow Black Rod back to the Lords, where they stand, looking mighty uncomfortable, at the opposite end of the Chamber throughout the speech. It is all a tad theatrical, but makes for great TV.

Back in Buckingham Palace Road, the copper outside the Royal Mews told me that if I legged it across St. James' Park I might just get across The Mall before the procession arrived and turned right into Horseguards' Parade.

In the end I was a little too slow, and was just about to make a dash for it, when the State Coach came clopping along, and I was brought to a halt by a police sergeant the size of a small tower block.

The Mall was lined with grey-coated, busby-hatted, gun-toting soldiers, who outnumbered spectators by about ten to one. In fact, by the time she got to the end of

The Mall, the only people left for our poor, dear Queen to wave at were three Japanese tourists, two joggers and an out of work actor. She looked a bit miffed, as well she might.

It was then I noticed the snipers, or rather they noticed me. Along the roofs of the buildings opposite, men in black, cradling sub-machine guns like breast feeding mothers, were eyeing me with disturbing curiosity. In my business there is only one thing worse than being recognised - and that is *not* being recognised - but in this instance I would have gladly remained anonymous. There was evidently something familiar about my face. I fervently hoped it was from TV, and not from mug-shots of suspected suicide bombers.

I decided to make no sudden movements, and under no circumstances to reach for my wallet. As the procession disappeared, I crossed The Mall and nonchalantly headed for Lower Regent Street. Close call, eh?

Mind you, it occurred to me, because of the current climate, that if I had been a suicide bomber, no security measures on earth could have stopped me from leaving quite a mess for Westminster City Council to clear up.

That alarming thought may to some extent explain the lack of public interest in what must have taken weeks of organisation to arrange. If fears about safety are going to increase, however, and crowds dwindle away to nothing, next year the Queen might well decide to opt for the relative anonymity of a London taxi.

"You'll never guess who I had in the back of this cab last week…"

David Roper

LA DONNA E MOBILE

'In days of old, when knights were bold,
And mankind was contented,
We roamed the earth quite undisturbed,
Then mobiles were invented.

Not long ago, the only sound
Would be the blackbirds singing.
Not anymore. They're drowned out now
By all that bloody ringing.

No more dawn chorus greets the sun,
No pattering of rain.
The sound that marks the break of day
Is, "Hi! I'm on the train."

No sooner have you parked your bum
And opened up The Times,
Than through the peaceful carriage scythes
A mobile's merry chimes.

You'd love to grab the sodding thing,
And through the window throw it,
Because you know it means the end
Of silence, as we know it.

An Actor's Life For Me

There's no escape. You're doomed to sit
And hear of others' lives.
Of where they are and where they've been,
And how they love their wives.

It wouldn't be so bad, I guess,
Acceptable, no doubt,
If they would just chat quietly but,
The buggers always shout.

It doesn't matter who has called,
Their office or their home,
They yell so loud it's hardly worth
Them bothering with a phone.

They scream about their holidays,
Their trip to Val d'Isere,
And how, when they were on the piste,
Prince Charles was also there.

You hear about their business deals,
Their profits and their losses.
How Sandra, the receptionist,
Has been through all the bosses.

You're privy to their darkest thoughts,
Their deepest hopes and fears.
How Sandra bedding the M.D
Was bound to end in tears.

They tell the world that it was her,
Who, through some strange mishap,
Gave Trev in Sales and Marketing
A painful dose of clap.

Then Trev gave it to Marjorie,
Who passed it on to Ken,
'Til finally he gave it back
To Sandra once again.

From Preston Park to Wivelsfield,
Past Gatwick to Victoria,
Inconsequential drivel will
Be guaranteed to bore ya.

But when you're sick of hearing how
They once met Sally Gunnell,
You breathe a sigh and say out loud,
"Thank God - a ruddy tunnel."

STRIKE ME, IT'S SANTA!

Going on strike is never an easy decision, and it has had a somewhat chequered history throughout its often violent life, it is true. Dependant on your point of view, or politics perhaps, a strike is either a totally justified stand against injustice, or else is a totally *un*justified intrusion into the daily lives of innocent hard working people.   Take your pick.

Usually, though certainly not exclusively, a strike has at its core some form of dissatisfaction with the relevant pay and/or conditions of whichever workforce is involved. Its sister form of 'industrial action', the sympathy strike, relies on the desire to demonstrate solidarity with whoever is actually withdrawing their labour. That is the situation we find ourselves in at the moment.

You see, David Roper has declared himself on strike in sympathy with Teaching Assistants. However, in order that you, dear reader, will not be deprived of your weekly 'fix', David has kindly allowed me access to this article.

My name is Santa Claus, aka Father Christmas. As usual, I will be visiting your city next Saturday with my sleigh and six reindeer. In the light of information from my little helpers in City Hall, may I have clarification on the following:

1) Will I need a tradesman's parking permit for the sleigh? If so, what time does the issuing office close on Christmas Eve? Last year's debacle resulted in three penalty points being slapped on my Trans-global sleigh licence, and Norwich Union quoting me very unhappy on my Christmas Party insurance.

2) Do reindeers come under the laws governing animals fouling pavements? As you can imagine, it will be a long night, and what with Rudolph's recent stomach upset, and Prancer's and Dancer's predilection for curry, accidents can happen. It is worth bearing in mind, in case you are out late that night, that these

'accidents' tragically involve the 'results' being dropped from a great height, so keep an eye out, if you know what I mean. Besides, have you any idea of the size of poop-bag needed to clear up behind an incontinent reindeer?

3) When is it chucking out time at the Night Clubs in Brighton? Last year I got caught up in the exodus and was mistaken for a festive taxi. The girls were quite pleasant, I must say, and did clear up most of their vomit from my hood. However, they had it away with several presents, when doing a runner at the traffic lights at the bottom of Edward Street. Still, I got my own back by switching their gifts of Revitalift for Tiger Balm. That must have warmed them up on Christmas morning.

4) I couldn't help noticing that Chris Eubank's Christmas list included a heart-rending plea for funding to restore the West Pier. Although this is not in my gift, I do think Chris has a point, and something should be done about this Grade 1 listed lump of rusting metal. The fact that the year-on-year decaying West Pier seems to always feature in the background of every single TV report from Brighton & Hove, does the city no good at all, I can tell you.

(Chris. Re: Item four on your list - the Eddie Stobart artic - delivery will be on Boxing Day. Appropriate for you, or what? S.C.)

5) What time does Burger King, North Street, shut? I often use it for a quick snack, as Mrs. Claus insists on going to Bingo on Christmas Eve and refuses to make me a reindeer and pickle sandwich.

6) In last week's local newspaper (I have it delivered) there was a disturbing report about the paucity of Brighton and Hove's Christmas decorations. This is just not on. There is simply no excuse for the Council skimping on the physical manifestations of the festive season. So come on, lads, pull your fingers out from where you have obviously stuck your heads, and give us a few lights.

7) Finally, I really must protest at losing my pitch in Churchill Square. Debenham's is so handy for a six-piece breakfast, cheap at twice the price (excluding drinks, of course), and the adjacent Superdrug is where I always get Mrs. Claus's cut-price perfume (Shalimar by Guerlain).

I look forward to hearing from you before the big day, so get your letters in to me. Let's face it, you wouldn't want me to go on strike, would you?

SHAGGY DOG STORY

It has come round again, I am afraid. Yes, it is that time of year once more, when we all dust off the old address book and pop along to WH Smith's to shell out a small fortune on a collection of Christmas cards that we wouldn't be seen dead receiving, and which are covered in robins, snow and muffled up Victorians.

Christmas cards, invented by Sir Henry Cole in 1843, and designed by John Horsley were originally intended to highlight the plight of the poor. Not any more. These days, they seem to be more of an advert for the sender's generosity or stinginess, depending on the quality of the card and/or whether or not the price has been deliberately left on the back. I would never do that. Would you? 'Course not.

It is a sad fact, though, that many people view the writing and sending of Christmas cards as one enormous, time-consuming bore. Not only that, but there is a school of thought that holds that 'Christmas' is too religious a concept in a multi-religion world, and is therefore replaced by 'Winter Wishes' or some such. So, while it is supposed to be a pleasure, the whole business ends up being a real grind for many of us.

However, not for all God's creatures, it seems, for I can now reveal with impunity that last week our dog, Poppy, received a Christmas card from David Blunkett's guide dog. Inside was a note.

Dear Poppy,

Merry Christmas! I don't know if your owners let you watch TV at all, but if you happen to have caught the news during December, you won't be surprised when I tell you that life with the ex-Home Secretary has been somewhat of a roller coaster existence, to say the least. It has certainly taken its physical and mental toll on me, I can tell you.

What with dragging him in and out of the Commons, on and off chat shows and up and down Blair's stairs to Tony's office, I have been losing weight hand over fist - or should I say claw over paw? None of that would have been too bad, but I have also had to sit at his feet in countless restaurants, without a bite to eat, while he wined and dined his 'morceau sur le cote', as the French have it - and they usually do - wine and dine their 'bit on the side', I mean.

On top of that, when we all get home I find myself stuck to the bedpost overnight like a piece of chewing gum. What human beings get up to behind closed doors is no spectator sport, Poppy, believe me. All you can do is keep schtum and listen out for when they start talking about the 'doggie position', because that is the time to leg it and quick. To tell the truth, come breakfast time I would be starving. No favours, just a bit quicker with the old Pedigree Chum is all I wanted. Let's face it - you wouldn't treat a human like that, would you?

Having said all that, life has not been too bad, I must admit. With unlimited entry to every shop in the West End, all the TV exposure and the fast-tracking of my graduation from the blind dog school, I have been given certain advantages over your average Labrador, I must confess.

But I honestly don't think I could face sitting under the back benches and not being able to see anything. When David B. was Home Secretary I could at least amuse myself by sniffing Gordon Brown's socks, and by watching the entire Tory front bench falling asleep and scratching themselves at alarmingly regular intervals - and they think we dogs are obsessed!

I would miss the cut and thrust of life with David B., naturally, but then I am not alone there, am I? Winalot have offered me a seat on the board (well, a basket, actually), and I am at present in negotiation with the Royal National Institute for the Blind about becoming their director of training, so there are opportunities in the private sector for a dog of my experience, on leaving public life.

To cut a long story short, I have finally decided to hang up my harness, return to the real world and enjoy a leash-free life of long walks and lamp posts.

Anyway, all the best for the New Year, and, if you have any trouble with your pet passport, I still have connections!

Keep wagging it!

Yours faithfully, of course, David B's doggie xxx

GET A LIFE

I have a confession to make, and not before time, I dare say. My confession involves me coming clean and openly admitting that all my life I have been somewhat of a dinosaur as far as technology is concerned; my generic name being Roperus Technophobus. I find each revolutionary innovation in technology, which is, no doubt, designed to ease some burden of everyday life, to be merely an addition to the mind-numbing catalogue of technological hurdles that I find it impossible to overcome.

It all started with the general introduction of the hand held calculator way back in the early 1960s. The first one I ever came across belonged to a Trans-Atlantic neighbour of ours. He had brought this tiny machine (about the size of a fag packet) from America, needless to say, and was mightily amused at the astonishment with which it was greeted by the indigenous population of West Yorkshire, and the by rest of the UK, too, no doubt. Nevertheless, these new-fangled gadgets were quickly seized upon, and soon they were appearing everywhere.

At the time, I was a student accountant in Bradford, and we were not allowed to use these innovative little machines either in the office or especially during our exams. Even the smuggling of an abacus into the exam room was met with a sound rebuke. Therefore, we had to do all additions and calculations in our heads, resulting in me acquiring a deep and lasting prejudice against using any of the 20th century's technological innovations. That irrational prejudice became stamped on my mind, and the imprint of it exists to this day. So steeped am I in the mathematical strictures of those days that I still automatically add up in my head my purchases at our local Coop. Yes, I do. Oh, get a life, David.

It wasn't just calculators that aroused such deep feelings in me, either. Throughout the 1970s, I battled manfully against the pressure to buy a washing machine. Instead, I would bag up my smelly clothes each week and take them round the launderette. There, a cuddly little lady, whose life's work was dealing with other people's smalls, would wash and iron them, thus sparing me the horror of facing man's greatest fear - his congenital aversion to all aspects of washing, particularly ironing. If only that lady had put a crease in my boxer shorts, I would have married her on the spot.

By the 1980s, though, I had succumbed to the pressure and had bought an AEG washer-dryer. As if to prove my inbred unsuitability to all things technical, I immediately did something that is tantamount impossible - I set fire to it.

I had decided that my blue shag pile rug needed a clean, so I set the machine to wash it and, consecutively, to dry it, since it was, after all, a washer/dryer. Unfortunately, the spinning cycle, in a tribute to the ferocity of German technology, stripped the rug of its pile, which got lodged in the holes in the drum and started smouldering in the heat of the equally ferocious drying cycle. The machine never fully recovered - neither did the rug - neither did I.

There does exist, however, one piece of domestic technology for which I have a touching and almost fatherly affection - the dishwasher. As recently as the early 1990s, I could be heard poo-pooing this machine as an expensive, unnecessary luxury and a further example of post-Communist Capitalism's decline into decadence. But when I finally experienced a dishwasher's life enhancing qualities, I fell hopelessly in love, and am now a world authority on dishwasher salt, Rinse-aid and Finish tablets (Three-in-one with Powerball, for preference).

This potted history of my love/hate relationship with technology has arisen because this column is the first one in over a hundred that I have actually e-mailed. After years of eschewing my computer's capabilities and parking illegally, while sprinting in to deliver my weekly offering and to exchange friendly banter with the charming ladies on Reception, I have finally been dragged kicking and screaming into the 21st century.

Just one caveat. If you open your paper this morning and find this column blank, then I have failed miserably.

WELL, BLOW ME DOWN

Forget riding the Grand National big dipper at Blackpool's pleasure beach; forget landing a two-seater Cessna at Shoreham airport in a thunderstorm; you can even forget that feeling of impending doom as the Duke of Edinburgh opens his mouth and puts his foot in it at the Kami Kazi pilots' (ground staff only) reunion dinner.

No, for sheer unadulterated terror there is nothing to beat sitting on the top of a No. 27A double-decker from Saltdean to Brighton, as it heaves to starboard, like a storm-tossed galleon in a force 8 cross wind, along the A259 and passed Colditz Castle (Roedean School, to the uninitiated). There is a point on that perilous journey where the edge of the cliff is only a little more than the height of a double-decker from the wheels of the bus you are travelling on, raising the alarming prospect that, if the bus were to be blown over, we might slide over the cliff and end up splattered all over Brighton's nudist beach. Now there's a thought.

The whole fearful experience and the potentially, if admittedly unlikely, horrific consequences, happened to me on one particular morning last week. I had braved the elements, in the gloom of a slowly lightening dawn, to buy a £2.60 adult saver (£2.40 in shops and Post Offices), for my trip on the 07.05 omnibus to Brighton station on my way to rehearsals for 'An Inspector Calls'. I had to start so early because rehearsals were in East London, a journey involving the Brighton bus to the station, a train to London Bridge and then a half hour walk through the crowds of commuters. All in all nothing short of a two and a half hour slog.

As I waited at the bus stop, I was delighted to find that the 27A was on time. I got on, sorted out my return ticket and we all proceeded towards Brighton along the cliff edge.

That was when the wind hit. The four of us, who had bravely, if ill-advisedly, climbed the stairs to take our seats on the top deck, gripped the hand rail in front of us, our knuckles whitening by the second, and rode out the buffeting wind like contestants in the Vendee Globe round the world yacht race. Ellen McArthur eat your heart out! Our journey made the rounding of Cape Horn seem like a Sunday afternoon row on a park lake.

We bounced along like this for over two miles, smiling nervously at each other, as the pounding sea and our past lives flashed before us, until we reached the relative calm and safety of the Old Steine. Dawn was finally breaking as other passengers joined us, blissfully unaware of why we ashen-faced four looked like Scott of the Antarctic and his mates.

But all was not over. What none of us had realized, was that the bus was being driven by an ex-Formula One racing driver. I couldn't fault him on safety and speed (we arrived bang on time), the problem was the way he treated every 'Bus Stopping' sign as an opportunity to show off his pit-stop technique.

He would approach each group of waiting passengers as if he were going to drive straight passed them. At the last minute, almost the last second, he would swing his bus to the left, straighten up and come to a halt exactly opposite the head of the queue. Precision driving, you could say. The doors would hiss open, the passengers would pile on and he would be off just as the last one flashed his pass.

What this meant in the first instance was that those descending the stairs to get off would suddenly find themselves ricocheting down the stairwell, as if it were the Cresta Run.

My stop was approaching, and I tentatively made my way to the top of the stairs. As Schumacher made his final approach to the Pits, I turned to the assembled passengers on the top deck and, with the stiffest of upper lips, I quietly said, "I may be some time."

REMEMBRANCE DAY

By the time you read this, our three weeks of rehearsals in London for the national tour of J.B. Priestley's 'An Inspector Calls' will be over, and we will be heading for Birmingham and next Friday's opening night (flowers and cards to the stage door, thanks, but please don't say 'break a leg.')

Normally, the rehearsal period is for learning about the play, finding out about the other members of the cast and for exercising the actor's eternal paranoia over how much better everybody else is, and how much more they are being paid.

With this particular play, though, the situation is somewhat different. There are some new members of the cast and crew, true, but there are several of us who were with the tour two years ago and who know each other extremely well. The three lead parts, for example, Mr. Birling, Mrs. Birling and the eponymous Inspector (played by me, Sandra Duncan and Nick Day, respectively) are all hangovers, and I use the word advisedly, from the last tour, as is Edna, the maid (Elizabeth Ross).

So, while the three new youngsters in the cast (Mark Healy, Katie McGuiness and Nick Barber) are off exploring the play and forming embryonic friendships, which will no doubt flourish over the coming six months, we trio of 'wrinklies' are content to settle into that comfortable pair of slippers, represented by our knowledge of the play and of each other.

That is not to say that our cosy familiarity has bred complacency. Far from it. We are acutely aware of the enthusiasm being brought to rehearsals by the new cast members, and we are grateful for the fact that their freshness is a constant reminder to we 'old hands' that we must guard against cruising along in a sea of bad habits just because we have navigated this stretch of theatrical water before. I can't believe that I managed to avoid a mixed metaphor just then, can you?

However, all things considered, I don't think anybody would begrudge us our memories, as we look back on our common history and reminisce about what we all went through together.

Actors on tour don't necessarily socialize all the time, although this company did used to get together at a local restaurant every Thursday after the show for what came to be known as 'Nosh Night', arranged and booked by Nick Day. Thanks, Nick.

Along with memories of those meals, we remember that night when the Inspector had to stop the play in Bradford and utter the immortal line "Is there a doctor in the house?" - there wasn't.

We remember when the fire alarm went off in Llandudno, and we spent twenty minutes outside in the street, chatting to the theatre crew, the fire crew and cadging fags off the audience. Not a good idea, though, to ask the Chief Fire Officer for a light for my cigarette.

And we remember that fateful June afternoon in Norwich, during the last week of Wimbledon, when I whispered to the girls on stage, "Serena's in the lead - three, love," and completely threw the Inspector's concentration on his big speech - naughty! I did apologize later, after I was roundly scolded for being unprofessional.

Most of all, though, we remember how much fun it was to spend four days and nights in a new town, with people we liked, doing a play we respected and with the prospect of going home on the Saturday for the majority of three days and nights with our families.

The reason we could enjoy that sort of time off was because the play didn't open each week until the Tuesday evening, meaning that everybody could usually get back home late on Saturday night, but not have to leave again until late Tuesday morning. The other 'perk' of this particular job was that the play had no interval, and lasted one hour and three quarters, meaning that on a 7.30pm start, the play would end at about 9.15pm and you could be in the pub by 9.30pm. That routine will no doubt continue throughout this second tour.

So, here we go again. I wonder what the next six months will bring. I will let you know.

A LITTLE LEARNING...

During the last three weeks, as I have been trolling up and down to London on the 07.33 train from Brighton to attend rehearsals for the imminent opening and tour of 'An Inspector Calls', I have learned a lot. No, I don't mean that I have been studying the script of the play and committing to memory all the lines I will have to say. What I mean is how much there was to learn about the ins and outs of commuting.

Lesson one:

My comparatively short stint of daily rail travel, the end of which was always in sight, was a mere walk in the park compared with the year in, year out, never ending slog of the professional commuter. It must take some advanced form of dedication, or do I mean desperation, to spend nearly half your working life stuffed into an elongated metal tube along with a couple of hundred others, all of you travelling at up to 100 miles per hour and being subjected to the eternal repetition of disembodied and mind numbingly banal announcements.

Lesson two:

There was an awful lot to learn about the apparently simple act of travelling to and from work by train, and I was in the presence of the experts. You see, what those lads on the 07.33 don't know about the tricks of the train, you could write on the back of a season ticket. I can only assume that their expertise is the result of the vast experience they have gained from hours; days; weeks of enforced travel up and down to the big City.

Consider seating strategy. You or I would just plonk ourselves down and be done with it, but not these past masters of the art of spatial distribution. No way! Take an empty pair of seats, for example. The practised commuter will always sit in the aisle seat, never the window seat. This has the dual effect of deterring other passengers from disturbing you to get to the window seat and, even if they do, you are still left with the upper hand when it comes to the inevitable dash for the door at London Bridge.

Then there is the four seater chess move (fool's mate, to the expert). Faced with a table and four empty seats, our expert commuter will always choose a seat facing the direction of travel and next to the window. Why? Because the next person to come along will always choose the aisle seat opposite (for comfort and leg room), thereby forcing the next person to choose the other aisle seat, which will leave our expert with all the leg room in the world, and with only a slim chance of anyone bothering to climb over into the opposite window seat. Check mate.

Carriage choice is also crucial to successful commuting, and is often a question of compromise. Choose the rear carriage on the 07.33 and yes, you will be served coffee first, if available, but you will end up being about three miles from the exit barrier when the train arrives at London Bridge. (Small footnote here: this rear carriage is also very popular with commuters to East Croydon, as it ends up dead opposite the exit ramp - front carriage applies on return journey – hope you are taking notes.)

If you think I am kidding about all this, or maybe exaggerating for effect, perish the thought, consider the onward journey by tube and exactly where to stand on the Underground platform. The ace commuter knows, almost from birth it seems, exactly where the door will be when the tube train stops, so he and his fellow expert travellers can walk straight on. You can see these lads, clustered like Antarctic penguins keeping warm, ready to waddle on as soon as the doors open.

In my three short weeks I tried to grasp some of these essential travel survival tips, but without a great deal of success, I am afraid. I would always end up wedged into a corner by someone on the way to Gatwick with their worldly goods piled up on their knees, just as the coffee trolley rattled past.

I don't think I am cut out for commuting by rail. Anybody know the way to Pool Valley coach station?

IT'S ALL THE SAME TO ME

Revisiting your old haunts is one thing, reliving a whole tranche of your past life is quite another. The latter is what I was doing all last week, by returning to Birmingham to start on rehearsals for 'An Inspector Calls' for the second time.

Same town; same tour; same time of year.

So, on Monday at 09.00 I set off on the same journey I made two years ago, almost to the day. Up the M23, clockwise round the M25, off onto the M40 and follow your nose more or less straight into the heart of Birmingham.

As I drove, everything around me looked just as it was the first time: the same lifeless, leafless trees; the same hint of fog around Gatwick; and, yes, you guessed it, the same endless queue on the M25 between the M3 and M4. I swear that even the driver of the Mitsubishi Shogun, next to me in the middle lane, was the same bloke I spotted two years ago. It must have been him, because he was still exploring the deepest recesses of his nasal cavity with his index finger. What is it about sitting in a car that makes a grown man behave like a schoolboy? There will be a law against it one of these days, you know.

As the traffic was slowly gathering speed around the M4 exit, and I was trying not to get distracted by the jets taking off overhead, I spotted an intriguing number plate on a rather large, expensive looking car. The number was PRO 147. I thought,

"Just a minute. PRO 147? If that car doesn't belong to a snooker player, I'll eat my cue!"

In case you don't know: PRO = professional and 147 = the maximum break in a frame of snooker!

Of course, it had to be a professional snooker player! I caught a glimpse of the driver's profile, and that clinched it. It was Willie Thorne, one of the troop of pros who have regularly appeared on the snooker circuit over the years. That may not mean a lot to you, dear reader, but for me it made my journey all the more memorable. Thanks, Willie. Having got over that exciting interlude, the rest of the journey was relatively uneventful, and I made it to Birmingham in good time.

Believe it or not, my digs there were the same, too. Same landlady; same room; same four digit code for the burglar alarm, which I never did remember. I unpacked all my gear and hung up my collection of shirts that had been meticulously ironed by Andrea, and set off for the theatre. I walked along the same streets, passed the same shops, averting my gaze, of course, as I skirted the same lap dancing clubs, and arrived at the same stage door.

Only one or two tiny differences stopped me from believing that I really had gone back in time. The new Sainsbury's Local half way along Broad Street, for instance, was obviously a recent addition. These kind of supermarket versions of the old corner shop seem to be springing up all over the place. The only reason I can offer for this is that the big chains have spotted a niche in the market, which has been left by the closure of all those small corner shops that the big chains themselves forced out of business in the first place. Talk about creative business!

Another difference, albeit small, in the Birmingham landscape was that McDonald's have now started to open their doors at half past six in the morning. Don't ask. No doubt their tempting ploy of 'one free hot drink, per person, between 6.30am and 7.00am' will have the inhabitants of Moseley and Edgbaston leaping from their beds at the crack of dawn and rushing headlong for Broad Street to take advantage of this offer of a lifetime. Bit of a bummer, though, if your alarm doesn't go off and you arrive at 7.01am, eh?

So here I am, in the same dressing room, writing the same column, before going on the same stage to perform the same part in the same play. And they call this Variety!

PEDAL POWER RULES

If you recall, last week I was banging on about how everything was the same on my return to Birmingham with 'An Inspector Calls'. Well, whilst there is indeed much continuity here, on reflection there is also much change.

The biggest change in the vicinity of The Repertory Theatre, where we are appearing, is that the dramatic statue of a group of working class people, which used to dominate Centenary Square, is no longer. It was dramatically burned down. Yes, actually burned down, if you can believe it, by a group of working class people in an act of symbolic self-immolation, the significance of which has escaped everybody, including, I suspect, the perpetrators themselves.

Still, this act of urban terrorism has had the benefit of clearing the way, literally and metaphorically, for the City Council to sanction the erection of a giant Ferris wheel on the vacant lot. From this quite stunning addition to the Birmingham sky line it is possible, so they say, to get a bird's eye view of the queues of traffic along Broad Street, by day, and of the queues of scantily clad teenagers outside the lap dancing clubs, by night.

The only trouble with this Brummie version of the London Eye is that, at its full height, it is still quite a lot shorter than the top of the Hyatt hotel next door. What this lack of foresight in the Ferris wheel's positioning means is that a good 25% of its panoramic view is totally obscured by the Hyatt, which in any case affords a far better view over the city from its top floor rooms in the first place. Although, it has to be said, the exorbitant cost of simply occupying one of those rooms for an hour or so, just to cop the view, might not make the investment really worthwhile.

There has also been a quite radical change in the Birmingham Police Force's Traffic Division policy vis-a-vis transport for its officers. Since the completion of the Bull Ring development (complete with a larger than life-size metal charging bull, modestly deprived of one essential part of its anatomy, thank goodness, but good for a selfie, if you are that way inclined), a vast area of the City Centre has become almost entirely pedestrianised.

At the same time as easing the congestion on the pavements, and thus allowing pedestrians to spill on to the roads that were previously clogged up with cars, the Council has, at a stroke, turned the whole Bull Ring shopping experience into nothing short of a pleasure. And it is not only the shoppers themselves who can now enjoy the freedom thus afforded them, the shopkeepers and department store owners, too, are thrilled to bits, as they have a constant stream of potential customers strolling slowly by, and all too ready to part with their hard earned cash.

On the downside, and there is one, I'm afraid, this attempt at a vehicle free environment has made it somewhat difficult for police Panda cars to attend incidents quickly, or to give chase effectively, if needed, without endangering the lives of hundreds of innocent shoppers going about their lawful business.

So, in a move that Norman Tebbit's dad would have heartily approved of, the Birmingham Police Traffic Division have 'got on their bikes', or Panda bikes to give them their proper name. These machines are state of the art pedal cycles, souped up to outstrip any fleeing felon, and the officers atop them are equipped with the latest in aerodynamic helmets for that extra burst of speed.

Thus, New Street, the Brummie equivalent of a pedestrianised Western Road, Brighton, say, resembles nothing less than the final stage of the Tour de France, even down to the yellow blousons that all the pedaling peelers wear.

The result is that while Birmingham's shoplifters live in fear of the humiliation of being carted off on his pillion by the bobby on the bike, the rest of the population live in fear of being mown down by policemen pedaling, hell for leather, through their midst.

The introduction of flashing blue lights on their helmets, and hand held sirens is eagerly awaited!

A FOXING QUESTION

Did you awake this morning full of hope? Did you look forward to opening the letter from your Bank that promised to refund the ridiculous amount of £45 they charged you for going 25p overdrawn? Did you find yourself convinced that this would be the day when you would hear a politician actually answering a question? No? Then perhaps you were plunged into despair by the dawning realisation of today's momentous significance.

Depends where you stand on the big question, I suppose. The big question being:

Should the hunting and killing of animals, using other animals (organized and attended by humans) be banned? Well, it is from today. Needless to say, we are talking here about fox-hunting, basically.

My reaction to this debate is, and always has been, a resounding - Yes...

...and No. The reason for this ambivalence, or to put it bluntly outrageous fence-sitting, is that there seems to me to be a certain amount of confusion as to what exactly is being banned here.

Is it simply the hunting of one animal by another, which arguably is part of Nature's natural order of things, in the first place?

Or, is it the fact that the 'sport' is organized by, and for the pleasure of, human beings, who have scant consideration for any of the animas involved?

Or, is it some manifestation of class division that is being banned?

With hare coursing, say, the 'anti' argument seems fairly clear. Protesters object to the deliberate act of placing a hare in a relatively confined space, and at the mercy of two greyhounds that compete to see which is first to catch the poor animal and, presumably, rip it to shreds. Supporters contend that the odds are, in fact, stacked in the hare's favour, because only 126 were caught and ripped to pieces in the last year i.e. a mere 10.5 per month - yippee! You try telling that to some terrified bunny, waiting in the wings to make its final appearance. Why don't these 'sportsmen' go to the Coral dog track instead, have a nice meal, a bottle of house wine and watch exactly the same event without the attendant bloodshed? If they had a bet, they might even go home with a few quid extra in their pockets, which they could donate to some animal welfare charity.

All that, by the way, brings me to my confusion over fox hunting. Protesters seem to object as much to the dressing up and clopping around as they do to the fate of the fox. And hunters say that their sport is the most humane way of controlling foxes, while also saying they rarely catch one - so what is the point? Are protesters actually waging some kind of class war, and are hunters simply dressing their bloodlust and themselves in the colours of humane environmentalism?

Perhaps the solution is to rehabilitate blood sports in the same way as, say, throwing the javelin has become an acceptable Olympic event. I mean, originally, the javelin was an instrument of death, wasn't it, and the ability to throw it and stick it into the chest of an oncoming enemy was quite an advantage. As a sport we have taken the sting out of the javelin's lethal capability, except maybe for the odd one that spears an inattentive Official, and we now concentrate on the strength and skill of the thrower. In the same way, hare coursing has a humane counterpart in greyhound racing. We have simply replaced the one with the other.

So, why not apply a similar rule to fox hunting? If a large part of the fun in hounding foxes till they drop, is actually rooted in the social aspect of putting on costumes, blowing horns and chasing the pack of hounds, then why don't they do just that? I see no problem there. One of the 'hunters' could be supplied with a couple of tins of Pedigree Chum and be sent off, while the glasses of sherry were being dished out, so he could to lay an appropriately Chummy-smelling trail, while the scarlet-clad cavalry downed their Amontillados, or whatever, and followed at the gallop. To be fair, I think that happens, in some form or other, already, but only when all the local foxes have twigged what is about to happen, and have hoofed it over the hills and far away.

Everybody would have fun, nobody would protest (except maybe the bait, if he was a tad slow), and I will bet you that foxes would be queuing up in their thousands to watch him get caught. That would keep them away from our chickens.

PARTING IS SUCH SWEET SORROW

As you settle down with your morning coffee today and dunk your donut, agog to know what gems I am about to impart, I shall, in fact, be packing up to leave Stoke-on-Trent. It has to be said that the leaving of it has been the highlight of many a trip to Stoke-on-Trent, and my departure is no exception.

You see, we were here two years ago with 'An Inspector Calls', and I must say it was one of the most miserable weeks I have ever spent anywhere. You will get a flavour of what life is like in this dismal, life-sapping place, when I tell you that Stoke is not twinned with a foreign town, but has a suicide pact with Beirut. On Friday and Saturday nights the Stoke constabulary holds an informal get-together in the town centre. They stand around as if at some al fresco cocktail party, eyeing the assembled drunken youths and fondling their truncheons longingly. Anybody with any sense leaves this urban squalor, heads for home and watches a video about...urban squalor.

Well, that was what this article was intended to be about. I was going to have a right good old moan up about its physical deficiencies, and then make several witty cracks at the expense of the limited nature of cultural Stoke, if that is not a contradiction in terms.

However, I have been stopped in my tracks - literally. To start with, when I got back from Birmingham late last Saturday night, after bombing down the M40, I discovered that Andrea had invited three girlfriends round for dinner (I had the left-overs, and very nice they were, too, dear). To be honest, I had totally forgotten about this arrangement, but then Andrea says I never listen to her - at least I think that's what she said.

However, what really came as a shock was that this series of articles is to end today. In tabloid parlance, I have been axed.

Ok, I have had a good run for your money, it's true, and I have enjoyed every minute of it. Nothing has given me greater pleasure than trying to entertain you, so that is what I am going to try next - nothing.

The response I have had from all you has been fantastic. Therefore, I feel it is my duty to sign off with all the dignity and humour I can summon. Not for me regrets and recriminations. Far from it. I have too many people to thank to get bogged down in the minutiae of whys and wherefores.

Most of all, I must thank you, dear readers, for doing that very thing - reading. Thanks to the dozens of you who have told me how much you have enjoyed my articles. Special thanks to the trio of lads who dubbed me 'The Brighton Bryson' and who would compare notes on each offering.

Thanks, everybody, and all I can say is, "I shall be sorry to see you go."

DAVID ROPER
Shoreham by Sea
October, 2019

PS: My vote of thanks, contained in the above article, was supposed to make up that final chapter, which all books seem to have, and which you never bother to read.

However, I decided,

"No thanks. I think I'll have my Appendix taken out."

Printed in Poland
by Amazon Fulfillment
Poland Sp. z o.o., Wrocław